The Systems Approach
and Its Enemies

THE SYSTEMS APPROACH AND ITS ENEMIES

C. West Churchman

BASIC BOOKS, INC., PUBLISHERS

NEW YORK

Library of Congress Cataloging in Publication Data

Churchman, C. West, 1913–
   The systems approach and its enemies.

   Includes index.
   1.   Social systems.   2.   System theory.   3.   Social
sciences—Methodology.   I.   Title.
HM24.C49   300′.1   78-19937
ISBN: 0-465-08342-0

To all those
who over the past fourteen years
have attended "West's seminar"
in 652 Barrows Hall
at the University of California
at Berkeley

"And thus while we do not comprehend the practical unconditional necessity of the moral imperative, we yet comprehend its
incomprehensibility, and this is all that can fairly be demanded
of a philosophy which strives to carry its principles up to the
very limit of human reason."

I. Kant,
Foundations of the Metaphysics of Morals

CONTENTS

PREFACE

THIS BOOK has taken a long time to write. I sometimes suspect that its beginnings lie in my Ph.D. thesis, which was called "Towards a General Logic of Propositions." There I discovered how extraordinarily difficult it was to design a general logic, if one took the adjective *general* seriously, as had my mentor H. B. Smith. (For Smith the propositional logic of Russell and Whitehead's *Principia Mathematica*° was definitely *not* general.) This book is just another step in the search for the meaning of *generality*, in this case a general design of social systems.

There are lots of themes that can be used to describe this search. Perhaps the best one is the discovery that the usual dichotomy of *x or not x* never seems to display the general, because *neither of the above* is always so prominent an aspect of the general social system. Thus there is an immense part of social systems reality that is none of the following popular dichotomies in the current literature: rational–irrational, objective–subjective, hierarchical–nonhierarchical, teleological–ateleological, deductive–nondeductive reasoning (for example, inductive or dialectical), ineffable–effable.

In the text I have used the word *enemy* to connote this immense land of social systems that has remained largely unexplored by "hard" systems analysts, who thereby reveal a distinct softness of living by avoiding the dangers of exploring unmapped lands.

Some will inevitably think that I have "sold out" to the enemy, that is, to those who claim that the *none of the above* is, in fact, all that there is to reality; certainly such a viewpoint is very popular among today's "radical" intellectuals. But my point is that if you have never explored the intricacies of trying to model reality within a mathematical language, then you, too, have missed the generality of reality. It is really quite inappropriate to claim that a mathematical model cannot represent reality when you have no idea at all as to what a *mathematical model* is.

Of course (an "of course" that is strictly my own), I lay down no claim that the land of the enemies, here described in four parts, is accurately mapped,

---

° Russell, B. and Whitehead, A. N., *Principia Mathematica*, 1910.

because I suspect that the land is also beyond that dichotomy, accuracy–inaccuracy, which is so beloved by today's "scientists."

No author of a book that has taken so long to write could possibly acknowledge all those who have contributed to its writing. In the dedication and in the text I have acknowledged that a great many of my teachers have gone under the highly deceptive label of student, but I have found no legal basis for preventing this deception on their part. And I have been immensely helped by people with other labels: friend, editor, wife, son, colleague, etc. Perhaps of all these I should single out Tom Cowan, but if I did I should emphasize that he inspired a great deal but is not legally responsible for any of it.

Christmas Eve, Mill Valley, California, 1978

The Systems Approach
and Its Enemies

CHAPTER I

On Systems and Their Design

DESPITE the incredible amount of technical jargon that surrounds the word "system," it has a plain meaning for most of us in our everyday lives. Suppose we have made a list of items we need to purchase from the store. This puts us right away into the "shopping system," which consists (at least) of two major components: transportation (to and from the shopping center) and the shop itself. But each of these has a rather large number of subcomponents. Transportation involves building, maintaining, and policing the streets, budgeting funds for all these, personnel hiring and firing, administration and management, etc. Similarly, the running of the shop involves financing, purchasing, construction, maintenance, personnel, management, etc. So our little shopping trip takes us into a rather large system made up of many interconnecting components.

Now there are several questions one can ask about these systems which we humans have created to serve our needs and desires. For example, precisely who created them? Or, more to the point of this book, were they created well or badly, and do they function well or badly today? I take it for granted that the correct response to this question is that however well designed the systems might have been, today the vast majority (perhaps all) function poorly, harmfully, dangerously. The next question is, What can be done about it? I regard this question to be a matter of the design (or redesign) of human systems.

This first chapter is intended to show that the proper design is not a simple matter of fixing up some messes within the system. I want to let reflection show that simple, direct, head-on attempts to "solve" systems problems don't work and, indeed, often turn out to be downright dangerous.

The Environmental Fallacy

The simplistic approach to systems design says that there is a clear and urgent necessity to do something about our systems, else we perish: we must create more resources of food and energy, we must reduce the pollution of air and water, we must reduce our population—or else no environment will sustain us. The other approach says that above all we must think through the consequences of any proposal for action, because otherwise the "clear and urgent necessity" will lead us down the pathway of disaster: we create more farm land and irretrievably destroy its future productivity, we eliminate pollution of waters by enacting laws that therefore prohibit industry in impoverished areas, we attempt to stop population growth by attacking deeply embedded religions and cultural values.

Strangely enough, the two approaches rarely confront each other. The battles seem to be mainly civil wars, between those who see different "clear and urgent necessities," or between those who see different ways of "thinking through." In one "peaceful" seaside town in California, there is a fierce battle between those who see that there is an urgent need to build high-rise hotels on the beach, and those who see that there is an urgent need not to build them. Or between those who see an urgent need to control drugs by means of search and seizure even in private homes, and those who see the urgent need to stop such brutal police action. But few of these antagonists ever think through the broader implications of the particular action they are fighting for. For example, those who see drug abuse as a real danger talk about the ruined lives of people who succumb to the habit. But the action they propose is police search and seizure to enforce the law. This action, among other things, leads to an underworld drug market, which profits in proportion to the "success" of law enforcement, so that the price of drugs goes up, necessitating robbery and even murder on the part of the drug abuser. Yet the proponent of law enforcement rarely thinks through the consequences of his action proposal— namely, that law enforcement is directly responsible for the increase in crime. Instead, he goes on talking about the evils of drug abuse, a topic it is pointless to discuss since no one wants to argue with a tautology: "Drug abuse is bad" is equivalent to saying, "Too much is bad for you."

Then there are the prophets of doom, who scare us by "proving" that our environment will not sustain our lives twenty, fifty, or a hundred years from now. The argument is beautifully presented, with statistics for the growth of population and the resources of the environment. But then there is the delicate issue of what to do about such a situation. The response is that "we" must persuade or legally force people to stop having so many babies. Here again, the same blind tactic has been adopted as in the case of the enemies of drugs. First establish that x is bad for us; then propose to force people not to do x, thereby creating an underground movement that not only continues to do x but does so by means of force if necessary.

Why should we be so blind in our proposals for action? Our story, which is about rationality, about the hero who wants the world of humanity to act sanely, can therefore begin with anger, which is often the prelude to reasonableness. This is both heroic and intellectual anger, the anger of a hero who sees that his enemies are righteously bent on destroying the peaceful world of humanity.

The best way to express intellectual anger is by revealing a fallacy, as Aristotle did in his anger at the false and deceptive teachings of the Sophists. The fallacy in point can be called the "environmental fallacy"; it might be called the "fallacy of ignoring the environment," but this label doesn't have nearly the clout of the simpler one. One form of the environmental fallacy consists first of observing that x is growing (or declining) in a way that is dangerous, harmful, or potentially disastrous. Usually some critical point is identified as being definitely unsafe, really harmful, or disastrous. On the basis of these observations, an imperative is generated, usually either legal or technological. The imperative takes the form "Prevent x from growing." If x is the use of alcohol, then the (fallacious) imperative says, "Stop the consumption of alcohol by making it illegal," and we have prohibition, that most dangerously fallacious law designed to overcome the dangers of drinking. And, of course, we never learn our lesson from the experience; x is now consumption of marijuana: x is growing, growth of x is dangerous, and "hence" it is "imperative" to outlaw the consumption of marijuana.

Or, x can be population, which is growing alarmingly, and soon the disaster point of starvation will be reached. Hence what David Hertz calls the "technological imperative": create the pill, vasectomy, or whatever, to try to stop the growth. Or we can try the legal imperative, which will outlaw too many babies.

Fallacious, all too fallacious. Why? Because in the broader perspective of the systems approach no problem can be solved simply on its own basis. <u>Every problem has an "environment,"</u> to which it is inextricably united. If you stop x from growing (or declining), you will also make other things grow (or decline), and these changes you have created may very well be as serious, and as disastrous, as the growth of x.

The fallacy of the environment, says our hero, is far more serious than pollution, depletion of resources, and the like. These so-called ecological phenomena are easy enough to see, but the insidious pervasiveness of the fallacy of the environment seems not to be seen at all. Nothing the prophets of doom predict about population growth can equal the disasters that lie ahead as a result of our repeatedly basing large-scale social policies on the environmental fallacy. The environment of a problem is far more difficult and far more important to perceive than the physical environment of a city or a nation.

It is important to note the strong, nontrivial implication of the rather bland prescription to look at matters in as broad a way as possible. One finds these days a number of articles reporting some "facts" about the harmful effects of smoking marijuana. Presumably the research that led to these facts was impeccable by the existing standards of scientific inquiry. Yet the decision to publish these articles may well have committed the environmental fallacy, because the article may induce policy makers to put further irrational restrictions on the use of the drug. So the bland prescription questions the whole existing enterprise of science, which is based on the publication of findings arrived at by "acceptable" research methods. He who proposes to eliminate the environmental fallacy in today's society could be a very dangerous fellow—if anyone of importance would listen to him.

Note that the fallacy of the environment also occurs when x is growing and x is lovely, beneficial, world-saving. The National Aeronautics and Space Administration recently launched a satellite that takes images of the same area of the earth's surface every eighteen days. This is great, because we will virtually have an "instant" geological map of the world; it is beneficial, because we'll be able to detect changes in resources, the existence of hitherto unknown resources, the dangers to resources, and so on. So let x (the imagery) grow and grow! The environmental fallacy again. Why? Our suspicious neighbors to the south call it another United States "spy in the sky." They may be wrong, but that's irrelevant: they are more suspicious, and that's the critical point. Thus we've adopted the technological imperative to make more of x which is good, without considering that increasing x will also increase y (suspicion of developing countries), which may be far worse than the benefits of x. Again we've ignored x's environment.

One of the most glaring examples of the environmental fallacy of a growing x is nuclear energy, which it seems beneficial to increase, but which creates wastes that may kill our descendants in enormous numbers through bombs built by smart nihilists or through seepage into their drinking water. No one can now say how long the danger may last; estimates vary from seven hundred to three hundred thousand years. But in any event the "environment" of the nuclear energy problem is vast and obscure. *Our* generation may become the most abhorred of all generations!

Now our hero does *not* say that every dangerous growth should be fought indirectly; it may be that stopping *x*'s growth is the right step, but *not* on the basis of *x*'s growth alone. This is why the population-scare writers are so wrong in the eyes of our hero. You simply shouldn't publish a book citing statistics on the growth of population and the decline of food resources and let it go at that. If you do, you inspire policy makers to make the environmental fallacy.

A curious instance of the environmental fallacy arises in connection with the label "ecology" and its correlative "ecosystem," which surely must puzzle many readers these days. Some biologists regard these words as part of the basic vocabulary of biology, and hence as technical and esoteric. But the technical problem of creating, say, a stable ecosystem in a wilderness forest may have grave economic and social implications for a region or a nation. These implications must belong to the problem along with the biological definition of the "closed system." Etymologically "ecological" means "pertaining to the home," and the environmental fallacy occurs when the "home" is given a technical, esoteric definition within a discipline.

Thus the angry-hero-of-the-systems approach. You don't have to like him, and certainly you don't have to agree with him. But his reasoning or reasonableness is compelling, and you'd make a mistake if you didn't include him among those you appreciate—that is, those whose opinions you try to evaluate. Like all heroes, this hero at times does dumb things, for example, trying to get a computer to run an economy. But we all do dumb things, because that's human. And this hero is very human.

The Systems Approach

Our hero espouses something he calls the "systems approach," which is designed to avoid the environmental fallacy. In order to appreciate the systems approach, we should try to understand what it really is. Don't try to find out only by asking an advocate or a practitioner, because each will start by emphasizing his own special approach. One will talk incessantly about how the systems approach is linear programing; another will insist that it is nonlinear feedback modeling; yet a third, that it is the application of the homeostatic theory of the brain. You'd come away from such encounters feeling that since systems approachers don't agree—at least in the esoteric language they use—perhaps there is no systems approach after all. But that would be just as riduculous as inferring that art doesn't exist because no two artists describe it the same way.

On the broadest level, the systems approach belongs to a whole class of approaches to managing and planning our human affairs with the intent that we as a living species conduct ourselves properly in this world. Everyone adopts at least one such approach during her/his life, even if he/she is a recluse, an agnostic, a nihilist.

The systems approach is, therefore, only one approach to the way in which humans should respond to reality; but it is a "grand" approach, by which I mean "large," "gigantic," or "comprehensive." It is one of the approaches based on the fundamental principle that all aspects of the human world should be tied together in one grand rational scheme, just as astronomers believe that the whole universe is tied together by a set of coherent "laws."

Even so, this description hardly captures the richness of the systems approach. To go farther, we must do what any mind must do to understand a rich idea, which is rich because it involves so many connotations. Thus the pursuit of meaning must follow many pathways. In this book I've selected six pathways, all of which can be at least partially articulated. In order to understand what the systems approach means, we try to understand something about (1) its history or tradition, (2) its logical structure (i.e., its meaning of "reason"), (3) its ethics or theory of value, (4) its potential (i.e., what it claims it can do that no other approach can accomplish), and hence (5) its enemies (i.e., those other approaches that most fiercely challenge this contention), and finally (6) its future (i.e., its long-run perspective which links its past to its present and to the ages to come). Note that these six pathways toward meaning all borrow from the philosophy of the systems approach, in that they are all "grand" perceptions of an idea. If you feel that your understanding of the systems approach will be biased as a result of these pursuits, you should respect this feeling as being sound. But then if you are inquisitive, you might also ask yourself whether an unbiased appreciation of meaning is possible.

One further remark about the coming pages may be helpful. The underlying imagery of the book is that of a voyage, with pathways and concomitant dangers and joys. The writer is simply a guide. When I was a boy, I used to travel the Maine wilderness, and we always had a guide along (indeed, the law required one). He did know some things that we didn't know about the wilderness, and helped us here and there to find our way and to avoid setting fires or breaking our canoes in rapids. But we also came to know many things he did not know: the origin of a creek, the best fishing hole in a lake, a cave perhaps, or a place to worship. I think I know some things about the six trips we're about to take, but I hope you'll know a lot that I don't know. Otherwise, the journey will have few rewards.

My Personal Journey

But you have every right to know something about the guide—and at least to know how he comes to think he's professionally capable of the job.

I think my strongest claim to qualification lies in the fact that I was a convinced disciple of one strong systems approach, developed by E. A. Singer, Jr., in the first part of this century. I say it's a fact that I was a disciple, because Singer so named me at his retirement dinner, and hence it was "official." A disciple is one who has become convinced by another about the correct way of looking at reality, be that way religious, philosophical, economic, or whatever. His virtue lies in his dedication to as complete an understanding as possible, and as his understanding increases, so does his conviction. The conviction then takes on a life of its own and successfully repels any attacks on the so-well-understood viewpoint. There is usually one central theme that acts to suppress any strong doubts. Eventually the disciple must commit the environmental fallacy, since he believes that what is outside the position and the theme does not exist or is meaningless, ridiculous, inappropriate: his world view—for him—has no environment.

Singer's philosophical position had the theme of comprehensiveness, so that all aspects of the natural world were to be "swept in," in order to pursue humankind's endless quest for knowledge and control of Nature. Singer made no attempt to exclude values from science, as did so many of his contemporaries—for example, the logical positivists; indeed, he undertook to include values in explicit ways. Physical reality, psychological and social reality, ethical and moral reality, religious reality were all to be included under the generic label "science," or the quest for knowledge.

We'll be exploring Singer's land later on, but for the present it's germane to note how a disciple might react to such a theme of comprehensiveness. Since nothing could be left out of a program respecting all the serious facets of human learning, the disciples's mission was to see whether Singer's systems approach really worked—that is, whether it could be successfully applied to the study of real problems in the social world. Singer was a student of William James, whose philosophical position of pragmatism said, in loose terms, that truth is what "works out." But Singer's background in science would never permit him to leave matters in such loose terms. His world view was a precise elaboration of the theory of evidence required to determine whether something "works out." Only after all the relevancies have been "swept in" can we feel satisfied that a theory works well, and this means that we can never be fully satisfied. But we can make approximations; and to do so, we must go out into the real world to begin to make them.

Hence, all of Singer's students, who regarded themselves as philosophers, studied facets of the world in order to see how its features could be "swept in"; we went to biology, law, aesthetics, physics. To philosophize, we believed, is to philosophize about how the world fits together. My personal voyage was frustrating for a while. It started with symbolic logic (in order, I then thought, to understand the foundations of reason). But the discipline was (and still is) extremely limited, because its strong requirement for precision excludes such essential world features as how people reason psychologically or sociologically. I began to realize that the psychology of inconsistency is hardly captured by the symbolic logician's "p and not-p are both true." Also, symbolic logic, like many formal disciplines, is eternally bound in its own language, incapable of telling us about forms of inquiry other than its own. Or so it seemed to me, though logical positivists like Carnap° tried valiantly—and I still think futilely—to develop the method of induction out of the framework of symbolic logic.

But there was a discipline, mathematical statistics, which had tried hard to prescribe how the empirical sciences should inquire. They do so by "posing questions to nature"—that is, by formulating hypotheses and subjecting them to empirical test. This was no new way of putting things, but if one used Singer's deep insights, then the modern theory of statistical tests (e.g., as posed by Neyman and Pearson†) fitted in very well. Singer saw that inquiry must be an integrated "whole-system," and not a sequence of isolated and separable hypotheses.

In effect, all scientific inquiry is conducted by means of a set of strong

---

° R. Carnap, *Logical Foundations of Probability* (Chicago: University of Chicago Press) 1950.

† J. Neyman and E. Pearson, "Contributions to the Theory of Testing Statistical Hypotheses," *Statistical Research Memoirs* 1 (1936).

assumptions about reality, called a "Weltanschauung"; and this is so whether or not the individual scientist is aware of his assumption-making. An "experiment" is an attempt to put this set of assumptions to its most severe test. The fact that many so-called experiments do nothing of the kind is irrelevant: Singer's systems approach was never intended to be a description of how scientists behave, but it was intended as a prescription for how the inquiring system ought to behave.

Now the system obviously needs to be able to decide whether an experiment "passes" or "fails" the Weltanschauung. This has always been a problem of central concern to philosophers of science, and a great deal of nonsense has been written about it. For example, some innocents have claimed that there is such a thing as the "critical instance," which is an observed "fact" that may destroy the whole Weltanschauung. But, of course, no such critical instances ever exist in practice, nor should they, according to Singer. For one thing, all observation is subject to error; a "fact," to be established, requires the concurrence of an idenfinitely large number of qualified observers, most of whom are yet to be born. Furthermore, scientific inquiry can only estimate facts approximately, and the estimates differ in the final significant number (if they don't, one must take readings to a higher degree of precision).

This is why statistics turn out to be so critical in the design of inquiring systems—or apparently so. Statisticians like Neyman and Pearson thought that they could determine a prescriptive role for statistics. It takes only a little patience and common sense to see that the manager of an inquiring system is always faced with two possible errors (at least): he may reject some aspect of his Weltanschauung when it is "in fact" true, or he may accept it when it is "in fact" false. Neyman-Pearson assumed that the scientist-manager should set the probability of the first error, and that the statisticians should then minimize the probability of the second. Whether these are really the proper roles for manager and statistician is debatable, but it is rarely debated in the halls of statistics, I've found.

Of course, there are difficulties in applying such a theory of statistics. (What does "probable" mean? Since there are an infinite number of ways an assumption can be false, what then? What about the value loss in making either error? And so on.) But I soon became aware that I wasn't going to learn much about designing an inquiring system from statistical theory, because the really crucial issue was never addressed: this is the problem of selecting the right hypothesis to test. Compared with this problem, the problem of the right theory for testing a *given* hypothesis seems trivial. How does the inquiring system select the right question to study?

It is not difficult to appreciate the explosive power of this question. If you are working in a certain area of inquiry, as I was during World War II, then, of course, it is reasonable to ask what direction to take next. I had found that the probability of detonation of a certain chemical compound depended in a predictable way on its physical environment and specifically on the resistance of the object that was holding it. What next? Should I test for dependence on temperature? On the shape of the firing pin? In the long and unpressured process of scientific investigation, the issue does not seem very critical: temperature today, firing pin structure tomorrow, or vice versa. But then a more general question arises. Shouldn't I be trying to find out *why* a firing pin makes a compound go off in the first place; perhaps if I know why, I can formulate general laws that will automatically cover the special cases of temperature and firing-pin shape. To waste my time on the latter would then be to test the wrong hypothesis. But the explosive power of the question doesn't end there. Should I be inquiring into detonation at all? Isn't there some far "better" use of my inquiring time? Or should I be inquiring at all?

The consequence of these "system" questions seems clear enough: to *know* that I'm investigating the right question, I must know the total relevant system of my opportunities. And, of course, I cannot know the total relevant system, so I can't *know* I'm testing the right hypothesis. But I can *estimate* the right choice by trying as well as possible to estimate the relevant system of opportunities.

The trouble with the laboratory as a ground for studying the systems approach is that most laboratory scientists do not want to consider their work from a systems point of view. If the question they ask seems significant to themselves and their colleagues, and if it seems feasible to study the question by "legitimate" methods, that is enough. I came to suspect that the rationale for the disciplines was to provide a bulwark against raising the question of the right hypothesis beyond a certain level of generality; the disciplines are political, not "scientific."

This was a pretty radical thought and threatened my disciplehood. Singer had regarded the scientific community as essentially cooperative, with each scientist seeking goals that would aid others to seek theirs. He even speculated that the measure of performance of science might be provided by the probable error of some physical constant—for example, the velocity of light *in vacuo*. Just why it is valuable from a total-system point of view to become increasingly precise about light's behavior was not a serious question for him. But it has to be a serious question from the point of view of the systems approach.

In any event, I had come to realize that there are two "sciences": the one represented by the collection of the disciplines, and the other by the systems approach. The first contains a collection of ideas about methodology and is essentially isolated by its disciplinary politics. The other is an attempt to engage in those areas of inquiry which are most relevant to the social good.

Of course, this way of describing the distinction between the two meanings of "science" may not seem very radical or very new. After all, the pragmatists have always been saying that truth resides not in facts, or in hypothesis testing, or in any other data-based technique of verification, but rather in significance to our human enterprise. But there is in the distinction an implication that traditional pragmatism did not emphasize. The distinction is not just logical, but political. The "science" of the disciplines is an "enemy" of the science of the systems approach. What does "enemy" mean? For the moment I take the word to be dialectical—that is, a consortium of opposites. An enemy is someone who is distrusted and admired; loved and hated; respected and feared. Above all, an enemy is someone who holds powers, resources, capabilities that one desperately needs. Thus, disciplinary science must not be trusted by the science of the systems approach. Disciplinary science's insistence on a very narrow meaning of control in experimentation, for example, must be regarded by the systems approach with a great deal of suspicion; disciplinary science may very well be a political device to convert broad-minded Ph.D. students, who want to study big problems, into narrow-minded assistant professors, who study small problems in accordance with accepted standards of research. But, of course, disciplinary science must be admired by the systems approach science, because it has developed so many methods which are potentially useful in the total process of human learning: mathematics, the concept of control and adaptation, precision, measurement, etc. However, the point is that one is not likely to learn very much about the systems approach by dwelling in a discipline.

All of this was a long learning process for me, a lifetime of ambiguous relationships with many disciplines. It meant leaving the discipline of philosophy, because in virtually all contemporary philosophy departments the grand concept of the total system has been abandoned as a topic of discussion. Almost all of the philosophy of science today is philosophy of disciplinary science, with its worries about the meaning of theory, or verification, or paradigms. I was amazed that Kuhn's book, *The Structure of Scientific Revolutions*,[*] or the advent of Bayesian statistics,[†] could have created such a stir among the intellectuals! In the systems approach, all methods of inquiry,

[*] Thomas S. Kuhn, *The Structure of Scientific Revolutions* (Chicago: University of Chicago Press, 1970).

[†] Named after Thomas Bayes (1702–1761), who introduced the idea of "a priori" probabilities that are not estimated by empirical data.

all designs of inquiring systems are options of the inquirer; there is no a priori set of standards that dictate the preferable ones.

Since I was not going to learn about the systems approach in disciplinary science, it was only natural to look around for some other area of human effort which *was* attempting a systems approach. At first I and my colleagues thought a likely candidate was city planning; after all, a city planner is supposed to be looking at the "whole system"—education, recreation, industry, police, traffic, etc. But at that time (late 1940s) the planners seemed to be deep in the environmental fallacy. They looked around to find the "worst" aspect of the city and, not surprisingly, found the slums. There is x; x is bad; so eradicate it! Tear out the slums and replace them by "better" housing. There is no need to repeat the miserable story of that version of the environmental fallacy.

Labor unions seemed to be another likely group, because many of us felt that the basic social philosophy of labor was much more of a systems approach than the social philosophy of owners who emphasized "property rights." Whoever bases his idea of right and wrong on the unexamined principle that each person's legal property right must be upheld, commits the environmental fallacy.

But labor unions, since their revolution in the 1930s, apparently have created their own version of the environmental fallacy, a version that happens frequently in the professions as well. Obviously the prime client of a labor union must be its members, in the sense that the first priority among its objectives is to serve the members' objectives. But to bring about this happy state of affairs, a qualified leadership is required. In order for this leadership to work, a lot of a union's resources must be used to safeguard the leaders against political attacks within and without. Hence, the leadership becomes the top priority client in order, it is claimed, to serve best the rank and file. But this claim is rarely examined in any detail: it lies in the neglected environment of the leadership's problems. The same process happens in the professions. Obviously the client of a hospital is the patient. Obviously, too, the doctor knows how to serve this client's objective better than anyone else. So the surrogate top client becomes the doctor. Whether the ways in which the hospital serves the doctor actually serve the real client best tends to be an unexamined question of hospital operations. I'll quickly pass over the delicate question of whether a university's policy of making the faculty the highest priority client best serves the real client (students and society); the responses might be embarrassing.

Now you may want to express an obvious objection to this rather dismal account of our organizations and professions. After all, no one is required to be a union member; and furthermore, if he doesn't like the leadership, he can vote it out. But as you'll see, the obvious is usually a symptom of the environmental fallacy. The question is, what "opportunity costs"° occur when an individual relinquishes his membership? It's not as though he's on a peaceful walk through life and can take any pathway. The decision to resign brings with it a whole complex of other consequences. And as for changing the leadership, the systems question is, what social forces cause someone to rise in an organization to become a powerful candidate for leadership? The question is not well understood, but one might describe the resultant of these forces in the words of Ambrose Bierce:

President, n. The leading figure in a small group of men of whom—and of whom only—it is positively known that immense numbers of their countrymen did not want any of them for President.†

In any event, we did approach a labor union with the suggestion that we investigate why the rank and file so seldom attended meetings, except in the case of a crisis. We rather naïvely thought that such an inquiry would open up the question whether the leadership was really serving the prime client, the member. Our proposal was greeted with interest and rejection on the part of the union leadership.

In any search, after exploring likely places and exhausting most of them, one has to resort to opportunities, wherever they occur. And the opportunity lay in industry. Many American managers of industry are quite inquisitive; they keep wondering whether there isn't some better way to manage, especially when they come to realize that they don't really know how they manage at all. They love that heroine of fiction called Topsy, because, like her, their companies have just "grow'd." No one can explain the how and the why of a company's growth. But the reflective managers feel they ought to understand the how and the why.

During World War II, first in the United Kingdom and then the United States, some eager academic scientists offered to assist military operations in their desperate needs: early-warning radar, U-boat hunts, and the like. Why did these scientists, who were largely ignorant of military operations, think they could help? Mainly because they felt that *not* being bound by military background and precedent enabled them to ask some unusual but relevant questions. And when they did, and studied the questions, some remarkable results occurred. In a minor way they were attacking some of the environ-

---

° As we'll see, "opportunity costs" are basic to the systems approach; they describe the value of opportunities foregone once we decide to do one thing rather than another.

† Ambrose Bierce, *The Devil's Dictionary* (New York: Hill and Wang, 1961), p. 146.

mental fallacies of the military operations. .Since they studied operations, their activity was called "Operations Research," or "OR" ("Operational Research" in the United Kingdom, since the British much prefer not to run nouns together, even at the cost of printing one extra letter).

Since scientists performed OR, there was a tendency to think of OR as a "scientific" approach to military management. Hence our reflective managers in the post-World War II period naturally asked whether OR might not work for industrial management. One of them, John Kusik, vice-president of Finance of the Chesapeake and Ohio Railroad, went to the acting president of Case Institute of Technology and asked him what Case was doing about OR and whether the "C & O" could make use of the results. The story goes that the acting president hadn't the foggiest idea what OR was, but as a president he could easily tell John he'd "look into the matter." He did so by getting a copy of the only existing text by Morse and Kimball,* which describes some of the wartime OR work, and by calling me to see if I'd be interested in coming to Case. What I and my colleagues had been doing with city planning, labor unions, and the like we labeled the "Institute of Experimental Method," which, contrary to OR at that time, had a fairly well-developed philosophy based on Singer's work, but—again contrary to OR—no outstanding successes. A marriage of convenience clearly seemed called for, and since we were marrying OR, we took on its name and modestly dropped ours altogether.

The experience with industry at Case was all I could have hoped for in terms of learning more about the systems approach. "Learning" means not only the discovery of new things but a better understanding of the old. Singer, as I said earlier, had showed, to my complete satisfaction, that a single datum of science is both theory-loaded and value-loaded. It is theory-loaded because a datum is one reading in a total measurement process which, among other things, requires calibration of instruments, and all calibration requires estimates of causal laws of nature. It is value-loaded for the reasons stated earlier: to collect a datum is to make a commitment to one research opportunity versus another. In addition, Singer points out that the scientist's response to a question of fact is always in the imperative mood: "Let the measured length be taken as lying between a and b," where the strength of the imperative resides in the ethical values of the scientific enterprise.

This Singerian lesson becomes much easier to grasp in the OR studies in industry. Industrial managers show a natural and strong concern about costs; to them the true costs of doing something (making a product, conducting a

---

* P. M. Morse and G. E. Kimball, *Methods of Operations Research* (New York: John Wiley, 1951).

service, investing capital) are as crucial as the true measurement of a physical constant is to a physicist. Now industrial managers have lots of help in estimating costs: accountants, industrial engineers, and economists are the primary aides in this effort. But we found a peculiar aspect of the concept of cost relative to decision making. One of the first studies we conducted at Case was an attempt to determine the correct inventory of parts which a manufacturing firm should carry. The question can be stated in terms of costs: How much does it cost to carry an item in inventory, and how much does it cost not to carry it? These two costs can be broken down into subcosts, one of which will suffice to illustrate why Singer's lesson so obviously applies. This is the cost of holding dollars in inventory. If an item lies on a shelf for sixty days, and I've spent ten dollars in making it, what does the idle time of the item cost me? If you think about this question from the point of view of the economics of the firm, the proper response seems to be that the firm has forgone the use of ten dollars for sixty days, because the part that sits provides it with no economic benefit. (You should note as always that nothing is obvious in this book: I might be a miserly owner who loves to gloat—not over coins—but over my beautiful and precious nuts and bolts, in which case the idle part has great value of another kind.) If we accept the economic world view, then the problem of measuring the cost of keeping an item on the shelf depends on our ability to say how the inactive dollars should be spent if they had been available: that is, what is the best alternative use of the resource that has been captured by inventory? Note the word "should." As system designers we are interested not in how the firm does in fact use its money, because it may manage its money supply very badly, but in how it should do so. Hence, to be able to measure the cost of holding an item in inventory, we must know how money should be spent by the firm: that is, we need to know how the financial system of opportunities should work. All this may have a familiar ring to it; I discussed the problem of the right hypothesis in much the same terms.

Thus the cost that should interest the manager can only be known by knowing how his financial opportunity system ought to work; as in the case of science, so in industrial management, we cannot know the financial opportunity system precisely, but we hope we can estimate it. The cost data and other data in the systems approach are in effect "linkages" between systems; the cost of holding the dollars in inventory is a linkage between the inventory system and the financial system. Needless to say, the story of linkages doesn't end with just two systems; the financial cash flow system is linked to the marketing system, to the public relations system, to the personnel system, and so on.

As I said, there was nothing new to be learned here about measurement, because such linkages are well known in the physical sciences, and Singer had been well aware of them (though his careful nineteenth century style would probably have eschewed the crude word "linkage"). The way in which classical physics handled the problem of an exploding series of questions was by creating the idea of a "sufficiently closed system." For example, how is the laboratory technician, bent on measuring a weight on a bench, to know whether he should take into account the temperature, the altitude, or the phase of the moon? The only conceivable answer is that he or his boss must know—or estimate—how each of these variables influences weight. Depending on the phase of the moon, the technician may be gloomy or joyful: in gloom he sees everything as heavy; in joy, everything as light. The design of a good laboratory consists in understanding such relationships and in either eliminating them (e.g., by hiring a duller, more phlegmatic technician) or adjusting for them by means of physical laws. The design is successful if the scientist believes that no external cause influences his readings except in a random fashion; at such a point his belief becomes the imperative he judges to be right. "Let us accept the system as sufficiently closed"—an imperative that subsequent experience and reflections may cause him to modify.

In the world of the systems approach we have not yet found so satisfying a method to handle the problem of stable and reliable data. Instead, we usually operate under rather questionable assumptions. Those in a hurry use some existing rule of the firm to estimate costs—for example, the cost of borrowing money, which is really ridiculous because if it's always profitable for a firm to borrow money, then why doesn't it always borrow money? The more astute researchers assume that some managers somehow have enough experience and insight so that they can properly intuit a good estimate. This is really a fantastic compliment to the manager, considering that he is intuiting the whole system of relationships among the subsystems of the firm. But the assumption may be the best we have at the present time.

I see no reason to be discouraged by the monumental task of arriving at sensible estimates of costs, demands, and benefits; it's even exciting to see the enormous and mysterious problems we face. And I see no reason whatsoever to act as though these problems do not exist. I was surprised and delighted to learn that economists had long known about "opportunity costs," like the cost of a dollar sitting on an inventory shelf. I naturally expected that the literature of economics would be filled with methods of estimating such costs and with epistemological considerations about the validity of an economic theory when such costs are lacking. On the contrary, there is extremely little to be found, and what little there is on such matters as the cost of capital is of no help to the researcher in a practical inventory or marketing problem.

Many economists seem to have the odd idea that the methods of their discipline raise no serious philosophical problems. When they do write about epistemology, what comes out is a kind of naïve positivism or rationalism. For example, the economist Milton Friedman seems to think a theory is validated if it "works out in practice." But if a firm makes ten million dollars more than any other firm in its industry by "using" an economic theory, does this "validate" the theory? Surely not.

But quite apart from these irritating remarks from a philosopher, it would be truly astounding that a discipline devoted to generating sound economic policy could ignore the methodological problems of its data collection, if we did not realize that disciplines do not follow the rationality of the systems approach.

All that I've had to say in the past few pages concerns what I earlier called the "logic" of the systems approach, because that was what I was chiefly learning while working with industry. Before leaving the logic, I should say something about the discipline of mathematics, which has often been thought to be the foundation of the logic. In its original sense, in which mathematics meant "learning," mathematics does underly the systems approach, because everything I've said implies that the systems approach is an approach to learning. But in the last few centuries mathematics was "disciplined," just as were so many other topics like psychology, philosophy, and sociology. Most managers know a lot more about important aspects of all three of these last topics than do those residing in the respective disciplines. Disciplining mathematics has really been a rather sordid affair, which probably reached its apex in the time of Russell and Hilbert, who bled the subject of all its content and made it into a precisely regulated game with symbols. This scandalous situation even spread to the elementary schools in the form of the "new math."

None of this was particularly harmful, even though it effectively lost the spirit of mathematics as a learning process. But the question of relevance for this essay is whether formal mathematics as we know it today in models of decision making is an appropriate tool for improving the social system. Certainly the usual argument for justifying the use of models for management seems weak and even fallacious. The argument states that all management decisions, if rational, are based on a set of assertions about the real world, and that it is better to be precise and rigorous in using these assertions to justify decisions, rather than to be ambiguous and sloppy. But why? If they were honest, many advocates of models would have to reply "because an article which has rigorous and precise language gains more respect among my colleagues than one which is written altogether in ambiguous English."

In point of fact, there is a great deal of value in ambiguous language. In the first place, we usually don't know enough to be precise, nor would attempting to be more precise help us very much. A well-known example is the bald man: no one cares to specify the number of hairs, square inches of bare area, or whatever, that constitutes baldness. The realization that most management problems deal with sets which are vaguely specified led Professor Latva Zadeh, of the University of California at Berkeley, to create a theory of "fuzzy sets." Of course, the paradox of fuzzy set theory is that it runs the danger of becoming precise about fuzziness. The essential ambiguity of the decision maker's world lies much deeper than ambiguity about membership in a class.

I can illustrate the trap you may fall into if you espouse precision as a way of life. Suppose you are a manufacturer of sleds for kids. Of course, you want to make a profit, but you also want to make safe sleds. Precisely what do we mean by "safe"? Well, it's reasonable to say that "safety" is measured by the probability that something will break in such a way as to cause a serious injury: the higher this probability, the less safe the sled.

Now you're in the trap. First, we precisely relate this measure of safety to various factors of the sled and its manufacture: for example, the quality of the raw materials, the skill of the workers, and the amount of inspection. In each of these three cases we can estimate a fairly precise price: the price you pay for raw materials, workers, and inspection. We're now ready to spring the trap. By a bit of precise mathematics, from the price you pay we can deduce the "expected" dollar cost of a serious accident which you implicitly assume by paying these prices; say it's one thousand dollars. So you're the kind of louse who thinks a serious accident to a little kid is the equivalent of losing only one thousand dollars.

But notice how you fell into the trap of precision. You *could* have said that safety is not precisely definable and, in any event, is not expressed by an empirical probability. In other words, as always precision is an option— sometimes very good for learning, sometimes not. In most cases, a student of decision making should learn formal mathematics but should also learn when *not* to use mathematical language.

I've glided over this point quite rapidly, not because I think it's unimportant, but because most students of decision making have made up their minds totally and irrevocably on the subject. They fall into two classes. Some believe that in all rational decision making there is an implicit cost, or "price," for everything relevant, including loss of limb, life, or love. The othes believe that "quantifying" such things as life and love is morally outrageous. The first never want to argue why they are right, because they mainly talk to themselves, with whom they agree completely. The fact that their thesis (that everything relevant has a price) is probably a tautology never occurs to them; it's plausible to argue that the thesis follows from their definition of "decision" and "relevant." On the other hand, advocates of the position that quantifying some spiritual aspect of our lives is immoral rarely explore the basis of their very human feelings. They, too, meet in friendly circles where an outrageous shake of the head is sufficient to establish the point. Of course, I've just established myself as a member of a third—and superior—class of people who disagree with both of these. Such is the glory—or the foolhardiness—of reflection.

Next we come to ethics, the theory of the appropriate goals of a system. We're not likely to learn very much about the ethics of systems either in the disciplines or in industrial management, because neither spend much time on the subject. A pure scientist is willing to discuss (briefly) honesty and the ultimate value of knowledge. In the private sector of capitalist countries a manager will discuss (also briefly) the ultimate need of the firm to survive and make money, with a comment on its social responsibility. Neither scientist nor manager has spent much time on how pure knowledge or survival of the firm compare with other human values.

The best place to learn about the ethics of systems, I found, is in nonmilitary government, and this discovery in effect took my journey of inquiring back to planning. Each agency of the government is seeking fairly specific goals. The National Aeronautics and Space Administration, for example, was striving during the 1960s to put a man on the moon. The Fish and Wildlife Service is trying to preserve endangered species. The Office of Education is trying to upgrade K-12 education. I studied all three of these objectives, keeping in mind the question *"Why?"* What is the ethical justification for such goals?

During the 1960s and 1970s the United States government showed a strong interest in applying one ethical theory, called "utilitarianism" by philosophers, to determine whether such objectives are ethically justified. The method is called "cost-benefit analysis" (C-B). One attempts to estimate what the nation pays to put a man on the moon, to preserve a species, or to educate a child, and then to estimate the likely economic benefit of each of the programs. Bentham's "greatest good for the greatest number" becomes the prescription: fund those programs with the greatest social benefit minus cost. The method is plausible in the case of education—so plausible that a lot of federal money has been spent on applying it. The method is not plausible for wildlife without a considerable modification. It is ridiculous for NASA's objective, unless one wishes to argue that it was ethically correct for the nation to pay billions of dollars to have a TV program of man's first moon step.

In the 1970s some social scientists tried to bolster cost-benefit analysis by means of "social indicators." They weren't really changing the ethics at all, but were criticizing the purer economists who were neglecting some important benefits and costs just because of the difficulty of quantifying them.

As we'll see, Singer had a much more fully developed ethics of systems than has C-B analysis, especially because his ethical theory takes due regard for future generations and is not based on the rather wishy-washy idea of satisfaction which seems implicit in C-B. But as I thought about the objectives of the government agencies, I began to realize that there was the strong, but often hidden, theme of morality. In education kids are rewarded or punished in terms of what they do on standard tests. A "good student" is one who performs well on the tests, even though he may be a very bad student in terms of his moral conduct. It is absurd to conduct a cost-benefit analysis of a program to preserve the egret from the killers who want to sell its feathers; destroying the egret is morally reprehensible, that's all. NASA's satellites, which take images of the earth's surface, could be regarded as a "spy in the sky" for water or mine developers, or for the secret police or the military. If they are doing any of these things, the policy of keeping them up there is immoral.

Singer felt that morality could be swept into his ethical system. As he put it, there is no need for an ateleological ethics, one that ignores goals and ideals. Hence one can judge the ethics of destroying the egret, or testing and rewarding kids, or spying on people by means of the long-run implications for an ideal-seeking mankind. But I began to feel that there must be another voice in the matter which would not be stilled by astute arguments. It is the voice that says, "Don't eliminate the egret because it's immoral; it's also immoral to argue the matter." This voice is plausible and forceful. I became convinced that because the voice is real and had not been subsumed successfully under any version of the systems approach, including Singer's, it is necessary to heed its message.

This conviction was closely tied to another—namely, the importance of the psychological individual and of the ineffable qualities inherent in every individual. I came to this conviction as a result of a common middle-aged illness which especially attacks those who have believed their lives to be meaningful in their younger years: we come to question the meaningfulness of our lives, and the response is depressing, to say the least. So I went into Jungian analysis to find out more about this "life" I had thought so meaningful. To the Jungians, a meaningful life is a process of individuation, of the discovery of the individual in oneself.

To be sure, in the tradition of the systems approach there have been many attempts to capture the essence of the individual. British empiricism seems to have identified the individual with the ego, and crude Western economics found it convenient to regard the individual as a utility function which translates commodities into "utiles." Individuality, therefore, represents the assumption that the utility function behaves properly and gives unique utiles at a given time and for given commodities. No serious consideration of the inadequacies of this quaint version of psychology seems to have occurred in the economic literature, even though the major work of the psychoanalysts was taking place at the same time as the major work in utility theory. Kenneth Arrow was writing on the problem of going from individual utilities to social utilities° at about the same time that Jung was exploring the archetypes. Yet I daresay that practically no economist read Jung or saw the relevance of his work to the inadequacy of any concept of individual utilities, nor was any Jungian cognizant of Arrow's struggles. It's the Wonderland of the disciplines again!

I decided that Jung's journey was the starting point for learning about the individual and his/her relationship to the social system. And the journey brought to mind a paraphrase of Kant's famous dictum: "Two things fill my heart with never-ending awe: the social system without and the individual within." I began to give up another assumption which I think I got from Singer—namely, that the mind is a teleological entity whose characteristics can in principle be described by its potential behavior patterns. This assumption had led me to write a tome called *Psychologistics* with Russell Ackoff in the 1940s.† By means of some ingenious logic I concluded that the basic properties of an individual can be described in terms of his knowledge, his beliefs, his way of valuing acts for themselves, his way of valuing ends, and the manner in which his values change. I believed that his individuality in principle lay in the set of measures that describe these properties. It is always possible that two individuals could be exactly alike with respect to these measures, but they would differ by being in different places or times. One's uniqueness, in other words, follows from geometry and kinematics. Such nonsense, it all seems to me now!

° Kenneth J. Arrow, *Social Choice and Individual Values* (New York: John Wiley and Sons, Inc., 1951).

† C. West Churchman and Russell L. Ackoff, *Psychologistics* (mimeographed; University of Pennsylvania, 1946).

The Enemies of the Systems Approach, or
Learning from SA's Enemies

It was gradually dawning on me that there is another, totally different way of learning about the systems approach. The lessons I've been describing so far come from an *inner* critique—that is, from within the system. Then one day I was listening to a talk about the virtues of the world models which the Club of Rome had sponsored; the speaker was asking why the world's leaders had not more rapidly responded to the models' results. The answer came like a flash: "Because they're not 'in' the systems approach but rather live and decide 'outside' it." Thus was born my idea of the "enemies" of the systems approach. I threw away the speech I'd planned to give, and talked instead about the four enemies I'd identified: politics, morality, religion, and aesthetics. In each case the approach to human life is not comprehensive, holistic, or even "rational" in the sense of rationality which model builders use. What is common to all the enemies is that none of them accepts the reality of the "whole system": we do not exist in such a system. Furthermore, in the case of morality, religion, and aesthetics, at least a part of our reality as humans is not "in" any system, and yet it plays a central role in our lives.

To me these enemies provide a powerful way of learning about the systems approach, precisely because they enable the rational mind to step outside itself and to observe itself (from the vantage point of the enemies).

Of course there are many rational questions to be raised about the enemies: Are they truly enemies? Is the list exhaustive? How are they to be defined? What should the systems approach strategy be with respect to them? And so on.

First of all, I think they all defy "definition" in any of the senses of this word which reason has invented. But of course that conviction does not stop me from characterizing them.

POLITICS

Politics means primarily the way in which people gather together around issues of human living, food, shelter, education, patriotism, war, security, etc. Each such gathering together I call "forming polis." Although polis may look like a system at times, for its inhabitants its existence is not justified by some larger system—for example, by some cost-benefit analysis. Of course there is a systems approach to politics, and writers like Rapoport° have even tried to

---

° Anatol Rapoport, *Fights, Games and Debates* (Ann Arbor, Michigan: University of Michigan, 1960).

explain, in a rational mode, how political "fights, games and debates" are to be handled. But there is also a political approach to systems analysis—namely, the ways in which the appearance of rationality can be used to create political action.

MORALITY

Morality is the underlying spirit of all action that drives a person to act as he does. True, "spirit" and "drives" can be defined conceptually, and we systems thinkers can even codify the moral spirit into moral codes of conduct. But by so doing, we can justly be accused of destroying the spirit. The tradition of morality lies in the history of moral action, in wars, in crime and retribution, and especially in the many forms of revolution the moral human has invented: overthrows, strikes, civil dissent, voluntary starvation, and so on. A Marx can "explain" the history of revolution in terms of the inevitable dictatorship of the proletariat, but his is a systems approach to morality. There is also a moral approach to systems thinking—namely, consideration of whether the thoughts of the systems philosophers destroy or distort the moral spirit, as in strikes and revolutions.

RELIGION

Religion refers not only to the actions of organized religions but also to everyday human action in relation (often in worshiping relation) to something higher, more powerful, more knowing, more comprehensive than the action itself, or else to something fantastically small and refined. Such an account of human action can be described in systems terms, as I'll try to do when I come to theology. But there is also a religious appraoch to systems thinking. Perhaps the systems approach is one of man's finest ways of worshiping God; if so, should we dare to define "worshiping God" by rational concepts? The attempt may be sacrilegious.

AESTHETICS

Aesthetics is the core of all action, that which makes action "radiant" for us: beautiful, ugly, pleasurable, painful, comic, tragic, whatever. Since systems thinking is a kind of action, its significance lies in its aesthetics, and not in its "validity." Aesthetics is that which gives life to human action; perhaps the action of trying to define such "life" kills the liveliness.

Human history is a tapestry made up of the interplay of the four enemies. Politics is the background of human events, as people have formed themselves into communities and nations. Morality is the deep red hue of revolutions, dissent, and heroism. Religion is a pervasive tone, which melds into the background of politics by turning into doctrine and bureaucracy or into morality as the inspiration of religious wars. The history of aesthetics is rarely written, except in histories of art and (occasionally) in biographies, but the true essence of aesthetics is what gives the tapestry its meaning; what "really" happened to humans in history is an image of human joys, desperation, love, hate, opulence, and drudgery. Most histories recount the major political movements, just as most news journals emphasize the blending of morality (horror) and politics. Wouldn't it be a delightful change if someone were to write a history of "welcoming the stranger," the fantastic ways in which just plain folk have designed, aesthetically, a welcoming environment?

But are these four really enemies of the systems approach? The reflective mind of the rational systems planner can't help asking whether politics has improved matters over the years, whether our present-day moral revolutions are really better than the old ones, whether our religions and our aesthetic sensibilities have become more refined. Perhaps, after all, the best systems approach we humans can find is coping with issues, so that the total tapestry of political history does display a "holistic" integration. Of course, there is much to make the rational mind skeptical about any of these speculations. But the question whether these four are truly enemies will remain to the end. After all, if we really understood the enemies, we'd really understand ourselves, and *that's* not going to happen.

As to the exhaustiveness and exclusiveness of the four enemies, the proper response seems to be that the question is irrelevant, since these are not logical categories; indeed, they "unfold" into each other in fantastic ways. Another writer could easily make another list of enemies which would eventually unfold into mine.

One last remark on my learning journey, which is a reflection of older but not necessarily wiser years. The mood of the journey was serious, deadly serious. Now there is one thing we all must learn about seriousness—namely, that it is ridiculous. None of this story can be told without reconizing the underlying humor of the systems approach. It forever runs the risk of being caught with its pants down in Phoenix Park.

This must surely be enough of my journey to let you know what the guide is like, where he has been and not been, how he's likely to guide or misguide you. By this time it'll come as no surprise to you that the answer to what "it," the systems approach, really is, must be that it's a journey. Bon voyage!

PART ONE

THE SYSTEMS APPROACH

CHAPTER II

The Tradition

ACCORDING to our hero-rationalist, the advocate of the systems approach, one of the most flagrant examples of the environmental fallacy is the failure to recognize history as a part of our environment. We act as though the past has no relevance to the concerns of the present. Indeed, people have developed a kind of universal pride in today's plight: "No other age," they boast, "has ever faced problems of such complexity."

This is a strange situation with paradoxical overtones. On the one hand, people are becoming more and more concerned about the future as a part of their environment and are devoting a modest amount of our resources in attempting to predict what the world will be like technologically and socially in the year 2000, or 2050. But the implication of this concern is obvious enough—that the society of the year 2050 will have to look back to the 1970s as part of its environment. If it is sensible, it will try to examine what we attempted to do with respect to its welfare, and learn the lessons from our mistakes and successes. Yet, on the other hand, we tend to regard every current crisis as essentially a novel one, and show little interest in its historical roots.

But from the systems point of view there is strong reason for a historical perspective. The basic idea behind the systems approach is that all relevant interests or values should be served by the kinds of change we can institute in our society and in nature. Of course, there are the questions of the total scope of these interests and whether the interests of those who have died are of relevance to our planning for change today. It is becoming almost common sense to say that the interests of humans of the future have considerable relevance with respect to today's planning. Should we also consider the interests, the expectations, and the hopes of the past? Yes, says the rationalist, simply because this is our own attitude with respect to the future—namely that *our* hopes, expectations, and interests will be reflected in what future generations will do. Our concern for our children does not perish when we perish. A departing rational soul does not say to itself, "Thank God, that's over with forever." The phrase "planning ahead" might seem redundant until one realizes that indeed there is some point to "planning behind."

Now you can appreciate the rationalist's inspiration in "putting it all together"; we, who live, are simply the existing caretakers in a grand scheme of caretaking. But what is the value of "caretaking"? What do we owe to the future or the past, and why should we caretake for either, when we've got plenty to do to take care of ourselves? Some (nonrational) wiseacres want to know what the future generations have ever done for us. The rational answer is that they have made us human—an integral part of human destiny. If we start taking care of ourselves only, we simply lose our human quality and become an ostracized species.

But what is human destiny? Some responses to this question are to be found, again, in history, in the history of ethics. The concern about the values of the past is one reason the history of ethics is so important to the systems approach. Ths history of ethics should be read not from the point of view of the specific answers that philosophers have suggested for the perplexing problems of human values, but rather for the display of different kinds of hopes, expectations, and interests which have been exhibited in both oriental and occidental cultures and over the millenniums in which we have discussed human values, both in writing and in talking among men and women. To ignore these reflections is to commit one of the worst forms of the environmental fallacy.

Thus, we see one reason why history is a necessity for understanding what the systems approach really is, just as it is for understanding any other important and universal idea.

There is a paradox here. If history is to enlighten us on the meaning of the systems approach, then we presumably need a meaning of the systems approach in order to identify historical figures and occasions. Which comes first—the meaning or the history? The response to this reasonable question is that the systems approach itself demands a systems approach to defining it. I suggested one in the last chapter—namely, that we begin by recognizing that we are on a learning journey, learning how to govern ourselves rationally. From the first chapter we can glean some clues as to what this rationality is: it is comprehensive, unified, all-encompassing. It sees the destiny of man—and all life—as coherent and ethically good. It also assumes that humans can make decisions that produce good or bad results as judged by the comprehensive ideals of our destiny. All this is vague, of course, but it excludes the pessimist, the pluralist, the relativist, the determinist or fatalist, the nihilist, the existentialist, the positivist, the disciplinarian. It excludes those who believe that the "whole system" is an illusion. This seems enough exclusion for our historical journey, at the end of which we expect to have better criteria for exclusion and inclusion.

There are many ways of taking an excursion into historical materials. One way is to attempt as deep a scholarly analysis as is necessary to understand exactly what the writers were trying to say. To an academic mind this may be the most attractive historical approach, but it runs into two serious systems problems. One is that it's doubtful from the systems point of view whether anyone really knows what he is trying to do in a particular context, and even more doubtful whether the writer of a text is really clear about his basic intention. But the second and more important point is that we are trying to use history as a means for understanding more deeply the systems approach of the past as we see it today for the sake of the future. This means in effect that your guide must undertake a rather personal excursion into history by trying to translate some of the ideas that were expressed historically into the language and attitudes of our generation. In effect, I am contrasting those who believe in a reality of our social past which is independent of our own reality, with those who see all realities as one and each age as doing its best to put the total story together. The first group of historians have little or no interest in the systems approach; for them the realities of the past exist in a pluralism of events, and not in a monism of our destiny. It's the same old theme: the rationalist sees no separation, wants to wipe out nonessential distinctions, and hence perceives history as a unity.

Also, your guide, like all guides, has to make a selection of historical episodes, since there are a large number of them. Bertalanffy° tried much the same thing as a guide into the land of General Systems Theory; his selections and mine differ radically but are nevertheless samples from essentially the same population.

° L. vonBertalanffy, *General Systems Theory* (New York: Braziller, 1968).

Origins

It's quite likely that the tradition of the systems approach goes back to primitive man. It is certainly not difficult to imagine that one of our early ancestors sat one evening within his well-defended cave and reflected that with his food supply, his defense, and his nearness to water, he was sufficiently well off not to have to worry further about other aspects of the total world. If he did so reflect, he was on his way to an early beginning of the systems approach, because he had done his very best to think about the "whole system" and specifically about its components, its boundaries, and his decision making relative to it.

As far as I know, the earliest document aiming at a systems approach to deicsion making was written in China in the second millennium B.C. This very early attempt—which, interestingly enough, became quite popular in the "radical culture" of the 1970s—is the *I Ching* or *Book of Changes.*° The *I Ching* has been given many interpretations in the history of thought, and much of it as we know it today consists of commentaries on the original writings, so that there are several authors of the book. For our purposes, however, it can be regarded as a fairly straightforward attempt to assist decision making by identifying the relevant characteristics of a problem situation and suggesting attitudes and lines of attack that would be appropriate for the "management process."

As in all systems approaches, the *I Ching* makes some fundamental judgments about the nature of reality. Essentially it assumes that the reality of decision making can be compartmentalized into sixty-four basic possibilities, each of which itself is rather general in nature. In each of these possibilities certain attitudes and guidelines are appropriate for the decision maker.

For the *I Ching* to be useful, therefore, it is necessary to know which of the sixty-four basic decision-making possibilities really obtains. One discovers this by having an appropriate person throw yarrow sticks according to a specific ritual. The yarrow was a sacred plant in China, and the basic philosophy of the *I Ching* is that certain "experts" can get in touch with the necessary sources of knowledge through the ways in which this plant behaves when thrown in an appropriate manner.

On the whole, I find the *I Ching* to be an amazingly astute systems management document. Just consider what it does in modern systems terms.

° There are several translations into English and a number of modern commentaries. As far as I know, I'm the only commentator to emphasize its "systems approach."

First of all, it assumes that the systems approach requires a comprehensive set of models of reality. Most contemporary attempts to apply the systems approach through models make just such an assumption. The fact that the *I Ching* contains a limited number of situational models certainly does not mitigate against its astuteness.

In both the *I Ching* and contemporary systems planning, an expert is needed to decide which model should be used.

Next, the *I Ching* recognizes that there must be an explicit way of gathering information and a computational technique based on the information to decide which model holds. In this regard the writers of the *I Ching* thought they had solved a problem that today is still unsolved. At the present time we lack any explicit way of gathering the data to tell us which model is appropriate.

Further, the *I Ching* assumes that it is essential to describe not only what model is applicable but also the *mood* of the situation. In this regard it goes well beyond present-day practices. Most planners and operations researchers feel no necessity to describe the mood of the organizational situation they have been studying, although the mood may indeed be the most important aspect of the matter. For each of the sixty-four sections of the *I Ching* there is not only a "judgment" that provides the basis for the decision, but there is also an "image" that provides appropriate mood or attitude. This mood or attitude is often described in terms familiar to the decision maker—for example, in terms of wind, fire, or water. For example, in the thirty-eighth hexagram, the image is "fire above, the lake below, the image of opposition. Thus amid all fellowship the superior man retains his individuality." Sometimes the image is more cheerful, as in the thirty-fifth hexagram: "The sun rises over the earth. The image of progress. Thus, the superior man himself brightens his bright virtue."

I was trying to get at very much the same idea in *Challenge to Reason* where I argued that the mood of inquiry is just as important as the factual or the theoretical results. To be sure, in a great deal of modern scientific inquiry the results are presented in a phlegmatic mood; but also, to be sure, in the earlier stages of inquiry there has been both joy and despair, as research seems first so promising and then so frustrating. For entirely subjective reasons the modern scientist has chosen to eliminate all but the phlegmatic in his presentation, even though the joy and despair may be the most important aspects of his research.

At this point I should mention that giving the *I Ching* a systems interpretation may seem unaesthetic because it ignores the radiance of the work. Indeed, this entire historical account may often be at odds with one or more of the enemies, since it may gloss over the inspirations arising from forming polis or from morality, religion, and aesthetics.

Next, in further dogged pursuance of the *I Ching's* rationality, I believe that it created the idea of dynamic models, a really remarkably modern concept. In the early stages of operations research, in the 1950s, we had to confine ourselves to "static" models that described a single situation simply because we didn't have the theoretical power to describe situations that moved over time. Today with our increased capability for constructing large models, the time dimension is becoming more and more important. In the *I Ching* each model provides a way of determining how a situation will change (or not change at all). The changing situation is described both in terms of changing facts as well as of changing moods. Sometimes the changes can be horrendous, as in the fifth hexagram, called "Waiting," where the judgment is to wait and have perseverance. One of the dynamic models indicates that the situation can become extremely dangerous, and the image is "waiting in blood"—that is, the decision maker is viewed as being in a pit of blood. "There is no going forward or backward; we are cut off as if in a pit." And thus the mood is one of standing fast.

Finally, the *I Ching's* method (as I mentioned earlier) is to provide not specific directions for action, but rather general precautions, warnings, exhortations, and the like, which the decision maker then applies to his own framework. In this regard the *I Ching* may become a more helpful guide than prescriptions written in precise and unambiguous language.

My thinking side refuses to swear by the *I Ching* and naturally has a lot of questions about its methodology. But I have to admit that these questions about *I Ching* are really not different in kind from the questions I raise about any attempt to apply models to decision making. The source of the data that directs us to the correct model is just as puzzling in today's methodology as it was in the method of the *I Ching*. In my own experience there have been an amazing number of instances where the *I Ching* has been remarkably helpful and I have no rational explanation for its success.

Also oriental, and to some extent much more difficult for Western minds to interpret, is the Hindu tradition as expressed, for example, in the Upanishads and the *Bhagavad-Gita.*° These writings can be interpreted as containing all of the elements of the systems approach that I discussed earlier and they also clearly indicate the necessity of man's coming in touch with a superior nature. The main purpose of meditation, which is taken to be the basis of all decision making, is to get in touch with the Atman, the universal being, who in some very real sense *is* the whole system.

°Again, there are many translations into English.

Nevertheless, as we will see when we come to discuss the enemies of the systems approach, some aspects of Hindu philosophy seem to run counter to teleology. For the ultimate aim of meditation is to remove teleology—that is, to remove purposive behavior. "The seer," says the *Bhagavad-Gita*, "acts without lust or scheming for the fruit of his action." In other words, the seer, who is at the highest level, no longer needs to have a purpose. Whether this should be regarded as essentially an interesting version of the systems approach—that is, one in which we should be striving to remove goal-oriented behavior—or whether this aspect of Hindu philosophy is antithetical to the systems approach, we can postpone for discussion when we examine the ways in which religious man is an enemy of the systems approach.

On a more general level the *Gita* reverses the usual form of the "technological imperative," which says, "Whenever there is a real need or desire, create the technology that will satisfy it." The *Gita's* message might be called the imperative of desire control: "Whenever there is a real need or desire, control the desire or need, by either reducing it, or changing it, or eliminating it." In other words, the systems approach is not necessarily an approach to satisfying human needs however they occur, It may well be an approach to the understanding and control of human desires. Of course, many Western systems planners have pointed to the starvation and general deprivation of populations in Hindu countries as a reductio ad absurdum of the *Gita's* position or as a proof that its doctrine is a means by which the rich exploit the poor.

But the other side of the coin shows the possibility of overcoming one of the most serious deficiencies of the systems approach to human affairs—namely, the implementation of the findings of a systems study. Very often the findings are completely ignored. But when they are regarded as potentially important for an organization, then politics, operating through the desires of the organization's members, will begin to form a polis that opposes the recommendations on the basis of a general distrust of the so-called systems experts. Now a common experience of meditators is that there is a remarkable reduction in the inclination to put distrust at the top of the list of their concerns and to allow reason and understanding to take its place. One might regard meditation, therefore, as an ally of the systems approach in its battle with politics. But, of course, getting managers to meditate may be as difficult as implementing any other recommendation.

In the *Gita's* emphasis on "desire control" rather than "resource control" we have a striking example of a dialectical process. Today this process is dramatically displayed in the field of energy. On the one hand, there is the approach of estimating future demand for energy, identifying the sources of energy (coal, water, nuclear, geothermal, solar, etc.), and developing those that most cheaply and safely satisfy the estimated demand. On the other hand, there is the "appropriate technology" approach (of Schumacher,° say), which eschews large-scale developments and argues for changing downward the pattern of energy demand. As is typical of dialectics in the public domain, advocates of both approaches "know" that their opponents are wrong and dangerous.

If this were a complete story, we should have to examine the varieties of the systems approach in Babylonian, Egyptian, and other cultures of the Near East. Instead, I'd like to skip to that most marvelous episode in the history of thought, the so-called pre-Socratics, a label that's a bit of a put-down. The basic idea of the pre-Socratics, perhaps created by Thales, is that one can ask what reality is made of and arrive at a plausible and recognizable answer. But there appears to have been more to the idea than simply satisfying intellectual curiosity. For if we can discover what the world of reality is made of, then presumably we should also be able to find what human minds are made of, and from this information be able to infer how we should most appropriately live our lives—that is, to infer an ethics for humanity. This form of the systems approach is, of course, drastically different from today's physics, though perhaps not too different from today's biology. From the results of theoretical and experimental research into particles and waves, it has usually not been possible to infer any conclusions concerning ethics, but certain biologists have been willing to infer an ethics from biological findings, as we shall see.

I have found that philosophers who have been captivated by the pre-Socratic period tend to have their favorites. Mine is Anaxagoras, because in his theme "in everything there is everything" I can find an important lesson for systems planning. Anaxagoras did not mean that everything is like everything. A chair is different from a table, and both are radically different from a lake or an ocean. But in a chair one would find the same elements that make up an ocean, but in different relative quantities. So, in systems planning, in any problem are to be found all other problems. This is not to say that all problems are alike. World malnutrition is a different problem from world militarism or from world energy. But in world malnutrition, as one explores it in depth, one will eventually be forced to recognize the relevance of militarism and energy and all other problems. This means that an appropriate style for the planner is to recognize the reality of specific problems in order thereby to obtain insight into all problems or the "whole problem."

° F. Schumacher, *Small is Beautiful* (New York: Harper and Row, 1973).

The pre-Socratics might better be labeled the "non-Socratics," because Socrates and Plato changed the metaphysical basis for systems planning. If I am right, the pre-Socratics took their clues for ethical doctrine from what the considered to be the nature of reality, whereas Socrates, and especially Plato, found their clues in the nature of rationality: reason, if allowed to respond freely to questions about virtue, would reveal the answers. Thus a dialectic was created that continues down the ages. Subsequently we'll see it as the debate between Bentham and Kant: for Bentham all ethical doctrine is to be inferred from man's hedonistic nature; whereas for Kant it is to be inferred from pure practical reason. As always the dialectic has created parties who scorn the opposites: so Nietzsche and Popper,° for quite different reasons, charge Socrates and Plato with the crime of having murdered the spirit of Greek philosophy.

Let's see how Plato proceeds in his *Republic,* an excellent example of design-by-reason. Plato regards the city-state as the whole system and tries to develop a design of such a system with its components and its overall purpose, which is justice. Justice is the unifying or monistic goal toward which all components of urban life are striving. Plato's form of rationalism is idealism: that is, he believes that we must get in touch with a higher being, in this case the world of ideas. Plato also sees clearly what I emphasized in the first chapter—namely, that the various components of the city-state should not be regarded separately any more than the functions of the body should be. One cannot simply add up the values of the goals of the workers, the military, and the rulers. The well-organized city-state will display a value greater than the sum of the values of the single components—a philosophy that sometimes goes under the label of "holism."

The *Republic* also raises one of the fundamental paradoxes of the systems approach—namely, the question of the role of the systems approacher himself. Many readers of the *Republic* have come to feel that Plato regarded himself as a kind of philosopher-king. The paradox arises from the problem of how to incorporate the systems approacher into the system without his turning into the individual on top of it all and representative of the final developed state. Thus, the dilemma: either the systems approacher is a servant of some set of individual decision makers who hire him, in which case he can hardly be called the designer of the system: or else the systems approacher does try to conceptualize the entire system, including the appropriate goals and ideals, in which case one can legitimately ask by what right he assumes such a role with respect to all of society. Indeed, if you attend a

° Karl Popper, *The Open Society and Its Enemies* (London: L. G. Routledge & Son, Ltd., 1945–62).

conference of systems approachers, you will find that they talk as though they were rulers of the world.° For the moment we can let this paradox rest in the arsenal of the enemies of the systems approach.

Aristotle, in effect, stands as one of the great heroes of the systems approach, because he encompassed the whole universal system in one intellect, his own. In a way, Aristotle returned to the pre-Socratic philosophy by inferring ethical doctrine, not from the world's physical nature, but rather from our biological nature. It is the emphasis on hierarchy of living beings which so strongly describes the Aristotelian system of philosophy. Thus, he used his own notions of biology as the basic theme of his systems approach and tried to describe the species in terms of lower and higher forms, of which the intellectual life is the highest. This concept of biological hierarchy became, therefore, the basis for defining higher and lower systems.

I am not sure whether Aristotle was the first philosopher to base his systems approach on biological hierarchy, but there is no question that he had a great number of followers, all eager to show in what way the human species is the pinnacle of living development. We think, we reflect, we write and speak, we know our past (somewhat) and we guess our future, and no other species does any of these glorious things. Unfortunately—or fortunately, depending on how you feel about us—all such systems thinking tends to be ridiculous, considering the terribly dangerous and destructive acts our fine intellects have invented. In any event, you should be aware that I have a bias that is against hierarchy as an essential aspect of systems or the systems approach; nonhierarchical system thinking is far more fruitful than hierarchical.

Aristotle also introduced in his own fashion a bit of control theory; that is, he recognized the desirability for individuals to maintain a type of biological control in their lives in order to develop their intellectual side. His principle of control is called the "mean between two extremes." In its qualitative form it is not really different from modern notions of systems control as they appear in, say, the design of machines.

Thus I can illustrate the power of a translation of Aristotle, not from ancient Greek into English, but from systems thought of Aristotle's day into current systems thinking, by reference to his discussion of virtue. Most freshmen in their first course in ethics are puzzled by the rather awkward prescription to choose the mean between two extremes. It makes sense when talking about food consumption, but what does it mean in, say, the case of kindness or friendship? I think Aristotle (and later Epicurus) would have been delighted by cybernetic (feedback) modeling, because it states in a clear language what they were struggling to express. The healthy body works

---

°A recent conference of such world planners, held in Paris under the auspices of the Institut de la Vie, was called "Towards a Plan of Action for Humanity."

through a homeostat, a device that returns the condition of the body to equilibrium, even when subjected to stimuli that disturb it. Aristotle's prescription, then, is to live a healthy life in which you attain the condition of homeostasis; this can only be done if there is an adequate feedback system, so that the body can send signals, often to the controlling conscious mind, whenever homeostasis is threatened. Also, kindness belongs to the social world: it is a homeostat for social relationships.

What I personally find most helpful in Aristotle is a lesson that later history, especially beginning with Renaissance science, seems to have unfortunately forgotten. This lesson is that in order to conceptualize social systems, one has to think of conceptualization in general, and therefore the ways in which we think about the psychological and social worlds. As is well known, Aristotle attempted to put all conceptualization into teleological form, so that even physical entities "seek out their proper places." Renaissance science and modern physical science has in effect assumed that one can describe the physical world without reference to teleology. This assumption of a separation of the two worlds, the world of the physical and the world of the social-psychological, was strongest in the physical sciences in the nineteenth century but still remains very strong in our own century. One of the first attacks on the separation seems to have occurred in the 1930s and 1940s, first with E. A. Singer, Jr., then later with Norbert Wiener and A. Rosenblueth.° The notion in both cases was that one could describe certain physical events quite usefully by means of teleological rather than mechanical categories. With the advent of the computer this facility of teleological explanation became even more pronounced, as in Wiener's *Cybernetics*.† But Singer, with his depth of analysis, also saw a real need to link physical imagery with socio-teleological imagery in order to overcome the great difficulties that psychologists and sociologists face in defining their terms. A typical example of the unfortunate struggle of psychologists to define some basic terms is the following: "Consciousness can be defined as awareness either of oneself or of something external to oneself." The definition does say something, but exactly what? First of all, consciousness is being defined in terms of another concept, awareness, which surely is no clearer than consciousness itself. Second is the trick of adding the expression "either of oneself or of something external to oneself," which in one sense adds nothing to the definition, though the definer of course is struggling to say something about the universe of discourse of consciousness.

But if we adopt the Aristotelian notion that the two domains of nature, the

---

° N. Wiener and A. Rosenblueth, "Purposeful and Non-Purposeful Behavior," *Philosophy of Science* 17, pp. 318–326.

† Norbert Wiener, *Cybernetics* 2nd ed. (New York: John Wiley & Sons, Inc., 1961).

physical and the social-psychological, are nonseparable, then as Singer and others have shown, we are in a much sounder position to define our terms, because we can link the findings of all the disciplines in order to explain what we mean.° I might parenthetically add that the once popular philosophy of operationalism, which believes that we can define our terms solely by the process of empirical observation, is fortunately becoming less popular simply because it is in the main an empty doctrine. The observational process itself has to be, and can only be, defined in terms of a larger concept of the whole system of inquiry.

Note again that all I have been saying refers to the nature of the systems approach designer, and specifically to his strategies of inquiry. The Aristotelian methodological point is that the entire conceptual scheme needs to be tied together and cannot be regarded in terms of separable components.

The tradition of the systems approach was certainly strong in the post-Aristotelian period, as it probably needed to be with the advent of the Roman large-scale empire system. The Stoics carried the pre-Socratic theme to the extreme, by arguing that the whole of nature operates in a rational and therefore deterministic fashion; hence there are no decision makers who can control either physical or social events. This idea *seems* to spell the end of any kind of design of a large-scale system. But the implication that the Stoics drew, and Spinoza later seconded, is that man's role in such a deterministic world is to understand the nature of the reason that governs the world. It is through understanding that we succeed in reaching the highest ethical level. The idealism of the position is obvious enough, since the whole of rational nature is certainly "superior" to any one of us. The perplexing aspect of the Stoic-Spinoza assumption has also been recognized many times: how is it possible for a man whose behavior is completely determined to change direction with respect to understanding? The problem is perplexing but such "freedom" is not necessarily contradictory to other assumptions in their system. It is really almost impossible to prove that a total philosophical system contains "contradictions," simply because a system is so tied together in terms of its concepts that any apparent contradiction can be removed by changes in definitions. In the case in point, obviously the Stoics, as well as Spinoza, had a different concept of free choice from the fairly simple one, according to which an individual can select different alternatives under the same circumstances. Rather the Stoic and the Spinoza emphasis was on persistency of choice, the ability to do the same thing under different circumstances.

° See E. A. Singer, Jr., *Experience and Reflection* (Philadelphia: University of Pennsylvania Press, 1957).

It would be impossible in this short journey to do justice to that magnificent period of the systems approach which begins, say, with Paul° through such tall figures as Plotinus, Boethius, Augustine, Anselm, Thomas Aquinas, Nicholas, Descartes, to Leibnitz, and beyond. The salient feature of this story is the question whether the "systems approach" requires a theology and, if so, what kind. The question is pervasive, seemingly in almost all cultures; what is remarkable about the Western European adventure is the depth and intricacy of its philosophical responses.

Out of the richness of this treasure I've selected two gifts. One is Paul's concept of the hierarchy of trusting relationships which we humans can hold with respect to the grand system: faith, hope, and love. Any systems planner who has worked actively with managers should quickly come to recognize the central importance of trust in this relationship, and therefore in the systems approach. What's bothersome to thinking types is that the prescription "Have trust" is both obvious and ineffable; therefore, the inclination is to say, "Of course trust has to exist, but that's all you can say about it." It may be that Paul's trio and its meaning constitute an enemy of the systems approach, terribly important but impossible to conceptualize.

The other treasure might be called "Augustine's muddle." If we accept the system's assumption that a Supreme Being exists, then we have the conceptual problem of describing (modeling) His relationship to the rest of reality. Two plausible hypotheses come to mind. The Augustinian hypothesis (in systems language) is that God is the designer of the real system, as well as its decision maker. We humans belong to the client class. But if an omnipotent and benevolent God is the designer *and* decision maker, how could He design such a mess? ("How is evil possible?" was Augustine's way of putting it. Ours would be "How is it possible that the measure of performance of the system be less than optimal?") The other hypothesis, the one chosen by Spinoza, is to say that God *is* the whole system: He is the most general system. The same problem remains, however: if God is omnipotent and benevolent, how can system performance be less than maximum? Spinoza's answer is like Augustine's: it is at its maximum, but we finite humans don't understand enough to see why this is so.

Of course, in one sense it is difficult to see how any systems approach can avoid the theological question of the existence of a God and our human relation to Him/Her/It. But in these times a common response is that God either does not exist or is an irrelevant concept for the systems approach. Once this rarely defended assumption has been made, theology can take its

° Romans, 5 and 12, Corinthians, 13.

place as just one more speculation of curious humans. We humans, according to this version of theology, must "go it alone," without expectation of God's help or hindrance.

For us today it was Descartes who posed the question most clearly, because he did not "confuse" the issue by relating it to Christ and the soul. His *Discourse on Method* and his *Meditations* are an exploration in the thinking process with the one most marvelous idea—namely, that the search for the understanding of the systems approach consists of a search for those propositions that lie beyond doubt. All young philosophers owe it to themselves to share this idea at the beginning of their intellectual lives. That the young philosopher as he matures gives up the idea by no means denies its greatness, any more than one can deny the greatness of empiricism which flourished on the other side of the English Channel with *its* most marvelous notion—namely, that the systems approach should begin with a set of unassailable observations about the natural world and about ourselves. Without rationalism and empiricism the tradition of the systems approach would never have moved through the essential part of its life, the search for its origin, either in reason or in observation. And without the vitality of that search for origins the later developments of the systems approach beginning with Kant could surely never have taken place.

In his quest for the indubitable propositions Descartes recognized the importance of the theological issue. He and his contemporaries realized that the heroes of the systems approach are always in need of a guarantor who assures that their adventure will come out successfully no matter how many erroneous pathways are selected. The guarantor that Descartes and Leibnitz selected was a being perfect in all respects. The specific answer they chose for the guarantor of the hero's journey is in some sense irrelevant compared with the broad question they raised.

For example, when we are honest, we admit that any example of the system approach is an "approximation" to a more fully developed analysis. Such a claim assumes that better approximations will exist; the Cartesian question is, simply, How do we know? What guarantees this chain of approximations? But more to the point, the systems approach assumes that reason and observation are the best guides to the betterment of society. When Descartes was considering grounds for doubting 2 plus 2 equals 4, he wondered whether a perverse God could be having a hilarious time watching us believe so strongly what isn't so. This may seem quaint, but try the same thing another way. We systems people are convinced that intelligence, reflection, reason, and observation are the highest expressions of living beings, even in the face of nuclear explosion, nuclear poisoning, pollution, slaughter by traffic, wars, and so on, all of them inventions of our intelligence. The Cartesian question is whether intelligence isn't the gift of a sardonic Creator.

I don't know why today's system thinkers have so sharply cut themselves off from this great systems approach tradition of humanity in search of its God. Part of the reason may be the politics of the disciplines, because the search is antidisciplinarian. And indeed one can detect an implicit theology in today's systems thinking which neatly takes care of Augustine's muddle while simultaneously introducing one of its own. Suppose one were to define "god" as the best systems design we humans can create at any period of time (we can safely drop the capitals in this account). Then "god exists" is just the same assumption we make when we say that there exists a set of values of the decision variables which optimizes. Such a god, furthermore, is not perfect, since at any period in our history we are incapable of finding a perfect design (to say the least). And god is not static; if we are hopeful, we can say that he learns or evolves, and that later on in his life he'll know a lot more than he does now. We can say all these things: our muddle is to find the evidence for such a grand anthropological theory. The problem is just another form of the guarantor problem: what is there about the human species which guarantees that its god learns? This is the question to be gleaned from seventeenth and eighteeenth century rationalism and empiricism: Does mankind have a destiny, and if so, what is its nature?

The Kantian Synthesis

Kant was the great synthesizer who set the stage for the methodology we use today in the systems approach, which has its foundation neither in observation alone nor in reason alone, but in some kind of complex inquiring system built out of the connections between these two sources.

One important contribution to the systems approach that Kant made in his *Critique of Pure Reason* is the notion that the way the world appears to our observation depends very much on our basic theory about the structure of the world. It seems to me to matter little that Kant himself was unable to supply us with the final answer about the theory of reality. The point he makes in the *Critique of Pure Reason* is the one that needs making over and over again today—namely, that in order to do our job as systems approachers, we must construct a theory of reality which will then guide us in the observations we make, which in turn will guide us in the revision of our theory of reality. Surprisingly, Kant's very elementary point that he makes in the *Critique of Pure Reason* is frequently ignored in the current writings on the systems approach. Many planners and operations researchers act as though there are data banks that need to be "plugged into" a model of a system. What they don't understand is the point Kant was so clearly trying to make—namely, that both modeling and observation are themselves based on a much more fundamental Weltanschauung (or "world view") of the system.°

After Kant—Systems Versus Models

Strangely enough, I have to go back to the eighteenth century to pick up the main threads of the systems approach tradition today, as I conceive it. The reason for this lies in my perception of how the majority of so-called systems builders misconceived their task in the nineteenth and especially the twentieth century. I am talking not about the great visionaries like Marx and Schopenhauer, but rather about those who believed that the road to comprehensiveness is through greater and greater precision. The phrase we have come to use for this approach is "model building." The vast majority of those who call themselves "systems analysts," "operations researchers," or "management scientists," regard model building to be necessary, and often sufficient, for a systems approach, whereas I believe, following the theme of its tradition throughout the centuries, that model building is neither necessary nor sufficient, at least in the sense in which it is used today, where optimization techniques are central in the method of model building.

Of course, the idea of reaching comprehensive understanding through precision goes way back; Euclid's *Elements* is an example in geometry. But I am interested here in the use of precision in making decisions. Although even this approach goes back at least to the early accountants in the Renaissance, as far as I know the use of "precision," meaning fairly sophisticated mathematics (e.g., at the level of the calculus) began with Cournot's work on the economics of the firm in the 1830s. For example, if one assumes that a firm's costs are linear in the number of items it produces, and that the demand for

---

° In other words, in tracing the tradition of the systems approach, up to the present, I must describe an aberration, which, though important, is not central. I return to the central theme in the next chapters.

items is linear (with a negative coefficient) in the price it asks in the market, then one can use the differential calculus to deduce the "optimal" price—that is, the price that maximizes profit. Although this simple model is not enough for understanding the system called a "firm," certainly many of Cournot's followers believed that generalizations of his model *was* the way to go to attain comprehension of how a firm should operate.

Indeed, it is remarkable how intuition and common sense cooperate to convince the mind that success in being precise about one sector of reality implies that one is becoming more precise about the reality of the whole system, and that the first steps are "approximations" to the whole system.

Consider, for example, probability theory as we know it today. Does it provide an accurate and precise account of how a manager should weigh the uncertainties associated with his decisions? Erlang,° around 1910, thought it could, at least in one sector of decision making.

Erlang's work dealt with the central office of a telephone company. He assumed that since a client does not make a call on a schedule (as would be the case, for example, in a doctor's office), the total behavior of all clients could be described as "calls at random." From this he was able to deduce such properties of the system as the average waiting time of customers, length of waiting line, average idle time of an operator, etc., given that there are one, two . . . ,n operators in the central station. Note that Erlang's "model" was highly selective; it did not describe the frustrations of waiting customers, the irritations of the operators, or the joys of two parted lovers meeting over the wires. Nor did it really say anything about how long customers should have to wait, or operators be idle waiting for calls. But the intuitive assumption was that all these factors, once measured and if relevant, could be included in a broader model.

The same remarks can be made about the inventory model developed around 1915, which attempted to guide the manager of inventories by estimating the "optimal" amount to be ordered, given demand. This model made "approximating" assumptions about demand over time very simple, so that the use of some elementary calculus enabled one to compute the "economic order quantity" (EOQ).

Almost totally ignored in the literature was the question of appropriate "data" of these simple inventory models.† To use the model, one must gather three kinds of "data": the cost of holding inventory, the cost of ordering, and the demand on inventory as a function of time. I've put quotes around the

° See E. Brockmeyer, et al., *The Life and Work of A. K. Erlang* (Copenhagen: Copenhagen Telephone Company, 1948).
† This point is also discussed on pp. 17–18.

word "data," because etymologically it is derived from "things which are given." But none of the required data for the models is "given." Nowhere is the cost of holding inventory to be found in the accountant's books, and for good reason. The conceptual basis of this cost is the idea that a dollar tied in inventory earns nothing, and that if it were released, it could earn, say 12 percent per annum. The "cost" is therefore the lost opportunity of using the dollar for gain. To estimate this cost, one should determine, not what the manager would do with the extra dollar, but what he *should* do—that is, what his optimal use of financial resources should be. But accountants tend to seek historical cost data, not optimal managerial cost data.

A similar theme can be built around demand "data." Here it is tempting to look into historical records, because the student has been drilled in constructing probability distributions from historical frequencies. But the correct demand "data" are to be inferred from a theory of "optimal" demand, assuming that the manager can partially control demand—for example, in the open market by pricing.

Now we can understand why the intuitive, commonsense belief that precision about the description of a sector leads to precision about the larger system, may be wrong—indeed, seriously wrong. In applying Erlang's model (the so-called waiting line model), one uses historical data about how customers make their calls over time. But suppose the company management can influence the behavior of their customers, as, in fact, later telephone companies did by lowering the rates for calls after 6 P.M. Then we ought not to use historical data, no matter how carefully we have fitted them to a probability distribution curve; and the use of probability theory would not be an "approximation" to the real uncertainties of the manager. The same remarks apply to the data being used in the large-scale models mentioned above: the implicit assumption of many energy models is that the way energy was produced and consumed in a geographical region in the past is the correct way.

The systemic implication of the inventory models is that one cannot adequately determine inventory policy without determining financial and marketing policies; these latter policies will also require personnel, investment, and political policies for the firm. Thus, all so-called subsystems, like inventory or service units, are really not "sub" at all and are strongly nonseparable from the whole system.

Another, and perhaps more dramatic, way of putting this conclusion is to say that a necessary condition for solving the inventory or the waiting line problem is that one solve the firm's overall problem: if you really know how to control inventory and service, you know how to run the firm. The point is that in some general sense it does not matter where we begin in our search for ways of improving the human condition, because every specific problem unfolds into the general problem. Thus, reflection on managerial models shows why Anaxagoras' theme must hold: in every problem—considered reflectively—is to be found all other problems. Indeed, if a problem does not unfold in this manner, then one can expect to find that reflection has been "cut off at the pass."

Finally—and also neglected—is the point that any "cost saving" for an organization generates a benefit-cost "trace," much as any environmental change creates a physical or biological trace. If the cost saving is based on having fewer orders, then perhaps this means fewer clerks to handle the paper work—that is, job losses for people. If it is based on requiring less space to store inventory, then the renter of space may suffer a loss.

The Flight from Human Values

These examples are all based on human values, of course, and they have been largely ignored because of this century's strenuous effort to keep the deeper problems of values out of social system design.

To see how this can happen, consider the Shewhart° and the Neyman-Pearson approaches to statistics in the 1920s and 1930s. Before Shewhart, the typical way of controlling a manufacturing process was to set "engineering tolerances" on certain critical dimensions of the product (e.g., weight, thickness, hardness, etc.). If the product's dimension went outside these tolerances, the machine would be shut down and adjusted. This was a "feedback" system, but not a very adequate one, because there was no guarantee that the tolerance limits were not set too narrowly (so that adjustments were being made when the machine was still behaving normally) or too broadly (so that the machine was deteriorating significantly long before it was adjusted). Shewhart showed how to design an adequate feedback system, which he called "statistical quality control" (SQC). Essentially the design assumes that items from a machine are tested at random, and that therefore, according to statistical theory, the averages of samples of five will

°Walter A. Shewhart, *Economic Control of Quality of Manufactured Products* (New York: D. Van Nostrand, 1931).

be distributed, approximately, in a normal distribution; the standard deviation of the sample averages can then be estimated and used to determine whether there are "significant" changes in the machine's outputs. The term "cybernetics," first introduced by Wiener in the late 1940s, is fully applicable to Shewhart's scheme. Shewhart recognized that the designer of his SQC system had to balance two risks: the risk of adjusting a machine that is still operating correctly, and the risk of not adjusting a defective machine. Actually the determination of the correct balance is a value problem, based on the economics of the firm and, to some extent, on the welfare of the customers.

The welfare of the customers becomes critical as we pass from the process inspection of SQC to final inspection. Yet, on the whole, the cadre of experts who designed SQC and final-inspection procedures during the 1930s and 1940s cleverly avoided the value question, either by an arbitrary decision based on "how others do it" or by passing the burden onto the manager. The arbitrary and customary decision was to set the "bands" of the SQC chart at plus or minus two standard deviations, which, in effect, set the probability of trying to adjust a good machine at .05. As we shall see, the sanctity of the magic number .05 was (still is!) pervasive.

The other tactic, putting the onus of the value judgment on the manager, often led to hilarious scenes between the SQC designer and the production manager. A typical SQC manual told the budding inspection designer to ask the manager, presumably in as polite a manner as possible, what he considered to be an acceptable probability of shipping out a "bad" lot (e.g., a lot with 1 percent defectives). Of course, the typical production manager, somewhat red in the face, would begin shouting that his plant never shipped out defective materials. The statistician would politely but doggedly point out that there was always some risk of issuing defective material, and that this did not detract from the manager's capability. Neither of the parties ever got to the point of asking what the question really meant.

It was incredible to me how often the arbitrary method was used without reflection. Thus, the final-inspection custom was to test a sample of one hundred and if all were OK, to accept the lot; if one defective was found, to test two hundred, and if all were OK, to accept the lot; otherwise, reject. During World War II, I found that this arbitrary procedure was being applied to testing small arms ammunition. A little elementary calculation showed me that a lot with 1 percent misfires could easily be accepted (about a one-third chance). But 1 percent misfires in the field would have been disastrous. It took only three years to persuade Army Ordnance to change the method. Luckily the manufacturers were making excellent ammunition; the point is that final inspection was no control at all on quality.

A similar attempt to avoid value (ethical) issues occurred in the 1930s in connection with scientific research. In the early 1930s Neyman and Pearson developed a theory of testing hypotheses that was based on the idea of the (statistical) "power" of a test. Again, as in inspection, it was essential to recognize that there were two risks of error—of rejecting a true hypothesis or accepting a false one. The basis of their theory was to find a test that, for a given probability of the first error, would somehow minimize the probability of the second. There were many technical difficulties with their theory, but the practical difficulty was how to select the probability of the first error. Again, the arbitrary answer was almost universally accepted, as countless hypothesis testers among students of all sorts of disciplines used the sacred .05, often not knowing—or caring—why. I know of one psychology department whose faculty decreed that unless the Ph.D. student rejected some hypothesis at the ".05 level," his thesis could not be accepted. Sometimes the eager student would almost go into ecstasy as he declared, rather meaninglessly, "not only is the hypothesis rejected at the .05 level, but also at the .001 level!" Since the vast majority of hypotheses did not matter one whit to humanity, the riskless "risks" probably should have been set arbitrarily.

It was, of course, tempting to regard the methods of inspection and hypothesis testing as generalizable into a theory of how all decisions under risk should eventually be treated. If a manager is faced with the question of whether or not to do x, isn't it obvious that he can make just two fundamental mistakes—doing x when he shouldn't and not doing x when he should? And isn't his problem one of using the available evidence, or collecting new evidence in such a manner that he balances the probabilities of the two risks appropriately? As I've tried to show, the generalization requires some ethical justification of what "appropriately" means. But there is also the question whether "x or not-x?" is the correct question for the manager to address. He may, in fact, be testing the wrong hypothesis. If so, his use of probability theory is not even "approximately" correct.

I'd like to end this discussion of attempts to reach comprehension through precision by one more example—mathematical programming. It has always been part of the common sense of the economist to regard management as the disposition of resources for some economic objective, usually cost minimization or profit maximization. In mathematical terms, then, the manager is engaged in minimizing or maximizing some function—subject, of course to economic, physical, legal, and perhaps moral constraints. The function the manger is dealing with is called the "objective function." The variables in the function are the resources at the manager's disposal: manpower hours for a set of jobs, investments, etc. Thus, the task of being comprehensive about the management of our human affairs through precision is to express the objective function in mathematical terms, as well as the constraints, and then, using the classical methods of minimization (or maximization) of a function subject to constraints, to "solve" the manager's problem, at least approximately.

But the same data problems already discussed apply equally to mathematical programming. There is a helpful connection between the data that describe the constraints and the data that provide the coefficients in the objective function, so that one can often check whether a constraint, like a budget figure, has been properly set; but this method works only if the coefficients in the objective function, as well as the variable that should be maximized, are reliable.

All this has not prevented many planners from visualizing the whole world of decision making through the imagery of mathematical programming. A friend of mine, one of the most renowned figures in this area, and I had been attending a meeting on energy, in which the appropriate objective function for the United States energy system had been discussed at length. He said that in his experience it was always possible to get people with different viewpoints on this topic together in a room and generate a consensus that was "good enough." "But what if someone says that there is no appropriate objective function?" I asked. He literally could not hear my question. Mathematical programming had become for him a political ideology (see p. 157).

Of course, when a sector of Operations Research (OR) turned academic during the 1950s, it was natural for a certain class of model builders to avoid the problem of reality (as well as ethics) altogether. (For more or less political reasons an equivalent label, "management science," was also introduced, and the field is often labeled "OR-MS.") Academics like to be able to judge the quality of a piece of research. The trouble with most practical OR studies is that they are messy, in the sense that plausible criticisms can always be made. As I've tried to show, even a nice "clean" inventory study may leave out the most important considerations. But when someone offers a new model, it is not so difficult to determine whether it is new, whether he properly derived the result he claims, or even whether the result is "trivial."

I'm not saying that all academics agreed on standards of quality in model building; indeed, some of my friends became lifelong enemies over issues that did not strike me as earthshaking. But, on the whole, model building was far easier to judge than was its practical application, as I found as editor of one of the first journals in the OR-MS field. I could never get my referees to agree on an applied study; their typical comment was, "This paper has nothing new to offer," because the fact that someone had been able to persuade an organization to do the study—and possibly implement its results—was not "new." Furthermore, the majority of "application" articles ended with a presentation of the model; even the authors could not say whether the study mattered to anyone except themselves as they climbed the academic ladder.

Much of the model building in this period (the late 50s and the 60s) was based on the designer's imagination. For example, extensions of Erlang's work were many, as one can easily understand once he imagines all the events that can happen in a service organization: balking customers, fighting customers, stalled cars, sick servers, irritable servers, etc., etc.

As another example of the free play of imagination, one article of research-and-development modeling began: "We assume that the costs of an R-and-D project are linear in time." It's the fact that the costs are *not* linear in time that creates the headaches of R-and-D managers!

In many cases the game was to create new computational techniques, as the growth of model building was matched by the growth of computers. The computer also was a playground for large-scale "simulations," in which one got it to act out in a matter in minutes a possible fifty-year future of a segment of human society. The enthusiasts also had a heyday with such things as risk analysis, multidimensional utility models, game-theoretic situations, and the like. Imagination had rich materials to mold in ever more complex patterns.

I want to close this personal review of recent history by asking what a "realistic model" of management should be in the systems approach. I've found it annoying how often textbooks in OR-MS° repeat the "definition" that a model is a "representation of reality," without further explanation. What exactly does it take to design something as a representation of reality? A good beginning point may be photography—say, the pictures the satellite sends back these days in infrared. What does it take to say that such a photograph is a "representation of reality"? The requirements are quite strong and difficult:

There must be two images, the picture and the image of reality.

Each image must have identifiable space-time properties.

There must be an interpreter who comprehends the properties of both images (e.g., a red, a yellow, or a blue blotch on the photograph, and alfalfa, grass, or rocks in a field on the earth, described by numerical data).

The interpreter needs rules that tell him the one-to-one correspondence between the individuated items of the photograph and the field data.

° Other labels appeared in this period; "systems science," "systems analysis," "systems design," "general systems theory" are examples, each label having its own motivation. The last, for example, was Bertalanffy and Boulding's label for a general theory of systems, *not* a theory of general systems as this book is.

To determine whether the photograph is a representation of the field data, the interpreter needs to know which correspondences are important (e.g., for what purposes).

I've used infrared satellite photographs, because with ordinary photographs we are quite unaware of our own interpretative function; but in the case of infrared, the need for interpretation is obvious because so much of the photograph is meaningless to an untrained eye.

Now, suppose we consider a linear program "model" of an organization. Presumably the mathematical model is analogous to the photograph. The interpreter is the model designer. The field data are analogous to a description of the organization. But therein lies the rub. Where is the authority for a proffered description of the organization? Indeed, if the description is accurate, why do we need a model? Well, let's say that the description is "static," whereas the model enables us to change variables to see what would happen if certain new policies were created. Out of the frying pan! If the model does this, is it a "representation of reality," especially since now the reality (the static description of the organization) no longer exists?

Perhaps we used the wrong analogy, because a photograph doesn't "move." Let's try a planetarium instead. Now the planets, suns, galaxies change in various ways, and, assuming the planetarium is well designed, there will be a one-to-one correspondence over time between a planet, say, and a speck of light on the space-time frame of the planetarium's ceiling.

But here again the analogy won't do. The astronomer makes no plans for the heavenly bodies; these are God's design. But the model builder wishes to construct a model that tells him what the social world of humans would be like if it were changed thus and so. The "would be" is not a description; no set of data is there for the interpreter to examine for correspondences. The model, for the purposes for which it was built, is not a "representation of reality," for the reality may never be, most probably will not be.

Still the myth persists. One can easily understand why it does, because "sense of reality" is one thing that common sense offers us so strongly: we tend to suppose that reality is offered to us directly, without reflection.

This book is as much about reality as it is about any other topic. The reality that interests me is the reality of the planner. We can see the strong role that the concept of reality played in the history of the systems approach. To employ the *I Ching*, one needs to know what situation really holds and what it will really change into. The doctrine of the *Gita* is entirely a doctrine of the nature of reality, and it is *not* a commonsense doctrine, at least not to Western minds. The pre-Socratics believed that if we could grasp the nature of reality, we'd understand ourselves and our destiny. And so on.

In the succeeding chapters, we'll be searching for a meaning of reality deep enough to justify the systems approach. Models will play a role in this search, but not as representations of reality, but rather as methods of trying to measure reality, to approximate it. The chaper on ethics deals with the attempt of the systems approach to understand the reality of human values. Finally, we must face the reality that the enemies offer: what's really happening in the human world is politics, or morality, or religion, or aesthetics. This confrontation with reality is totally different from the rational approach, because the reality of the enemies cannot be conceptualized, approximated, or measured. At least this is the reasonable claim of the enemies. For them it is absurd to say that any model is a representation of *their* reality.

CHAPTER III

Logic: General

THE TERM "logic" calls—indeed, shouts—for definition. In this book I follow Kant's concept of logic as the basic justification for what we take to be true or false. Thus, there is an ethical dimension to logic. We are not so much interested in the ways in which people do accept, or have accepted, statements as true or false; rather, we assume that some of these ways can be "justified," and some cannot. Since none of us knows whether any specified statement is true or false with unshakable certainty, the justification itself is never certain. It is, at any given state in the human learning process, the best that we know how to do. If your regressive mind now recognizes that we also never know what is "best," you're on the right track because you'll see the need for a lot more reflection.

This reflection is done here in two parts. This chapter provides a broad perspective of the logic of the systems approach, primarily for those who are interested less in the detailed structure than they are in the general idea. The next chapter is meant to be a contribution to the underlying methodology of the systems approach; it uses Kant's *Critique of Pure Reason* as a model to guide in the construction of the logic.

In this chapter I'll concentrate on the meaning of "logic" inherent in the concept of comprehensiveness, which is based on the assumption that the facts of nature are in reality tied together in a well-knit whole, and hence that the logic of nature's existence consists of dealing with the whole in terms of various ways of knitting together the facts. The word "explanatory" is helpful here. We see that the events we observe are all in need of "explanation," which is essentially a searching for the reasons why things happen the way they do in the natural world. The "why" is then explained by what can be called the "fact net" of nature's world. If I wonder why heavy bodies fall when released, this is explained by the "fact" of gravitation. If I wonder why the fact of gravitation holds, this is explained by a general theory of the motion of masses. If I wonder why we live in a world where such a theory holds, I may then search for some more ultimate explanation. One should be careful with the words "more ultimate," which seem to imply that eventually we come to *the* ultimate, the deepest untouchable truths. But science in the last few centuries has learned that the explanatory whole of nature's facts is really more adequately viewed as a vast circle or a spiral lattice network in which it is not possible to identify "the basic facts" of nature. It is tempting to use "consistency," as well as "comprehensiveness" in describing the logic underlying the systems approach, but the word "consistent" as currently used fails to capture the intended richness. Normally we say that someone is inconsistent if, for example, he declares x to be true and then later in the same context says that x is false. One might feel that inconsistency from the point of view of the logic of nature is intolerable, and in some sense this is true. But actually inconsistency of the rigorous sort just mentioned is as difficult to identify as a pure chemical in a bed of rocks. There are so many ways in which one can "explain" apparent inconsistencies in nature's fact net that one hardly captures the sense of its logic by simply saying that nature is above all consistent.

For example, ancient astronomers first said that the planets sweep around the earth in large smooth circles. But astronomers observed that the planet Mars seemed to sweep along happily enough on its circle but then stopped and went the other way for a while, and then changed its mind and went back to its circle. Thus, if we put this fact of nature together with the astronomers' alleged fact, it looks like a contradiction. Not at all. What we need to do is think of the planets as still sweeping around but in circles that are themselves attached to a larger circle. The apparent inconsistency is removed by simply enriching the imagery. Science of course has played this game over and over again in its history. Again and again it has been possible to account for the apparent inconsistencies of nature in a richer network of explanation.

Accepting for the moment that the meaning of logic is roughly displayed by the idea of an explanatory fact net, let's turn back to the traditional systems approach as described in Chapter II. In many systems approaches of the past the ultimate logic lay in the mind of an all-powerful God whose grand scheme of things flows according to His grand design. The logic of the systems approach in such cases requires that somehow we should get in touch with God, either through revelation, meditation, or some intellectual understanding of His properties. This solution to the systems approach's logic is extremely appealing, because by one grand "fact" it explains the nature of the "whole system."

Today, however, the vast majority of those who are interested in the systems approach to human problems have elected to drop the notion of an all-powerful being in whom the grand scheme takes place, and instead to adopt the "scientific" attitude which was developed most specifically in the West from the seventeenth century down to the present. This attitude is based in large part on the classical writings of men like Galileo, who in his *Dialogues* sets forth the basic logic of the "scientific laboratory," an idea that was given its philosophical justification by many subsequent writers.

In effect, the scientific laboratory replaces God's design in the logic of inquiry; the answers to questions about nature are to be found, not by listening to the revelations of a divine will, but by methodically testing various hypotheses, in order to arrive at approximately correct responses. Of course, one could say that God speaks to us through the medium of the scientific laboratory, but such a saying leaves out the spirit and awesomeness of an all-powerful godhead.

What is the classical scientific laboratory? In many science texts the classical laboratory is misrepresented, because the authors assert that the scientist in the laboratory "starts" with facts and only carefully generalizes from the facts to theories, and that if a single fact contradicts a hypothesis or theory, he must abandon the hypothesis or theory.

Here is a more accurate account. Let us assume that a scientist is interested in whether a certain sentence does or does not accurately describe a fact of nature—for example, whether the pressure of a gas rises as the temperature of the gas is increased. He brings his problem to the classical laboratory, which is designed as a system that essentially keeps out of his investigation all the nuisance variables that would cloud the issue. In other words, to the extent possible, he wishes to find himself in an environment where he can vary the temperature of the gas and can ideally be concerned only with the variation in pressure. If he suspects that in the environment which may be influencing the pressure, there are other variables, then he has to find what these variables are and either take them into account or eliminate them from his laboratory.

This is the essential idea behind "controls" in the classical laboratory. The environment of the laboratory is often described as a "sufficiently closed system," meaning that the only variables of importance are the ones that are being observed by the scientist. It is only under the assumption that he is in a sufficiently enclosed environment that the scientist can begin to vary the variables under his control and to "test" whether the experimental variables like pressure are changing in the way in which his hypothesis indicates they should.

In this very brief description of the classical laboratory several things are important to note with respect to our discussion of the systems approach. First of all, one could argue that the origin of the hypothesis that interests the scientist is really a matter of indifference as far as its test is concerned. In systems language one might try to say that the origin of the hypothesis is "separable" from the test of the hypothesis. Of course the interest that the scientific community may have in a hypothesis is of critical importance. But it does not matter who proposes the hypothesis so long as it is proposed in such a way that it can be tested within a classical laboratory. The second thing to note is that the observer in the classical laboratory is not part of the experiment, or ideally he should not be. Now of course the observer may get involved in the experiment, because his anxiety to have his results come out the way he wants them to may make him see things in the wrong way or "forget" certain observations that seem counter to his pet theory. But the ideal of the classical laboratory is that the observer is apart from that which is being observed. We say in this regard that the observer needs to take an "objective" attitude with respect to his experiment.

Finally, we should note the basic metaphysical assumption of the classical laboratory—namely, that nature is neither capricious nor secretive. If nature were capricious, she would tell one observer one thing and another observer a quite different thing. Of course any observer may try to repeat the experiment that another has run, and he may arrive at radically different observations. This happens quite frequently, as the history of parapsychology shows. This is why one so-called counterfact does *not* imply the rejection of a general theory. But the metaphysical assumption says that the fault lies, not in the capriciousness of nature, but in human deception, and that eventually the process of checking experimental results will eliminate the deception. Also, nature is not secretive, in the sense that she will not forever hide certain aspects of her being. Galileo captured the idea in his often quoted statement regarding the purpose of the classical laboratory: "to measure or to make measurable that which has hitherto been not measurable."

These two metaphysical assumptions of the classical laboratory constitute its basic theory of comprehensiveness: all aspects of the fact net can eventually be identified, even though the process may appear to be incredibly slow. I should also note that this principle is the basis for the nonsecrecy of nature, for if nature permitted some secret (inexplicable) force to operate—for example, extrasensory perception—then the whole business of the classical laboratory collapses, for it could never state its theories without also stating the intolerably vague phrase: "so long as no secret force is operating."

I should also mention briefly that in areas of inquiry like astronomy, geology, or archeology, there appears to be no "laboratory" as such, except what nature supplies, and in particular no feasible way of manipulating variables. Hence, in a more general description of the method we would have to discuss the design of a study from which the ability to manipulate variables is dropped. But we would find the same set of careful controls, in which nuisance variables and observer interference were eliminated.

Let's suppose for a minute in a mood of fantasy that we were to imagine how this description of the classical laboratory might be applied to a matter of environmental importance—for example, to smog control. We wish to find out whether a law requiring a certain smog control device on an automobile will result in a significant decline in smog in congested areas. In other words, we are to think of this experiment on smog control as very much like the pressure-temperature experiment. If we lower the temperature, we expect less pressure; and if we increase the amount of legislation for a particular smog control device, we can expect less smog. Note that in both cases the experimenter does not necessarily know how the result will turn out.° In the early experiments on pressure and temperature there were only weak a priori grounds for believing that pressure would rise with temperature; and in the case of smog control devices we have no ultimate reason for believing that just because a state legislature passes a law requiring smog control devices, consumers will use them or that their response will necessarily produce less smog.

The analogy then suggests that we create a classical laboratory to experiment on smog control ordinances—for example, that we take states where there are strong ordinances entailing severe penalties for individuals who fail to comply, and other states where the enforcement of the smog control laws is less, or states where it does not exist. We then observe in each one of these experimental states the measurable amounts of smog in congested areas. If the hypothesis is borne out, we will expect to find that in states with stronger enforcement there is less smog as a result of the ordinances, whereas in the states with less severe law enforcement or none at all, the smog will be correspondingly increased.

Fortunately or unfortunately, depending on how you look at the matter,

---

° In the history of experimental science there were notable occasions when the investigator did believe there were a priori grounds for accepting a hypothesis, perhaps the most notable being Galileo's rational arguments for uniform motion; the famous experiments with falling and rolling bodies were addenda to the basic argument.

this fantasy does not work in the real world. First of all, it is quite impossible for the experimenter to remove all the variables that might conceivably be affecting this experimental variable. In states where it is possible to get severe enforcement penalties through the legislature, one may expect that other smog control ordinances will also be enacted. Certainly the state itself is not going to wait patiently for three years, with no change in its smog ordinances, for the experimental results to come through. Even the very existence of strong law and order in such states may have some effect on the way people regard themselves as drivers of automobiles. The strong law and order idea might arise from a fairly conservative constituency. One may then expect that the explanation for reduced smog has been produced by a much more conservative attitude on the part of the public.

All this amounts to saying that the planning laboratory cannot be decoupled from the rest of society. In the classical laboratory the astronomer does not change the motions of planets or stars, nor does the chemist change the general structure of the world's chemistry. Indeed, the classical laboratory itself was regarded by the rest of society as isolated, mysteriously isolated, wherein, in the public's imagination, many an evil scientist could create dangerous monsters. But the planner's laboratory is not just concerned with testing one hypothesis; it is also going about the business of transportation, education, nutrition, and protection. If an analogy is needed, it's as though the administrators of a hospital ruled that the laboratory and the cooking facilities must be combined, and that the cooks were free to use any of the equipment and material as they saw fit.

For the most part this chapter argues against the use of the classical experiment in planning, on technical and logical grounds. But it is immensely important to point out that the argument can also be based on moral grounds. In order to understand this point, it is important once again to review the control aspect of the classical experiment. Its design of control is based on the postulate that the "dependent" variable(s) is a function of a set of variables which can be carefully controlled; these "independent" variables account for all the changes in the dependent variable, except for random fluctuations. If this postulate is not met by the design—for example, when an unexpected variable causes change—then the design is defective; and there are various ways of checking for the defectiveness of experimental designs.

Now in the last two decades we have become acutely aware that something has to be added to the conditions for designing experiments where human subjects are involved. Many experimenters have treated their human subjects in a thoroughly inhuman manner—for example, by administering electric shock or drugs, or by threatening their health permanently, or (in my case) by simply trying to deceive them, and many still do.° Though it is true that knowledge might be secured by these methods, there was a growing feeling that the methods were immoral, because they ignored the humanity of the subjects. In Kant's terms, they treated the subjects as "means only."

I'd like to introduce a term that helps describe the human quality of people: "ingenuity." Apparently, in the seventeenth century, English writers confused two adjectives, "ingenuous" and "ingenious," so that "ingenuity" reflected this confusion. "Ingenuous" meant free—for example, free of bondage of various sorts; it later came to mean naïve, but I'm retaining the original meaning. "Ingenious" meant, as it does today, clever or able to circumvent opposition. Now when an occasion provides people the opportunity to partake of ingenuity, and their right is denied by someone else for that person's own ends only, then suspicion of immorality is justified. When the carefully controlled classical experiment is applied to people in decision-making situations, the experimenters, but often not the subjects, wish to test a hypothesis; when the freedom to be ingenuous and ingenious is closed off for the sake of the experimenter's goals, then suspicion of immorality is justified.

There's a lot more to be said about this suspicion. What if the subjects agree or are bribed by high pay into agreeing? I'm not sure this escapes the moral issue, because it's questionable whether many subjects understand what they are agreeing to. There have been times when I thought we should generate a profession of experimental subjects who are trained to understand the experimenters' goals and their appropriate role in the experimental environment. Even so, would such professionals be "representative" of humans? They'd probably be more representative than today's subjects, who are often well-fed undergraduates or graduates in colleges. Perhaps the greatest service such a profession of subjects could perform would be to do their damnedest to use their ingenuity to ruin the experiment. Certainly such subjects would be more "representative" of humanity than the more docile ones.

I am, of course, aiming criticism at fields of study like education and even nutrition, where there is a high degree of enthusiasm for conducting experiments on children, teachers, and eaters. I wish to throw a big wet blanket over this enthusiasm. I don't think that most of the experiments prove anything, nor that they are dignified. They force Ph.D. candidates into long and tedious hours of sifting through incredible quantities of computer printout, in the hope that some hypothesis will be rejected at the ".05 level," when no one (not even the candidate) really cares any more.

Do I mean that investigation into education and nutrition is a waste of time? No. As the rest of this chapter and the next try to argue, there is another

° See pp. 95–96 for a description of these experiments.

method of inquiry for planning which does not use the strong control methods of the classical laboratory. A paradox still lurks, because this method calls for observing a lot of human behavior, and this too might fall under the suspicion of immorality; planners can't help looking like voyeurs on occasion.

Now let's return to the theme of the comprehensiveness of the classical laboratory. It was not comprehensive in one very important sense: it did not justify its own existence in the social order, or rather it justified that existence in a nonrational, political manner, by the slogan "truth for truth's sake." The question was never raised whether human society should sacrifice other opportunities—for example, feeding half a billion malnourished people—rather than support the classical laboratory.

Another vitally important point in connection with the planner's mode of inquiry is that the origin of the hypothesis is extremely important and perhaps the most important aspect of the whole picture. If the originator of the hypothesis is primarily interested in the measure of smog in the urban community along some specific scale—as he might be, for example, if he is an engineer—then one might have reason to expect that his experiment is useless, because he will only provide a measure of smog along some physical scale, whereas the main point about smog in congested areas is what it does to people, whether it makes them unhealthy or neurotic or even, on the other side, more careful, more mature, or whatever.

Finally, what about the objectivity of the observer? Is it possible to say that the observer is independent of the system he is observing? If the relevant facts about smog deal with ways in which people react to the air around them, then how is it possible to describe the observer himself as being independent of the situation?

The question of objectivity is the key issue in today's struggle to make better decisions about human society and its resources and environment. In the United States there has been a concerted effort to maintain the spirit of the classical laboratory in developing what are regarded as the essential so-called base-line data for such developments as nuclear plants, strip mining, dams, military test sights, etc. The instrument for creating such data is usually called an "environmental impact report" (EIR). A typical EIR will contain such data as expected soil erosion, change in temperature, flow and quality of surface water, air temperature changes, etc. These data that are taken to "describe" the present condition of the environment are called base-line data, a labeling that is best described as part of the advertising campaign of EIR writers, for how could a responsible decision maker ignore base-line data? It would be like an architect who failed to design the foundations of a building, wouldn't it?

Among the voices that complain about the EIRs is our hero-planner. He points out that the most important "impact" of any development is the way it affects people, their style of life, their neighborhood feelings, their perspectives. If one accepts the tradition of the *I Ching*, then in addition to numbers that describe the environment, one also needs an image or a set of images. How can a set of numbers tell us whether a dam or a strip mine has destroyed the radiance of an environment? My next-door neighbor, Pirkle Jones, is a photographer. He and Dorothea Lange learned of the decision to flood a small valley in California, "a valley eleven miles long, two and one half miles wide, warm, sunny, and quiet," which had never had a crop failure. It contained one town, with one store, a small hotel, and a roadside spot. "The valley held generations in its palm." The two photographers took beautiful shots of the valley and its people before the bulldozers came, when they came, and the flood aftermath. Their book *Death of a Valley*,° has no quantitative data, only a minimum of English, no arguments pro or con, but it is one of the best "environmental impact" statements I've seen.

But there is no doubt that Jones and Lange were biased; they took no pictures of people drinking water or getting jobs because of water. They make no mention of trade-offs. The advocates of the dam would describe their book as "bleeding hearts."

The trouble with trying to include "people impact" in EIRs is that people tend to be confusing, unpredictable in their opinions and perspectives, conflicting in their values—in other words, "ingenuous and ingenious." The trouble with people is that they tend to be human. At the end of their book the photographers summarize the story in two "Voices." One says, "Everyone said they'd never flood it. Even when they talked about it, we never believed they'd flood it." The other says, "This valley and this land was good to us, but the water over it will be good for the *majority* of the people. We *have* to think that way."

The choices for the hero-planner seem clear. One option is to maintain the spirit of the classical laboratory by collecting just those data that appear relevant and can be obtained objectively; this means that other competent observers would essentially agree with their findings, even though these data are not "basic" in terms of human lives. The other option, the harder one, is to recognize that the unpredictable human is an essential aspect, and to begin to invent a methodology in which human bias is a central aspect. Will this methodology be "scientific"? No, if we doggedly stick to the assumption that the classical laboratory *is* the basis of science. Yes, if "science" means the creation of relevant knowledge about the human condition.

° Pirkle Jones and Dorothea Lange, *Death of a Valley* (Millerton, New York: Aperture Publications, 1960).

Let's examine some of the broad aspects of the methodology of the second option. Essentially the methodology is based on a schema that can be modified—for example, by expansion—as the planner learns more about reality, and especially about the reality of the human being. The schema tries to depict the system in terms of decision makers who have a capability of changing certain things in the natural world. These changes effected by the decision makers are often called "means." The number of things that a decision maker can change is of course limited in terms of his resources, his own personality, the laws of the land, and all the rest.

When the decision maker makes a change, then certain things begin to happen in the natural world. Some of these happenings are essentially matters of indifference for most humans, but some of them may be extremely important. Thus, if the manager of a plant decides to adopt a new manufacturing procedure that will greatly reduce his costs, then humans as a whole may be rather indifferent about what his new plant will look like, but quite concerned about the price of the product, and very concerned if the new production method means further polluting of one of the main recreational rivers in the area.

The schema thus pictures the world of the decision maker as stages in time. First there is an action; at the next stage are the "outcomes" of the action, the things that have been changed as a result of the action. Among these may be some outcomes that the decision maker intended to occur—for example, a reduction in cost. We call these the decision maker's "ends." But there may also be unintended outcomes—for example, the pollution of a river. A specific decision maker may concentrate only on his goals; the planner needs also to concentrate on the whole set of outcomes, intended or not.

The next thing to notice about the decision makers and their actions is that the ends never end. That is to say, if the second stage shows that the decision maker's action does indeed pollute a river, and this is of great importance to humans, then the pollution itself leads in the third stage to such things as demonstrations against the company, or to competitors' polluting other streams, or to individuals' getting better jobs because the decision maker is able to manufacture more products, and so on.

Thus, the system of means and ends is always expanding as the planner examines the second and subsequent stages.

To fill out the schema we need to talk about the environmental constraints on the decision maker. These are conditions that also are extremely important with respect to the ends produced by the decision maker's choices. But they are conditions that the decision maker himself does not control. For example, the success of our decision maker who decides on a new manufacturing procedure certainly depends on consumer attitudes, on the laws of the land,

and even on the condition of the total economy. None of these may be even partially controlled by the decision maker, and yet they definitely influence what happens as a result of his choices: that is, they influence the ends and the further ends of his choices. In systems approach language we often refer to those factors that are outside of the decision maker's control and yet are highly important with respect to ends as "environmental constraints."

I have been describing the "decision maker" as though he/she were a recognizable unit—for example, a person. But in reality the decision maker is often incredibly complicated. And even if we succeed in approximately identifying the process, "we," the planners, have always the question whether the decision maker is the appropriate one—that is, whether the process of making decisions is working well.

This question takes us to another type of individual in the schema, the planner. The planner is analogous to the observer in the classical laboratory, but the analogy is limited. The classical observer did not ask the ethical question whether a hypothesis *should* be true—for example, whether nature is designed appropriately. He did ask whether he was observing and recording his observations appropriately, and in this sense he had to design an ethical code of honesty and reliability. But he did not ask whether the observations were ethically sound.

The planner, on the other hand, is essentially interested in just such a question, and he requires some place on which to stand in order to respond to it. The choice of such a place constitutes the varieties of planning and distinguishes the heroes from the nonheroes. A rather safe choice consists of saying that the planner is a servant to a specific decision maker who can be identified by the fact that he pays the planner for his services. If this choice is made, then the planner's task is to determine the intended ends of the decision maker over a time interval given by the decision maker, and to determine the course of action that "maximizes" either the chance of attaining the ends or, if the ends can be quantified, the "expected" or average value or some other agreed-upon value. Such a choice on the part of the planner can be called "problem solving," because, just as do exercises in a textbook, it tends to close down on the issues. In the next chapter I'll call this "goal planning."

A somewhat broader choice is to introduce some constraints on the so-called solution: it should be legal, it should not be blatantly immoral even if legal, it should not create irreversible physical or biological damage, and so on. This I'll call "objective-planning."

The broadest choice seems to be one in which the planner asks the general question—Who should be served by the social system, and in what way?

Those who should be served are called the appropriate "clients" and may (probably should) include future and past generations. Once this question has been raised, then the other two questions—who should decide and how? and, who should plan, and how?—follow inevitably. Now the "ends" are to be identified no longer in terms of the intentions of decision makers who pay, but rather in terms of a general ethic. When such broad questions are allowed as part of the design of the inquiry, then we say that the "inquiring system" becomes a "systems approach," and the planning is "ideal-planning."

Thus, the important feature of the systems approach is that it is committed to ascertaining not simply whether the decision maker's choices lead to his desired ends, but whether they lead to ends that are ethically defensible. Therefore, in the systems approach today it is extremely important to understand which values are ethical and which are not, a matter to be discussed in Chapter VI.

The ambitions of the systems approach are enormous, going far beyond the classical laboratory's ambition to measure and test hypotheses. In its struggle to design inquiry to approximate its ambition, the approach uses what might be called a "semiclosed system." With all of the hope and faith in the world, the systems approacher assumes that the system he is dealing with is not about to blow apart and is sufficiently closed so that he can begin to do some things and learn from what he has done.

Therefore, today in the 1970s the methodological words for the systems approach are "adaptation," "learning," "correction," and the like. The systems approachers have given up the notion that they are simply in the business of solving specific problems one after another This is far too dangerous an attitude for them to adopt, because there is absolutely nowhere within the context of a single problem to determine whether one has accomplished anything positive with respect to values. Even if I succeed, for example, in improving the inventory system of a medium-size company with respect to its products in the sense that I reduce the cost of the system, I have no real way of knowing whether the company might have made considerably more money by using for other purposes the funds they paid me. If they could have done so, then in some sense I haven't really "helped" the company at all, and my efforts to improve their inventory system have in fact been deleterious to them.

But there is the broader question whether the use of resources to improve the operations of a company is ethically justifiable. Thus, we must continuously think of ourselves as in a whole stream or process, constantly trying to become more and more comprehensive in our perspective.

One finds in the systems approach literature a number of labels that suggest the ongoing process of investigation: "dynamic programming," "industrial" or "world programming," "cybernetics" (a term introduced by Norbert Wiener, to reflect the fact that the systems approach is similar in kind to the steersman's problem in a boat, which is a constant reaction and readjustment in terms of new information). Russell Ackoff has suggested the concept of "interactive management"—essentially a management that is interested in "redesigning the future" rather than in waiting passively for the future to occur and only then trying to cope with it on a problem-solving basis.

When used properly, "program planning and budgeting" is another kind of dynamic adaptive system. The programs represent the kinds of aims the manager has, and the budgets represent the monthly or yearly constraints on his behavior. In a well-run program planning-and-budgeting system there should be constant re-evaluation of the allocation of resources.

Others have used the term "incrementalism" to express their concept of adaptive behavior, by which they mean it is essential that the system take only small steps where it can readily move, and that these steps can then be examined, and additional small steps made and so on.

Similarly, a number of writers have suggested a cadre of "social change agents," people who are capable of enabling managers to bring about certain desired changes. I myself have been suggesting the use of "dialetics" as a learning method, a method based on the idea that managers should be capable of looking at their systems in quite radically different ways rather than in one somewhat arbitrary and habitual manner. We expect that such managers will be better able to "learn from experience," by directing their observations and their decisions to those critical differences in plausible, but conflicting, world views of their systems.

I should hasten to add that the fact that an investigator describes his method by using one of these labels by no means implies that his is a "systems approach." Dynamic programming and cybernetics are often used in very narrow ways; change agents frequently see their business as solely one of bringing about a change some manager wants, and not as an ethical evaluation of the change; incrementalists are often scornful of those who try to obtain a broad or "holistic" viewpoint. I have introduced the labels in order to emphasize the techniques of "ongoing" inquiry as opposed to problem solving; ongoing inquiry is a necessary, but far from sufficient, condition for a systems approach.

The systems approach has not dropped the basic idea of "scientific" method, because it does not accept the classical laboratory as the only way of conducting "scientific" inquiry. The ideal of comprehensiveness of the systems approach inquiry is in effect exactly the same in intent as the classical approach to science, in which it was expected that the scientific effort could tie together in a meaningful way the various facts of nature. Just as the classical physicists saw no reason why their fact nets could not eventually encompass the entire universe, so today in the systems approach its adherents see no reason why all matters of human concern should not be tied together in one grand imagery of purposeful behavior. Consequently, says the systems approach, all our goals can be tied together in a meaningful schema, and we do not have to resort to mysticism or some deep inexplicable human essence in order to describe them adequately.

Note, too, that the scheme of the systems approach can be endlessly expanded from the many ramifications of a single life to the many ramifications of all our lives. In a very narrow circumstance you may be wondering which of two alternative products to buy—for example, which of two automobiles will best serve your purposes. In this instance your purposes are well defined in terms, let's say, of a convenient and cheap way of getting back and forth to work. If, on the other hand, we wonder why you commute to work in the way you do, then we can expand the imagery of your goal seeking to include not only the purchase of the automobile but your selection of a job; and if we wonder why you seek certain financial goals, then we can translate these objectives into the broader objectives of your manner of living in terms of recreation, home, gifts, etc. And if we want to, we can raise the question of your life in comparison with other lives, or of the meaningfulness of a middle class job holder's life in today's society, in which case we look not just to your own goals but to those of your community, or the state, or the nation or the world, the future world, and even the past world.

The point can be illustrated by a recent issue of the journal *Interfaces,*° in which an operations research project was certified to save a significant amount of an airline company's fuel costs. The questions of what other airline companies would do when they read this study, and what would be the consequences for the national economy, were not raised. This omission may have been appropriate, because it can certainly be argued that the "professional responsibilities" of operations research do not include a systems approach. But then OR must be viewed as a narrow approach to human affairs.

As we shall see, the enemies of the systems approach try to attack the expanding monster, because they perceive the danger of being swallowed by it. The politician will point out that the systems approach ignores the fact that

° D. Wayne Darnell and Carolyn Loflin, "National Airlines Fuel Management and Allocation Model," *Interfaces* (February, 1977).

humans conduct their affairs in a political arena. But if this is the politician's objection to the systems approach, he is in serious danger of being swallowed by it, simply because there is in principle no reason why the systems approacher shouldn't expand his imagery to include political objectives of the citizens in a community or nation. Political behavior, says the systems approach, must also be purposeful, and we can include its purposes into our scheme if that is appropriate.

In mythology the hero is often depicted in terms of his weapons and his armor. In this case we can see what a fantastic armor and weapon our hero has. If his enemy approaches him with his own weapons, then the hero can assume the shape of the enemy, so that in a short time the enemy sees himself fighting himself, and his defeat is imminent.

Could such a successful hero have any enemies in the long run? Doesn't he possess the capability of persuading all reasonable men to accept his grand scheme of human behavior that will guide us through scientific inquiry to ever better solutions of the problems that plague us? Is there any possible chink in the armor of such a hero?

The anwer to this question is familiar to anyone who engages in competitive sports. If you are really an astute competitor, you do not restrict your observations of your enemy to the tactics he can adopt to trick you into losing, for if you do so restrict yourself, then your enemy can cleverly pretend to adopt a tactic, absorb you into his pretense, and conquer you accordingly. Now the astute competitor tries to see how his opponent conceives of the entire game, and then acts accordingly. For example, in chess certain players like Petrosian essentially conceive the game as an extremely carefully woven set of plays in which the objective is not to lose and wait patiently for the opportunity, if it is to occur, to win. In their last match Bobby Fischer was successful against Petrosian because he took into account not only the tactics that Petrosian could use, but also Petrosian's whole idea of the game of chess, and developed his own strategy to surround Petrosian's concept; he tried to find a line of play that was, so to speak, beyond Petrosian's whole conception of the game.

But if this bit of common sense from competitive sports holds, then one can indeed see a chink in the armor of the systems approacher. From his perspective of the game of life is that, above all, it must be "rational" and the gateway to rationality is always the reasonable. If someone seriously and reasonably questions some aspect of the systems approach, then the systems approach must be ready to respond. For example, the earlier discussion of values assumed that all values must be somehow integrated. Why? Is the statement a mere tautology, following from the systems approacher's definition of values? If so, is his definition correct or arbitrary? If correct, why? If arbitrary, why should humanity have to accept it? These are all *reasonable* questions, demanding rational answers.

Thus, as we shall see, the enemies will all be asking reasonable questions. Isn't politics the way matters are really decided, and isn't the rational systems approach simply one political device, to be used when politically expedient? Or, isn't morality essentially inexpressible in terms of concepts and words, and doesn't this essentially ineffable quality of our lives lead us humans to decide the way we do? Or, isn't religious imagery really the basis of all our perspectives and concepts, including the perspective of the systems approach? And what is it that carries the values we humans cherish? It is not the ego or the mind, but, say, our basic aesthetic feeling, which cannot be conceptualized. And finally, and most generally, why is a rational, holistic approach desirable for the human species, especially since it so often gets out of hand, missing the vital essence of the specific and individual, the here and now, encompassing "everything" to the exclusion of every thing?

Reasonable, all too reasonable. Can we comprehend such questions, we systems approachers? Or, as Kant says, can we rather comprehend their incomprehensiveness? Is this the "best" we can do with our theory of comprehensiveness?

In order to understand such questions better, we must delve deeper into the meaning of the systems approach, and there is no better beginning than to ask further about the reality of "systems." Are systems "out there," or are they simply "in the minds" of systems planners? Could the answer be, "neither of the above"?

The question is reminiscent of another time in the history of philosophy, when Berkeley suggested that there is no "out there" reality.° A chair or the moon, he said, is a perception, and perceptions reside in the mind. He split philosophical speculation into two camps, the hard-nosed realists and the softer idealists or perceptionists.

It was Kant who suggested that the proper response was "neither of the above," which I take to be the most plausible response for the question of the reality of systems. In succinct terms, his answer to Berkeley was that a mind that has no way of conceptualizing an "other than mind," an "outside the mind," lacks the ability to understand its own perceptions. The system is "out there" because that's the only way we can understand the process of planning intelligibly.

This much, I hope, will entice you into the rather difficult pathways of the next chapter, where I'll be using Kant's *Critique of Pure Reason* as a guide.

° George Berkeley *Collected Works*, ed. by George Sampson (London: George Bell and Sons, 1897).

CHAPTER IV

Logic: A Theory of Reality, or Kant for Planners

A PLANNER needs to know what is really happening, in order to determine whether reality should be changed. How should he go about his task?

Now the question, "What is real?" (or What is really going on?) often seems to have the most obvious, commonsense answer, until we begin reflecting on its meaning. We recall from Chapter II the two answers that the history of thought provides: if you want to know what really exists, then use either (1) reason or (2) observation to find out. Classic geometry is a way of finding the realities of space through reason; geography is a way of finding the realities of the earth through observation. A rationalist like Descartes believes he can establish his own existence through reason ("I think; therefore I am.") An empiricist like Locke believes that we establish the existence of things in the world through our senses.

Reason and observations share an important characteristic. If I say that there exists no cube of a positive integer which is equal to the sum of two positive integer cubes, reason has no direct way of immediately justifying a "true" or a "false" for this assertion. But if I say that x plus 2 equals 4, we're getting "closer," so to speak, to a "direct" proof of x's existence—that is, a proof requiring no prior knowledge. Similarly, if I say that the number of hairs on this man's head is really 10,479, observation may have no direct justification method, but if I say that the color of this spot of fabric is really blue, we appear to be getting closer to a direct justification.

What makes reason and observation radically different is that if reason can establish some justifiable assertions, such as the postulates of Euclidean geometry, then a whole amazing series of other assertions can also be justified. Or, consider that most remarkable feat of Guiseppe Peano, who in 1900 showed how one could derive arithmetic, with all its profound mysteries, from the axiom of mathematical induction plus some additional but simple assumptions. Whereas if observation virtually justifies that this spot is (now) blue, nothing significant follows, not even that it will also be blue soon in the future. Reason invites fantastic trips; observation stays put. This is the difference that fascinated and worried Kant. Kant's rationalist contemporaries were convinced that they could "justify" whole sciences by reason—not only arithmetic, geometry, and kinematics but also theology and cosmology. The empiricists, on the other hand, were discovering how little could be justified by observation: Berkeley found no empirical justification for a "world out there," and Hume no justification for assertions about the future. To be sure, "observation" had discovered many remarkable things about the world of humans and nonhumans, but unless one makes the very reasonable (rational?) assumption that the future will be like the past, apparently one cannot justify even eminently reasonable forecasts.

But reason runs a different kind of risk, namely that its generalizations turn into (empty) tautologies. Thus a whole rationalist economic theory was generated by the concept of a rational (economic) man; the theory is valid because of the way in which it defined rationality and not because it describes the realities of the human being. As we have seen, the same comment applies to academic model building. One defines an objective function to be thus and so. Then what "should be done" follows from the definition and has nothing to do with reality.

Since I'm going to use Kant's first *Critique*° as a guide in the search for the planner's meaning of reality, it may help the reader if I begin with a description of its contents and how I shall relate them to the planner's reality.

1. In his "Introduction" Kant talks about tautologies. His main interest was in the validity of sentences that are not tautologies and yet are not validated by observation. I take this opportunity to ask, "What can a tautology tell the planner about reality?"
2. The first ideas of the *Critique* (in the beginning chapter) were actually developed by Kant in his "Inaugural Dissertation," which appeared eleven years earlier. In it

° Immanuel Kant, *Critique of Pure Reason*, 1781. Translated by Norman K. Smith (New York: Macmillan and Co., Ltd., 1929).

he parted company from Leibnitz by arguing that space and time are real, and yet our basic knowledge about them does not come from observation. They provide the form of our experiences. I take the opportunity to discuss the very strong role that space and time play in the planner's notions of reality.

3. The main body of the *Critique* begins in the next section, which introduces the basic categories through which we humans make experience intelligible and therefore real for us. I argue that the intelligible reality of the planner is similarly based on a set of categories (of purposeful experience).

4. The next section deals with consciousness, and in particular with the manner in which we hold an experience in one unified field of consciousness, which Kant takes to be the function of the ego. I discuss the collective consciousness of the planners, which I take to be unified through a plural ego, the "we" of the planner's community.

5. Since all experience is subsumed under the basic categories, a set of universal principles arises, which describe reality and yet are not validated by observation. The next section discusses these, as I do for planning: they form the basic postulates of every planning exercise.

6. In the final section with which I'll deal, Kant discusses the all too human tendency to take reason beyond its proper limits, as he thought many of his contemporaries did. In one part of his discussion he introduces the "dialectical" method, which I use as the basis of a fundamental difference in strategy among planners: those who use the concept of the feasible to limit the scope of reality of planning, and those who do not. The first I call "objective-planners," and the second "ideal-planners." I've placed the dialectics in a separate chapter.

Kant believed that if we can classify assertions about reality in a satisfactory manner, we may more easily be able to decide which can be justified as true or false, and which require prior knowledge for their justification. The sentence I've just written illustrates a point: it is a tautology—that is, its truth (or falsity) follows from the definitions of its terms. What does "in a satisfactory manner" mean? It means that the classification enables us to do the job of justification more easily. A cynic might be inclined to conclude that a tautology "says nothing," but this is far from true, as we shall see.

In Kant's case the tautology itself suggests a useful classification of assertions; those that are tautologies (he calls them "analytic") or are contradictions of tautologies, and those that are not (he calls them "synthetic"). Kant adds to this classification another one: those assertions that are justified (or refuted) by observation (he calls them "a posteriori"), and those that are justified by some method independent of experience ("a priori"). The result is a fourfold classification of assertions. (See Table 1, which contains examples of each of the four sentences.) For Kant the class of tautologies is itself evidently a priori, so that there are no assertions in the class of a posteriori tautologies. As we shall see, we planners have good reason to question this (implicit) assumption on Kant's part.

TABLE 1
Classification of Assertions

	Tautologies	Nontautologies
A priori	Straight lines are straight	Every event has a cause
A Posteriori	Too much smoking is bad for you	The earth has one moon

The class of a posteriori synthetic assertions poses no immediate problem, because its members are to be justified by observation; but the question of how observation does the job of justification is important for Kant. Specifically he wants to understand whether, as Locke suggested, some observation sentences require no prior knowledge for their justification; his response is in the negative: all such sentences require prior knowledge. It follows that some aspect of our knowledge of reality does not come from observation alone but is supplied a priori.

The remaining class of assertions are the a priori synthetic, such as "Tomorrow the sun will shine in such-and-such a place." This is clearly not a posteriori, since we cannot observe "tomorrow" (is *this* an a priori synthetic or a tautology?). Of some historical interest is Kant's argument that arithmetical assertions like 7 plus 5 equals 12 are synthetic a priori. A little over a century later, mathematicians and logicians like David Hilbert and Bertrand Russell thought they had established once and for all that mathematics is a (grand) tautology, and scientists were taught by their elders that mathematics is not a science.

Since Kant believed that the class of synthetic a priori assertions has some very important members, he defines his problem: How can we justify the truth or falsity of this class? This is not Kant's way of putting it; he asks, "How are synthetic a priori assertions possible?" But I am not translating the *Critique* from German to English, but rather translating its significance from Kant's epistemology of phenomenal science to the modern day epistemology of planning. Do planners have to be concerned about this question? The response seems clearly affirmative. The justification of any aspect of a plan is based on assertions such as the following: "If action x is adopted, then a consequence will happen with value y; if any other action were adopted, the consequence would have lower value than y." Such assertions seem to be a priori, because of the reasonable assumption that the future cannot be observed. Furthermore, what kinds of observation justify our saying that one consequence has less value than another? Therefore, I take it that Kant's (translated) question has basic relevance for the logic of the systems approach, and that we should proceed on our journey with him.

Something more needs to be said about tautologies. If I catch you smoking another cigarette, I may be moved to assert that too much smoking is bad for you. From a sematic point of view my assertion is a tautology, because "too much" is to be assessed in terms of the damage to you, and all I have said is that what is bad for you is bad for you. But from a *pragmatic* (planning) point of view my assertion may be important and, indeed, may become beneficial for your health. The planner's sense of meaning lies in consequences, so that the syntactical form of a sentence does not necessarily reveal the pragmatic meaning.

Of what pragmatic value are tautologies? Consider the following: "We cannot afford to do everything nor can we afford to lack boldness as we meet the future—so together—we must simply do our best."° We can't "do" everything, because the meaning of "do" (action) implies that some opportunities are forgone; hence by the definition of "afford" we can't afford to do what we can't do. By the definition of "must"—given two choices, one "better" than the other—we "must" choose the better, and hence, by definition, if we know the best, we "must" choose it. So much for syntax or semantics. But pragmatically the effect of such utterances may be to create a mood of agreement, in which each person feels allied with his fellow citizens, but each feels free to expand the meaning as he wishes. For those concerned about the country's defense, the expanded meaning is that we cannot afford to let our defenses down but must push ahead in the arms race. For those concerned about the deteriorating environment, we cannot afford further rape of natural ecosystems. And so on.

As I've already pointed out, the "political approach" to the management of human affairs is "making polis (or community)." One of the essential conditions for making polis is the creation of an image of sharing and a breakdown of the ego-desire drive. Hence the "So together" of Carter's address, a togetherness feeling fed by a tautology.

Not all tautologies will make polis; whether they do is a matter of trial and error for those who strive consciously to design polis. Hence, in this sense there is an important class of tautological statements that are justified in part by observation. The bottom left box in Table 1 may contain many assertions; a tautology may tell us something significant about the reality of a polis.

° President Carter's Inaugural Address, January 20, 1977.

Space and Time

The next section of Kant's *Critique*, the "Transcendental Aesthetic" says that all observation must be shaped by two (a priori) images, space and time. The implications for planning are very significant. For some social system design, space is the comprehensive imagery of reality; all planning is perceived as spatial design. This is true not only for many architects but also for many city planners, who imagine the plan of the city in terms of what activities should take place in what locations—for example, the planning of a city involves zoning. Of course, I'm not saying that concepts are eliminated altogether in the basic planning of architects or zoners, but rather that there is a basic spatial image that needs to be filled with conceptual activities. A good contrast to the zoning planner is Plato: in the *Republic* there is little or no mention of what happens where, but there is almost total emphasis on the various functions of the just city-state and on who is qualified to perform what functions.

Another class of planners are overwhelmed by the image of time: to them the crucial question is what happens when. Whereas spatial imagery often seems to provide a natural boundary for the system being designed, time does not. How rapidly "five-year planning" has became "twenty-year planning" and now "two-hundred-year planning." Part of this expansion is based on the realization that what we do now (e.g., build nuclear plants, strip-mine, fill in marshes) has long-run implications. But part is also based on the conviction that time is what dominates our lives, as it did for example, for the Mayan planners where temples were filled in after fifty-two years regardless of what we would call their cost-benefit measure.

Much more could be said about the imagery of space and time in past and present social system design, but I want to turn to the key issue of the "Transcendental Aesthetic" for Kant: individuation and (implicitly for Kant) identification.

As will be seen, a number of dialectical themes are intertwined throughout this book: objective-subjective, happiness-equity, and so on. One of the major themes, which encompasses all the others, is the individual versus the collective or the social. This theme is central in any thoroughgoing exploration of individuation. The collective approach to individuation is based on "common sense," since common sense *is* the thought process of the collective. Kant poses for common sense the question how we humans—collectively— tell the difference between the objects of our experiences: houses, roads, animals, people, etc. In Kant's day there were two common-sense answers to this question: we tell differences by description of the properties of an object, and we tell differences by space-time coordinates. Both answers make good sense. For example, the human mind has an incredible facility for recognizing subtle clues in a person's voice or face that enable it to "tell the difference," though occasionally culture blots out these clues so that "they all look alike." Similarly, even though you live in Philadelphia on a street where the houses all look exactly alike, you can find your own by space coordinates, for example, by the number on the door.

But is one answer more basic than the other? The common-sense reply can be found in forensics. The accused is identified as being at the scene of the crime by a number of reliable witnesses; at the same time his defense can establish an impeccable alibi. Which holds sway? The common-sense response that Kant adopted is the alibi. This led him to say that the human mind is equipped a priori with the individuating imagery of space and time. As applied to the more refined experience of the scientist, we say that every "inquiring system" requires a geometry (or theory of space) and a kinematics (or theory of time).

The same common-sense reply occurs in planning, because all plans require maps (blueprint designs, geographical information, etc.) and histories-forecasts (the story told in time). People, of course, will be individuated by various properties: age, education, race, income, etc. But basically the planner needs to know where people will be (or should be) and when.

This is not the end of the matter, however, because in addition to individuating objects and people, we also need to identify them over time. The question posed to common sense is: How do we determine that this is the same object or person that was observed in some previous time? Here common sense has troubles, because there appears to be no "ultimate" test comparable to the alibi. Normally we use the clues just mentioned, where the mind determines the existence or the absence of subtle properties, although this method may break down.

To bolster our ability to identify, we use a historical pathway that describes the where-when of the individual over a period of time—as in astronomy, for example, where the heavenly bodies are identified by their regular motions. Thus the "identical" individual is a recognizable pathway through space and time. More accurately the identical individual is a set of potential pathways and consequences. If one adds teleology to the description of such an individual, then the pathways, actual and potential, can be used to define all the significant attributes of the human psychological individual, his beliefs, perceptions, consciousness, hopes, anxieties, aspirations, and even his love. Does this really capture the individuality of a person?

There was a time when I believed that this "collective" idea of the identical individual was right (see p. 23). At that time, Jung was developing his idea of the "process of individuation," which is the internal process of understanding one's self or one's psyche. Of course I could not understand why the word "inviduation" was used by Jung, since he apparently did *not* mean the method of distinguishing between people or even of identifying a person over time.

Now I can see the matter more clearly in terms of the theme of the individual versus the collective. There is a deep and recognizable sense in which the individual is not a collection of actual and potential behavior patterns over time, and the sense in which this is so is *not* "common." It is unique to each person, not classifiable, not even comparable. I'm talking about the enemies at this point, because what a person is as a moral being, a religious being, or an aesthetic being is not what common sense says he is.

I'm thankful, though, that I explored the collective meaning of the human psyche as thoroughly as I did. The two sides of the theme of individual versus collective rarely talk to each other. Those who have found the unique individual in some way don't even realize the richness of the collective imagery; at best they think it refers to the psychologist, John Watson, or later "behaviorists," who have narrow and even noncollective notions of the psyche. For example, they regard ordinary human passions as ephemeral, whereas the broad collective viewpoint takes the satisfactory definition of human feelings to be a central challenge to its method. It's the lack of touch with collective understanding that makes Husserl, Heidegger, and most phenomenologists and many psychoanalysts so difficult to read.

Understanding Experience

In the next section of the *Critique* Kant tries to explain the intelligibility of human experience. In effect, he denies the fundamental tenet of empiricism—namely, that there are simple experiences. Every experience, despite its appearance of simplicity, is complex, constituted by bringing together what is "given" with a priori "categories" that operate universally and enable us to understand what the experience is and even to communicate it to others. It is no easy matter to recognize these basic categories, because they are universally employed and hence do not stand apart, so to speak.

Kant used classical logic as his guide and arrived at a "table of categories," neatly set forth in four groups of three. In this highly creative process one can discern what might be called the "magic of numbers," because three and four have repeatedly showed up in classification schemes. Thus in Aristotelian logic there are four categorical forms ("all *a* is *b*," "some *a* is *b*," "some *a* is not *b*," and "no *a* is *b*"). The syllogism is made up of three parts, the major and the minor premises and the conclusion. There are four "figures" of the syllogism. Maria von Franz° tells the story of a group of Chinese generals who were trying to decide whether or not to attack the enemy; the vote was three for, sixteen against. So they attacked, since three is a perfect number. The three-four symbolism led Kant to include some strange categories like "totality" and "limitation," but in the main his list does have the appeal of common sense. In order that any experience be meaningful ("intelligible"), the experiencer must (implicitly) understand the difference between one and many, between reality and nonreality; he must understand substance (mass) and causality; he must understand the difference between the possible, the existent, and the necessary. This is collective wisdom.

The post-Kantian period saw a concerted effort to explain the collective convictions associated with the categories, in genetics, in culture, in the archetypes of the unconscious, and so on. One interesting philosophical reflection is that this search itself was based on the causality conviction: some thing or property must be causing the categories to be.

The other post-Kantian event was the discovery that the categories and space-time do not operate in exactly the same manner as the common sense of Kant's day assumed. Thus the nineteenth century introduced, first, non-Euclidean geometries, then non-Newtonian kinematics and mechanics. Kant's assumption of "necessity" no longer could be taken to hold in the strong sense he meant. But the lesson of nineteenth and twentieth century mathematical and physical developments is that mathematics and physics have moved away from collective, commonsense thought. The collective conviction of the manner in which causality works still holds sway among nonscientists, most engineers, doctors, lawyers, and almost all planners. Whether the noncollective imagery of today's mathematics and physics will become tomorrow's common sense is a moot point.

The planners, too, have strong collective convictions, which are tied to a set of categories of planning, and especially to teleological causes. If I were to ask typical planners what concept seems basic to their planning efforts, I'm sure many of them would reply "information," because they seem to spend most of their time gathering information. But this is not the response I want. One

---

° A Jungian psychoanalyst.

might be inclined to say that in Kant's case "experience" was *the* basic category, and of course it is in the sense that it is the overall idea that his *Critique* deals with. But Kant wanted to know how experience is formed, and it was the "forming categories" he sought to find. So, too, in the case of the planner, information is the overall idea, and the question is, What forms planning information? Information about what?

In the *Design of Inquiring Systems* I tried my hand at the categories and was also somewhat overwhelmed by the number three, so that the categories grouped themselves into three groups of three. This is essentially a report of the development of the planning categories since I first formulated the scheme.

The categories are based on the idea that people are the center of the planner's reality. There are three groups of people: those who should be served (the clients), those who should make the decision (the decision makers), and those who should plan (the planners). The categories are thus ethical in kind, but each carries its realistic counterpart, those who are served, do make decisions, do plan. As we'll see, all the categories break down into a "should-is" relationship. The remaining categories are used to fill in the relevant information about each of the three groups. For the client,° we need to know what purposes he should have (or has), and how the variety of his/her purposes should be (is) unified (under a measure of performance). For the decision maker, we need to know what he should be (is) able to use as resources (the components of his system), and what he should not (cannot) control which nonetheless matters (the "environment"). Finally, for the planner, we need to know how he should be (is) able to implement his plans, and finally what should be (is) the guarantor that his planning will "succeed"—that is, secure improvement in the human condition. Since Kant used a table, and I'm rewriting his scheme for planners, here's how the result looks.

I
Client
Purpose
Measure of Performance
II
Decision maker
Components
Environment

° The label suffers some confusion, primarily because "client" in the professions often means "those who pay for service," whereas here the client may be a helpless malnourished infant or even those who cannot possibly "pay money" because they're not yet born, although they may "pay" in other ways. "Beneficiary" is literally a better term, but its legal meanings in insurance and inheritance also tend to confuse.

III
Planner
Implementation
Guarantor

But since I wrote the *Design of Inquiring Systems*,° a fourth class of categories has emerged—namely, those relevant to writers of books like this one. If we call the people in this class "systems philosophers," then the fourth set is:

IV
Systems philosphers
Enemies of the systems approach
Significance

The last (I hope) is puzzling, but it is rational enough; when all's said and done, what is the significance of the whole effort? Is it tragic, so that the destiny of the human condition is the destruction of its values? Is it comic, so that the destiny doesn't matter, is circular? One wit remarked that the only trouble with progress is that it's lasted too long. Or is it glorious and grand, a worship of its creator? Or all these?

As I examine the categories, I'll be more interested in their process of unfolding rather than in their definitions. Definitions tend to hold a concept down, in order to keep it in place, whereas each of the categories of planning tends to expand its meaning so as to encompass the whole. In order to assist in explaining the unfolding of meaning, I'll use imagery, and specifically the imagery of striving-force and the opposite, passiveness-helplessness.

Thus if a careful logician wants to know whether the twelve categories are exhaustive or exclusive, the answer is that each strives to be exhaustive, and each avoids being exclusive: they are moving ideas, and the corresponding images are "moving pictures." Furthermore, they are twelve labels for understanding the process of comprehending reality; and, almost needless to say, other labels could be found to accomplish the same task.

THE CLIENT

Since the categories are oriented toward people, I'll begin with the "client"—that is, the category that makes intelligible the question of whom should be served.

The hero-planner's image of the client is helplessness; that is, it is an image of people who desperately need help and cannot help themselves. One way to picture the image is as a maiden tied to a tree, or as a drowning man, or since the environment is a threatening monster, as a man, hands tied behind him,

---

° C. West Churchman, *Design of Inquiring Systems* (New York: Basic Books, 1968).

whose chin is on the block and the axe has been swung on high. Of course these are not the only images that can depict the client, because image making is highly individualistic and not "common sense."

One way to unfold any of the categories is to try to describe what "in reality" it now represents—that is, to compare the "is" with the "ought." The searching for the "is" usually leads to a "map." In the case of the client the map traces out where the benefits and costs go.

Cost-benefit analyses usually report aggregate benefits and costs, but not the distribution, which, as we'll see in Chapter VI on the ethics of the systems approach, is a central concern. Benefit-cost tracing is really an endless task, but "endless task" is the common theme of all the categories. One illustration may suffice for the moment. In one of California's northern counties, Sonoma, a considerable geothermal resource was discovered a number of years ago in a rather remote section called the "Geyser Area." Subsequently the resource was tapped, and a number of plants, powered by the steam, were built to supply electricity to the neighboring areas. A research team attempted to trace benefits and costs of this development. Obviously benefits went to the consumers of electric energy. Obviously, too, there was a significant change in the environment in the Geyser Area, where the main recipients of the cost (the "victims") were plants, trees, and wildlife. Overhead wires constituted a human cost for those who lived near them. The companies that dug the wells and operated the plants received a monetary benefit, as did the owners of the land. Another trace occurs in the form of taxes to the county, amounting over a three-year period to nearly four million dollars. A significant portion of this amount went to the elementary and secondary schools, not as benefit to the children in terms of improved education, but rather as reduction in the district charges to property owners. Some of the trace was lost because the county followed the typical procedure of putting a proportion of the money in "general funds." It should be noted that all these traces have secondary and nth level pathways, as we ask how increased profits, property-owner relief, lessor receipts, were used to benefit others. One very important trace, often used to defend development, is that geothermal-run plants reduce the need for other types of energy production which are clearly harmful both to present and future generations: fossil fuels, nuclear, etc.

In the geothermal example the almost universal attitude of both state and federal government, as well as private companies, is to regard the underground steam as a resource, which, luckily for us humans, is cheap and remarkably safe (free of radiation, free of lead, mercury, and other dangerous by-products, not likely to explode, etc.). Therefore, according to this attitude, the residents should accept the facts, welcome development as a gift to their county, and let the wise and intelligent engineers develop it according to the best standards. What this attitude ignores is that many of the residents perceive their county as peaceful and free of industry, with its concomitant trucks, roads, overhead wires, and air-water pollution. The benefits of a peaceful, remote life may well be removed if full geothermal development takes place. Now I believe that there are ways in which a well-planned development need not clash with the "peaceful countryside" vision. If my belief is correct, then the present attitude of state and national government is immoral. It treats the residents who want to conserve the natural environment much as it treats the boulders that block the roads that will have to be built: as "things" to be gotten around as quickly as possible.

The manifest difficulties of planning well for those who should be served, perhaps explains why the client is not a natural beginning for many planners; they are inclined to begin with the category of purpose, which then enables them to avoid the underlying human values. Thus, health planning can address goals such as "minimization of addiction" without asking anything about the humanity of the addict, nor indeed asking whether addiction programs are aimed primarily to serve the addict, his family, or society. In most energy development the Environmental Impact Reports tend to measure physical impacts, with only a vague connection to people collectively. The purpose is defined as one of satisfying projected demands; there is little or no discussion about who is going to demand and through what human urge.

PURPOSE

The category of purpose has a commonsense meaning: it refers to future states of the world which can be partially shaped by decision making, and which are intended to occur by the decision maker (i.e., are not accidental or unanticipated). As I remarked earlier, this collective meaning needs a great deal of clarification, which a number of us have tried to provide in other places. But in the unfolding process it's often helpful to think in terms of three subcategories: goals, objectives, and ideals.

One common way of distinguishing among these ideas is to say that goals are short-run, objectives are longer-run, and ideals stretch indefinitely into the future. But it helps in the unfolding process to say rather that goals are the perceptions of a planner who takes most of the aspects of the plan to be given—that is, that information is data or a "data bank." Thus, the client and the decision maker are well defined, as are the alternative pathways. The time span for such goal planning may be very long, as when the planner tries to determine the best times for increasing generator capacity for an electric utility company.

Objective-planning, on the other hand, consists of trying to embed a "given" in a larger problem: for example, should the electric power come from this source or from that, or should the conversion be to direct or to alternating electricity? Objective-planning consists of an analysis of each "given," though usually on the basis of other givens, and especially of data about what is feasible or "realistic."

Most planning these days uses some form of objective-planning. But it must be emphasized that the feasible and the realistic are data, not information; that is, numbers and other descriptors are used to bound the problem, and the planner does not try to understand why these "realistic" boundaries hold. Ideal-planning drops the feasible and the realistic, and attempts to define purposes that could hold if such restraints were removed. In a sense it is "timeless" planning, because its vision may be forever a vision. But through it the unfolding can begin in earnest, because its questions become more and more comprehensive: Why so many malnourished babies? Why the military buildup? Why so many dreary lives? Because, says objective-planning, there is no feasible way of changing these conditions. Such a reply—to the ideal-planner—is based on a given, not on imagination.

Since the main point of ideal-planning is the unfolding process, it is not even relevant to ask whether the ideal is "right" in the same sense in which there is a right goal plan or a right objective-plan. Suppose our problem system is mental health. A goal plan might specify a significant reduction of dangerously insane individuals on the loose. The objective-planner might try to embed the mental health goal in a broader plan of national health. The ideal-planner, using his imagination, sees a world in which there are no mental health institutions, but rather one in which everyone is both a mental health case and a responsible citizen. How could such an ideal work? It would require an immense amount of trust and caring, as well as an openness in communication. Now the mental health "problem" begins unfolding into the vistas of possible human relationships. For one thing, the imagined ideal suggests that the biggest mental health problem we face is war, and that the severest "cases" of mental breakdown are those who perceive war as a necessity. True, war is a reality, and there are no feasible means to eliminate it; but to the ideal-planner this is not a critical objection, because he doesn't accept the "data." Note that it is really not very important whether his original imagination (about removing all mental health institutions) is "correct"; its vision did fuel the unfolding process.

MEASURE OF PERFORMANCE

The third category in the first group is the "measure of performance." It, too, can be viewed under the three subcategories of purpose. In goal planning the measure is the degree of attainment of the goal, sometimes measured by the probability of attainment (e.g., of winning at cards or chess), sometimes by the amount of attainment (e.g., amount earned on an investment). In objective-planning the planner seeks a broader measure which attempts to include relevant benefits and costs. Thus, a goal planner of the Army Corps of Engineers might try to determine the best way of controlling floods in a certain region. An objective-planner might ask whether the flood control measures would endanger farm lands or wildlife, or whether making the land "safer" would bring about a serious population shift. Such a planner would try to set up an economic measure, using some form of trade-off principle.

When we unfold the measure of performance to ideal-planning, matters become difficult. Indeed, though I've been reasonably well acquainted with a large number of systems in my lifetime, I've never seen one for which there is a thoroughly defensible ideal measure of performance. All ratios are suspect, because they make intersystem comparisons difficult or impossible; further-more, they run the danger of deception, because if the denominator is small, the measure may be large but insignificant (e.g., the lethal dose of a drug divided by proper dosage can be very large if the proper dose is nearly zero). All cost-benefit measures are terribly weak as we unfold toward future generations. We've long since learned that net profit in free enterprise systems works only for the few. As for transportation, it suffers the same fate as education, which is hopelessly bogged down in attempts to "measure" the quality of an educational program.

None of these "ideal" questionings stops decision makers (managers, administrators, politicians, etc.) from using a large assortment of measures of performance. Annual net profit and share of the market are common measures in the private sector, even though the first, when used comparative-ly with other years, hides the effect of inflation and in any event glosses over long-term investments, while the second is clearly influenced by the wish to "better the other guy," no matter what the cost. In education there has been a strong tendency to budget in terms of student credit hours, which implies that the more students there are in a course, the better the course. I have found a somewhat similar measure of performance on wildlife refuges: the more migratory birds in October, the better the refuge. The matter becomes even more absurd in the health area; the use of life expectancy as a measure of performance of a nation's health care system suggests that the best way to score high is put the whole population in suspended animation at age thirty.

Of course, from a political point of view, it's easy to understand why such measures are used; a good way to make polis is to get people together on the task of making some number bigger—more votes, more energy ("meg-awatts"), more travelers, more doctors, more whatever.

Nevertheless, the category of measure of performance is central in the life of the ideal planner, because to him it expresses the meaning of "improvement" in the human condition. If some situation appears to be clearly better than it was before, then rationality requires an argument to justify the appearance, and the argument has to be in terms of "measurement"—that is, in terms of information that holds valid for different people, in different times and places.

Although the word "measurement" often conjures up the image of a number, its basic, pragmatic meaning does not require numerical form. Syntatically, measurements may be classifications (e.g., the subspecies of a species), or rankings (e.g., grades of students), or satisfy various other syntactical rules (e.g., addition, division, etc.). Semantically, measurements need to say what is being measured. Pragmatically, measurements serve a definite purpose in human lives: they are information that has wide use over time and space for different people with different purposes. To return for the moment to statistics, the test of a hypothesis or the determination of a correlation coefficeient that will never be repeated or used again, is not measurement in the pragmatic sense, no matter how quantitative or careful the test.

To the ideal-planner there must "exist" at least the possibility of a measure of performance. The fact that no completely satisfactory measure exists is not discouraging to him; completely satisfactory meanings of all the categories remain as unattained ideals.

THE DECISION MAKER

The next group of categories begins with the "decision maker." The verb "to decide" comes from the Latin verb for "to cut" as in "to cut the knot." The original meaning is still in the imagery of a decision, because when one decides to do something, one also decides *not* to do a number of other things—that is, one "cuts off" a plethora of possible lives. To my poetic side the image is awesome; my actual biography is the realm of possibilities, the lives that were cut off by my decisions. "To decide" has also meant in the history of the English language to decide between two contestants, as in a court. Today's commonsense meaning of "I, and I alone, decide" or "to decide is the essence of loneliness" seems to have been late in coming, perhaps as late as the nineteenth century.

Here again we find a variety of ways in which planners conceptualize decision making. In goal planning the basic idea is to simplify the concept of decision making either by eliminating it altogether or by identifying a single unit (person, committee, board of supervisors, etc.) which can "choose" among an explicit set of alternatives. The goal planner eliminates decision making from his considerations by making a contract with someone who is willing to pay, to study the relevant consequences of an explicit set of alternative actions, and to state as reliably as possible what the contract stipulates. Once the contract is made, the goal planner performs his study and reports the results. His only concern with the "decision maker" is whether the latter will agree to the contract. What one does with the results is up to him who pays for them.

The goal planner may unfold the idea of decision making a bit by trying to understand what the person who contracts for his services "really wants." The point is that the contract may be poorly composed because of ignorance regarding certain aspects of the consequences. If the planner has a reasonably clear idea about what is wanted, he can modify the contract better to serve the contractor's interest. One way to do this is to conceive of the contractor as a unit that operates through a "utility function." If the unit has reasonably sufficient information, it will choose the alternative that "maximizes" utility as determined by this function. The planner's task is to supply this "reasonably sufficient information." The simplest example of a utility function is one that is linear in money, but the literature on utility functions is replete with various modifications, nonlinearity in money, uncertainty, risk, etc.

I've used the word "unit" in this description because the goal planner regards the contracting person's mind as a computer, albeit a complicated and sometimes unpredictable one. According to the goal planner, decision making is the process by which the mind takes bits of data, plugs them into a utility function, and selects ("prints out") the action with the highest utility. If the "bits of data" are wrong, then the print-out is likely to be wrong. The goal planner's role is to upgrade the data. But to do so, he has to have a reasonably good idea of the utility function.

The next unfolding (toward objective-planning) is to ask whether one can apply such thinking to a group of people. The answer seems to be affirmative if they are all "of one mind"—for example, members of a religious commune with common objectives. Goal planners were fascinated when Arrow (see page 23), in the early 1950s, apparently showed that no reasonable (meaning "democratic") "social utility function" can be derived from differing individual utilities. Neither Arrow, nor as far as I know, any one since has considered the strategy that most goal planners use in practice—namely, the use of discussion to bring about a convergence toward a common utility function. Perhaps they avoided this idea in order to keep out of the fire, because once such a strategy is admitted, it brings up the issue of the proper mode of discussion (lest one forceful person dominate, for example) and thus introduces messy ethical considerations which goal planners do their best to avoid.

There are many ways in which the category of decision making can unfold, but for present purposes it will be most useful to introduce implementation, a subject which takes us into objective-planning. The relevant phenomenon is this: a contract is written, a utility function is established, the relevant data are collected, the "best" alternative is identified, the report is written or a briefing held, and—nothing happens.

Implementation is a basic category of planning inquiry, for it is the battleground of the decision maker and the planner, and its unfolding leads into strange pathways. Here, however, we need only unfold its meaning with respect to the concept of decision making. The idea of a single decision maker breaks down as soon as we go to organizational decision making. (It probably breaks down on its own, because, as we shall see, the individual person is not a "unit," and many external forces impinge on his/her decision making). Even in highly authoritative organizations there are all kinds of forces that can block or modify proposed actions. Here I need to unfold another aspect of decision making, which Singer labeled "producer-product." Something is a producer of an event if at least one description of the event would be different were the producer not there. Obviously there are many producers of any event that occurs in nature; in the case of organizational decision making, the coproducers are many but often operate in subtle and nonformalized manners. In fact, part of an organization's "unconscious" is the existence of coproducers who block implementation of "good" ideas but are never mentioned. For example, the fact that a proposed plan means firing one or more people may never arise in the discussions of the plan, although it is a highly important matter; indeed, those whose jobs are threatened coproduce the blocking of the plan, even though they never appear at the managers' meeting, never say anything, are never mentioned in the arguments. As another example, many a young assistant professor has become puzzled about why a certain course is kept on the required list, since the arguments for retaining it seem so irrelevant; no one explains to him that were the course removed, Professor X would have few or no students.

The objective-planner thus sees the need of bringing the organization's collective unconscious up to the conscious level. But in doing so, he has to cope with another aspect of decision making: a decision not only produces an event, but it does so in a manipulative way. The most significant aspect of "manipulation" lies in the perceptions of people: a manipulative decision maker is perceived to be one who is responsible for changing other people's lives. Once the objective-planner understands this phenomenon, he sees the necessity of reducing the perception of manipulation and his ally role with the decision maker. This leads him into participatory planning and, in the public sector at least, into "public involvement," both of which are aimed at eliminating the perception of manipulation.

At this point in the drama the snickers and the disgust of the enemy can be heard. Politics points out that the objective-planner at long last is catching on to the main point: that all planning is political maneuvering. Morality, on the other hand, is outraged, which is one of its typical moods. The planner is servant to the manipulator, a clever servant who uses magician's tricks to hide what is really there: people manipulating people. Shame!

Enter the ideal-planner. He starts with the real, in this case a "decision map"—that is, a mapping of all those who either influence (coproduce) a decision, or whose intent is to do so. In the geothermal example earlier, the map includes at least a dozen federal agencies, a similar number of state agencies, three county government bodies, public utility commissions, quite a number of environmental groups, a number of private companies, a regional planning committee, two citizens associations, quite a few individuals working on their own. Of course such a listing gives only an outline of the decision map; to fill in the details, one must describe what groups have what legal powers to decide: that is, the recognized or conscious level of decision making, and the manner in which the other groups are attempting to change the conscious policies of the legal decision-making process. I suspect that a similar decision-making "mess" exists even in dictatorial and in socialist countries.

To complicate matters still further, one should examine the relationship between benefit tracing and decision mapping. In the next chapter I'll discuss Kant's famous dictum (see pp. 126–27): "Never treat humanity in yourself or another as means only, but as an end withal." But to whom is this moral imperative addressed? In the context of the unfolding category of decision making, it is addressed to the participants in the total decision map; if some are benefiting by using people as means, then their role in the decision map may be judged immoral, even though they tend to produce a higher aggregate of economic wealth.

Our systems (ideal) planner now needs to decide what would be a nonmessy, or rational, approach to decision making. It may help to sketch the extremes of the spectrum of responses to this design question. At one end there is the argument that the present system, despite its messy appearance, is as near to being the right one as we humans can attain. It permits all interested parties to "input" facts and values as they perceive them to the legal decision-making process, which then constructs competing fact nets and selects that one that is believed to be the closest to representing the majority of interests, and deduces from the selected fact net the "appropriate" decision. Furthermore, if the legal decision-making process is perceived by many to be defective, then it can be modified by sufficient pressure, by changing the laws, or by legal decision-making bodies. Perhaps a suitable analogy would be a crowd of people pushing a large round ball on a field. The legal process is the shape and weight of the ball, which remains relatively stable. Where the ball goes is the result of the various forces impinging on its surface, or forces that impinge on impingers, so that one person may deflect another's attempt to move the ball. Note that this analogy is radically different from the analogy of the steersman of a ship, who strives to respond to forces that impinge on the ship, by eliminating their potential deflection from his chosen course. Note also that according to this account of appropriate decision making, wherever the ball moves is correct, unless the crowd, at recess, decides it is not and consequently decides to redesign its shape or weight.

But where is the ideal-planner in such an account? He can only be one of the "influencing" parties. His voice is not necessarily different from the voice of someone who is short-sighted and motivated by greed.

At the other end of the spectrum is the response that the social system needs to move in a direction that best serves humanity (or all species), and (because the dead and the yet-to-be-born cannot feasibly be here to push the ball) that we need to have overseers who represent their interests as well as to collect information from the living. In the past such overseers wrote the *I Ching*, the *Bhagavad-Gita*, were the philosopher-kings of Plato's *Republic*, the reflective Christian saints, the modern prophets of human society, Hobbes, Locke, Rousseau, Kant, Marx, etc., etc. Here is another dialectical theme that will run throughout this book: the locus of the rational planner in the decision-making process.

COMPONENTS AND ENVIRONMENT

The next two categories, the components (aspects of reality that the decision maker can change) and the environment (aspects of reality that the decision maker cannot change) are correlatives. A falling man has nothing but an environment; an all-powerful God has no environment.

A good way to begin unfolding these two categories is to recall the discussion on page 49 concerning mathematical programming (MP). The mathematical problem is to maximize a function, z, subject to a set of constraints. One plausible interpretation of the problem in planning is that z is the measure of performance of the system, the variables in the objective function are the components that can be set by the decision maker at various levels, and the boundaries in the constraint equations constitute the environment.°

°As I have already pointed out, this interpretation may not always work, because the decision maker may in fact be able to alter the boundaries in the constraint equations.

As we have seen, the philosophical questions about this account of decision making abound. In terms of one of our basic themes, comprehensiveness, there is the question of whether MP is supposed to describe or to prescribe the decision-making problem completely, or partially, or approximately. We have already discussed the problem of approximation (p. 46). Still, might we not say that z, the measure of performance—although forever subject to error—is an approximate measure comparable to physical measurements in this regard?

Singer, in *Experience and Reflection*, spent some time on the concept of approximation in physics.° He was impressed by the mathematician's ability to define a series of numbers, each of which is an "approximation" to some limit—for example, ½, ¾, ⅞ . . . is such a series, the limit being one, which is never reached but can be approximated within any small amount by selecting the right n. On the other hand, in physical measurement there is a "series" in the sense that the "probable error" of the measurement is decreasing. Thus, in the history of the measurement of the velocity of optical light, the probable error was 5,000 kilometers/second in 1728, 50 km/sec in 1879, 9 km/sec in 1941, 0.1 km/sec in 1965. One might now say with some feeling of confidence that the mean measurement is "converging" on the true value, and that the true value is a "limit" in much the sense in which 1 is the limit of the mathematical series. There still remain interesting philosophical questions: What guarantees that the probable error may converge not to 0, but rather to a very small but positive constant, or that it may start to increase? The arguments against either of these possibilities must be different in kind from the mathematician's arguments about 1 being the true limit. Indeed, in the history of measurement, the measuring world was shocked in the 1920s by the theory that the simultaneous measure of the velocity and the mass of a particle did have a positive constant limit of error.

But these refinements of measurement in physics are minor compared with the measurement of "optimal z" in mathematical programming. We simply have no way of estimating an error for this measurement, nor do we have any way of assuring ourselves that one attempt is a "closer approximation" than another. Nor is the "size" of the programs an indication of increased accuracy.†

° E. A. Singer, Jr., *Experience and Reflection* (Philadelphia: University of Pennsylvania Press, 1959).

† I should append a footnote on the matter of "sensitivity" analysis. There are explicit methods for testing the sensitivity of a parameter of the model by determining how different the "optimal z" would be if the parameter were seriously in error. This seems to provide the modeler with some linkage to reality, because he can determine those aspects of his model that are crucial and those that are not, in the sense that were reality quite different from what the model says, in

The same remarks apply to the "boundaries" of a system. The human being seems beset by the idea of bounding things. He bounds nations, states, cities, properties—even oceans and stars. In goal planning and objective-planning one of the first problems is to decide what system is to be studied; once the system has been identified, then the boundaries can be set. But what are the boundaries? In the case of MP, it's tempting to say that they are the constraint constants in the constraint equations. Indeed, when the program is given a geometrical interpretation, the representation is a bounded region in n-dimensional space. Thus, if for budgetary reasons the manager can hire only ten workers for a task, each producing, say, two thousand man-hours, then the "boundary" is twenty thousand man-hours for the task. But there is the reasonable question whether this boundary is "correct"—that is, whether the budget properly restricts the size of the work force. There is an "inner method" for answering this question, because one can formulate a "dual" in which the optimal boundaries can be deduced. But, of course, the dual is no better or worse than the "primal." If either leaves out some significant aspect of the system, so will the other.

From the point of view of ideal-planning, the question of the proper boundaries has no plausible, common-sense answer. It's like all the other questions, about clients, purposes, measure of performance, etc. The idea is not to find an answer but to foster the process of unfolding. What are the boundaries of the geothermal system? They are certainly not the boundaries of the county, since geothermal development is important for energy development in the state and the nation. Nor should energy bound the problem, because energy is a part of transportation, education, manufacturing, etc.

This is why—to the ideal-planner—most national governments appear absurd in their decision-making organization; the assumption seems to be that one can subdivide national problems into defense, education, energy, international affairs, etc., even though all of these are strongly linked. The designs are incredibly messy and don't even use the same logical method of classification: "energy" and "defense" are supposedly labels for two problem areas, whereas "interior" refers to the location of problems.

Now inevitably the objective-planner responds to such criticisms by point-

some regards this might be very important while in other regards it might not. The idea behind sensitivity analysis is quite important, for it suggests that the compulsive drive for ever more precision in information may be neurotic, if the increased precision means very little in relation to the way of improving the measure of performance. But sensitivity analysis is what I'll call an "inner method"; its results are valid to the extent that the model is valid. If the model leaves out some very important features—for example, the welfare of the aged in a health services model—sensitivity analysis will not reveal the gap: models only "know" what their designers have assumed into them.

ing out that unless the system is bounded, it will be impossible to study it except endlessly, and hence no recommendation for action will ever occur. This criticism is an important one for ideal-planning, because it emphasizes a difference between the objective-planner's and the ideal-planner's notions of implementation. The objective-planner loves to spell out the "stages" of planning, which in most texts have this kind of format:

1. formulation of the problem;
2. data gathering;
3. model construction;
4. model testing and verification;
5. formulation of recommendations; and
6. implementation and evaluation.

The last step is to take place within a prescribed time period and is the "action" phase of objective-planning. (I might note in passing that goal planning often stops with step 5.) The ideal-planner tends to shun orderly "phases" with their corresponding "PERT" charts. Were he forced into writing a comparable series of steps, it might look as follows:

1. implementation concerns;
2. determination of the client and benefit-cost mapping;
3. determination of the decision maker and decision mapping;
4. recommendation for action;
5. based on the action, a dialectical formulation of the problem;
6. etc.

Of course, since the ideal-planner lives in a world where the funds for planning studies are in the hands of objective-planners with their dry "RFPs" (Request for Proposals), the ideal-planner who needs money will revert to the first list, albeit somewhat sadly. If the second list seems odd for having implementation concerns at the top, a little reflection will show that it is very reasonable: if, for example, the planner can foresee that no matter what he does in his inquiry, nothing will change, then he may reasonably judge that the proposed planning study is futile and another design is called for, or else that the project be abandoned. (A man falling from the fortieth floor of a building has no need to "formulate the problem" as he passes the thirtieth.)

It is important to mention other philosophical issues surrounding mathematical programming (MP), because MP gives the appearance of being comprehensive. I've already mentioned the concept of manipulative causality which is inherent in every MP, although at the present time its meaning is quite obscure. A similar topic is the "separability" assumption of some MP's. If, for example, $z = 3x_1 + 7x_2$, where x_1 and x_2 are, say, man-hours on two tasks, then the contribution of x_1 is "separable" from the contribution of x_2. As

I tried to argue in *Design of Inquiring Systems*, one should also consider "design separability"—that is, the question whether x_1 or x_2 should be done at all, and whether z is worthwhile in the larger system; if this kind of ideal-planning question is raised, then all aspects of any system are strongly nonseparable. Finally, from the definitions of "components" and "environment" it is doubtful whether the relation "x is in system S" can be described adequately by "x is a part of system S," where "is a part of" obeys the rules of the algebra of classes. If a company can influence a government agency to do something beneficial for the company, then the agency is a component of the company system; if the agency can influence the company to do something that furthers the agency's goals, then the company is a component of the agency's system. However, in class logic, if x is a part of y, and y a part of x, then x and y are equivalent. But if x is a component of y, and y a component of x, from the example it apparently does not follow that x and y are the same system. To be clearer on the matter, we should have to work out a "system logic" that sets forth the necessary and sufficient conditions for something to be a "system" logically.

The image of the decision maker is of a warrior, ill equipped with a broken spear or a blunt sword, which are his "components." The environment is an amorphous green monster, in whose innards can vaguely be seen a skeleton resembling an input-output chart.

THE PLANNER

We come (at last) to the category of the planner, but of course we have long since come to it, as it plays a critical role in the unfolding process of each of the other categories. For example, there seems to be no reason why we should add another map, the planning map, because almost all decision makers are also planning, so that the two maps often are coextensive. But now we should examine the question of who *should* plan. This question unfolds in several ways. First of all, it seems that as humans any of us can employ the human intellect in an attempt to secure improvement in the human condition; perhaps our right to do so arises from the fact that it is virtually impossible to prevent us from doing so, even in very oppressive societies. At the opposite end of this unfolding is the position that only a very few can plan adequately. This surely would be the professional goal planner's claim: doctors, lawyers, engineers, educators, all have an expertise that "ought" to be used, the right being based on the "common good." For example, the public should not be allowed to vote on whether a certain drug should be used for patients with cancer, or on the conduct of the courts, nor should they vote on the proper structure for a bridge or on the content of a college course in history. In all these matters, planning with the intent to act on the plan should be restricted to those who know how.

This goal planner response unfolds into other issues: Who should plan for and decide about the expert's qualifications, the problem of licensing? Or, if the expert fails, who should plan for and decide about the consequences, the problem of professional malpractice?

But there are other questions that unfold a different aspect. Organizations tend to become bureaucracies with a tough structure that is difficult to change. In recent years a group of "experts" has come into existence who have found ways of creating change through astute methods of intervention. This new breed of planners, called "change agents," can guide the ambitious manager in making changes without destroying his organization. But, of course, their very unfortunate label, "intervention," immediately produces ethical concerns in both the objective- and the ideal-planner.

Finally (but not exhaustively) there is the model builder, someone who has the competence to build models and (usually with the aid of his midnight friend, the computer) can compute answers to the puzzling problems of human society. We still don't know how to judge his competence; there are no licensing procedures that I know of; and rarely, if ever, has he been taken to court for malpractice. As in the Club of Rome world-modeling projects, his colleagues may rant and rave, or applaud, but the only punishment or reward is irritation or an ego glow.

The most significant unfolding of the question, Who should plan? is the issue, Who should decide on goals, objectives, and ideals? Here common sense says that the unfolding should take place in reverse: first determine the ideals of humanity, and from them derive the objectives and goals. This recourse, in fact, will be the theme of the chapter on the ethics of the systems approach, where a dialectic will emerge between the ideal of human well-being and the ideal that no one be forced to lead a life that others choose for him. In the first ideal, experts play an important role, especially those who can perceive the larger system; in the second, everyone is an expert.

IMPLEMENTATION

These remarks bring us to the category of implementation, the tragedy and comedy of planning. Perhaps here it is best to begin with the image. As a beginning of the unfolding, "implementation" means the transformation into action of an intellectually conceived plan. This is the common-sense meaning, so common that it's an integral part of what Gertrude Stein called "daily island living." As I prepare my breakfast, I see we're out of salt, low on bacon and milk. So I find a piece of paper and start writing down items; this is my plan. Later I implement the plan by going to a store and buying bacon, milk, etc. But I forget to buy salt. Implementation means the transformation into action of an intellectually conceived but partially incorrect plan.

The objective, professional planner has been led to ask: "Why are so many plans well paid for but never implemented?" The goal planner might reply, "Because so many managers are bureaucrats who love to pay for up-to-date, computer-based, large-model plans, which they have no intention of implementing. As long as they pay me, that's *their* business."

But the objective-planner wants to make this a part of *his* business. If the goal planner is right, then he should recognize that big corporate plans are meant for the glorification of the managers, and he should then attempt to maximize glorification minus cost. But he suspects that there are deeper, hidden reasons for implementation failure. In the *Design of Inquiring Systems* and *The Systems Approach*° I explored some of these reasons. At one point in my planning life, in the early 1960s, I despaired of finding plausible reasons in the reality of complex organizations, and decided to "purify" the experience by designing a laboratory for investigating the phenomenon of implementation failure. Five subjects (usually MBAs) were told that they were to run a small business firm. Each period they had to decide on the prices to ask for each of their products, the production schedules, the purchase quantities, and the investment of extra cash (a nonexistent task, since they almost always lost money). Each of these tasks was assigned to a subject, who, to boost his ego, was called "sales vice president" or "production vice president," etc. There was also a "chief executive" who did not decide anything, although he did have the power to change a decision his subordinates proposed, or even to fire them. The subjects were given complete information, in the sense that it was possible to deduce from the information we gave them at the start of the experiment, the decisions that would maximize net profit each period. The deduction required the solution of a cubic equation by an iterative process, and hence for the mathematically naïve it was not simple.

Unbeknownst to the subjects, among their group was a "stooge" who did understand the solution. The experiment consisted of testing some "strategy of implementation" the stooge could use to convince the others that his was the right solution (of course one strategy that was ruled out was to inform the others that he was a stooge). The strategies included such ideas as a forceful ("arrogant") stooge, a compliant, pleasing stooge, a stooge who could use another "ideal" company as an example, etc.

° C. West Churchman, *The Systems Approach* (New York: Delacorte Press, 1968).

It was both pleasing and frustrating to find that even in this "simple" experiment the phenomenon of implementation failure occurred over and over. My favorite way of summarizing the overall picture is to point out that when we compared the average earnings of the experimental groups with the earnings of the control groups (where there was no stooge), the control groups did better; apparently the stooge was an irritant who reduced the performance measure.

We did discover some interesting, and perhaps useful, things about implementation failure. It was clear that in a very short time the subjects formed "polis," the term I've been using in discussing politics as an enemy of the systems approach. They felt that they should decide together, and not independently. Hence, even though they might be impressed by the stooge's arguments, each did not want to change his decision unless the rest did. This result was confirmed when we tried the strategy of a "friendly" stooge, someone they all admired. In this case implementation of the solution took place, whereas when the stooge was someone they did not admire, we found implementation failure. But just how useful this result may be is debatable; should we have a course in the curriculum on how to be a friendly planner?

But my real interest is in the meaning of implementation for the ideal-planner. Here the image is metamorphosis, for if the plan is implemented, it becomes a decision, and the planner is thereby changed into a decision maker.

But the prospect of this metamorphosis is awesome to the ideal-planner, for the one image he has of real decision making is that it is fraught with errors—often disastrous errors. Why shouldn't this apply to his own decision making?

We can see the difference here between the life of the objective-planner and the life of the ideal-planner. For example, demographers and world modelers agree that there are too many babies in the world, and that a reasonable objective for humanity is to decrease drastically the number of births. Let's imagine that the Club of Rome succeeds in uniting the governments of the world in a collective agreement to decrease population. An objective-planner, who has pressed for this agreement, might feel a sense of personal pride. An ideal-planner, who also might have argued for the policy, would be aghast if the world governments agreed to act on it, for now he sees the awesome unfolding: What atrocities will governments invent to implement the policy? What methods will be necessary to force people to have fewer babies? Will having babies become a bootleg operation? What will be done to the parents and babies once the "crime" has been detected? But much more to the point: suppose (as has happened in some affluent countries) that people willingly reduce reproduction because of an induced fear of overpopulation. How can the ideal-planner morally justify his manipulation of human reproductive behavior, especially when that behavior has deep religious and aesthetic meaning to many of us? This is the burden of metamorphosis: the ideal-planner must now carry the total weight of action, rather than the light burden of his vision.

And yet the metamorphosis must happen, or else the ideal-planner is only a dreamer. At the end of *In Search of a Way of Life*, Singer put it this way: "And that is all; one thinks these things out as best one can, and that is all."°

However, something more needs to unfold. For even though we try our hardest, by what right can we claim that this is enough, that the "way of life" we propose for mankind makes any sense in the long run? Indeed, in Chapter IX, I suggest that a Singerian world might be a world of gross immorality.

THE GUARANTOR

Enter the ninth category, the guarantor. I first formulated the idea for planners when the Operations Research Society of America, no doubt feeling its growing pains, labeled one of its annual meetings "The State of the Art." Russell Ackoff, with his typical wit, asked me to give a luncheon talk on: "The Art of the State." By some tortuous mental pathway I turned that topic into: What state are we in, and is it truly "artistic," in the sense that operations research is a skill, and therefore beneficial to mankind? This reflection sent me back to the readings on human progress, and especially to reviving Singer's theory of progress in science, where, as I mentioned above, he used the probable error of a physical measurement as an indicator of human progress. But Singer was writing before the world had good reason to suspect that modern physics may not be altogether a human blessing: sometimes the truth may hurt. But I couldn't find any obvious substitute: longevity, average annual real income, freedom to vote, percentage employed, none of these and their like seemed even plausible measures of human progress.

I was reminded of Descartes' "dangerous voyage" of doubt, and his search for a guarantor, and of Kant's vision, in the second *Critique*,† of humanity's gradually reconciling virtue and happiness, and the need to postulate a guarantor of this endless search. Thus, I argued, to show that the state is truly an art—that is, that OR is a valid human skill—we must postulate that despite its manifest errors in practice, OR is a progressive step, and to do this we must postulate a guarantor. Armed with this thesis, I gave my luncheon address, which fell unheeded into the pool, except for one ripple. The ripple was Wroe

° E. A. Singer, Jr., *In Search of a Way of Life* (New York: Columbia University Press, 1948), p. 90.

† Immanuel Kant, *Critique of Pure Practical Reason*, 1787.

Alderson,° who, delighted, suggested a slight addition, "guarantor of desti-ny"—or, in these days when everything has its acronym, GOD.

It was nice, after a number of years away from the topic, to return to theology once more. I was brought up a Catholic, a faith whose mark on the soul can never be fully eradicated. One reason for my leaving Catholicism, I think, was a sense of unfairness about its doctrine; it would be utterly unfair of God to reveal Himself to a relatively few people, leaving the rest to spend eternity in a limbo less satisfying than heaven.

But as I began to become a youthful philosopher, I was fascinated by the "proofs" for the existence of God, especially that most marvelous invention attributed to Saint Anselm, the ontological proof. When I was nineteen, I wrote in my journal: "Having read so much of late about the proofs (especially the ontological†) for the existence of God, I thought I would put down my concept." I then got to speculating about whether, if God is perfect, He might not be perfectly evil. I finally concluded: "He is the guarantor that all our good deeds will be rewarded—that is, he assures us that by maturing our ego [my own discovery of the 'process of individuation'], we will reap the benefits of it in an afterworld." So the later "discovery" of the guarantor category was a rediscovery, not surprising, though, because this young man and this old man were reading the same texts, especially Kant.

Now, of course, the category of the guarantor does not "prove" the existence of God or any of the gods. The guarantor is an idea that appears necessary if the ideal-planner is to make any sense—namely, if the destiny of all conscientious human planning is to be realized. Since each of the categories unfolds by asking its basic ethical question—Who is and who should be the client? What is and what should be the purpose? etc.—so here we can ask, What is the guarantor, and what should it be? And the answer to the second part, as in any of the previous examples, may be, "There should be no guarantor of planning for human destiny."

° One of the leading authors in marketing during the 1950s.

† My present version of the ontological proof goes as follows. A descriptor of an object is a "property" if (1) it obeys at least the laws of ranking (e.g., more or less powerful, more or less intelligent, etc.); if (2) the highest rank (x_{max}) exists; if (3) "more" along the ranking implies "better," *ceteris paribus*. Define an object (God) which is x_{max} for all properties. For such an object, existence is a property because existence is "more" than nonexistence, and hence better than nonexistence. Hence God exists. This formulation is interesting because, among other things, it's quite likely that the class of properties is empty, as my discussion of the environmental fallacy in Chapter I indicates (making more of x—or less of x—does not improve matters); *ceteris paribus* presents some tricky definitional problems, to say the least. What's interesting about this refutation of the ontological proof is that it attacks the definition (which defines that which cannot exist) rather than the notion of existence as a property (which was Kant's objection).

Actually I think only a logical mind could regard the ontological proof as marvelous; when I've tried to get students to appreciate it, they have rated it R, for ridiculous. It's marvelous for a logical mind, because it attempts to use logic alone to prove something of tremendous importance to mankind, probably the most important aspect of reality.

Just as each of the categories is reflected in specific systems, like health and education, so is the guarantor. It seems to me that students of organizations and their management should have a keen interest in the guarantor, because most organizations are components of larger systems which, as far as we can judge, ought to survive. Consider the U.S. Fish and Wildlife Service. If we ideal-plan for the service, we must consider those aspects of reality which guarantee its continuance, because those of us who are dedicated to its work see no end to the task of helping humans properly to relate to the other species. One hypothesis says that humans have a natural, or biological, concern for the survival of all species; this natural concern "guarantees" the survival of the service. But this hypothesis ignores the fact that humanity, in destroying itself, may well destroy all species; one report has it that only cockroaches will survive the neutron bomb. In any event, the appropriate guarantor of the Wildlife Service should include the guarantor of human survival, whatever that may be. In similar fashion, the service needs an "informed" public, because an ignorant public might rush to use its refuges for camping and boating. This means that the guarantor of the service should include the guarantor of public education. And so it goes: the guarantor of one system will always unfold into guarantors of other systems—eventually of all other systems. Now it seems reasonable to me to call the ultimate unfolding of the guarantor category "God," who, like all the ultimates of the categorical unfoldings, is a design concept, but also a "reality."

I'd not drop the name "theology" for the study of system guarantors, though I wouldn't press hard for it either. The label is a useful tease. My colleagues like to argue endlessly as to what should be required courses for our MBAs. My answer is that I have grave doubts about making any of the existing ones required, but that I have no doubt that we should require a basic course in theology. But naturally I don't mean a course that analyzes the Old Testament or Christian doctrines about Jesus' divinity. I mean a course that deals with the theory of the survival of systems, including the theory of whether they should survive. Surely, in their lifetime, our MBAs will never face a more important question as managers.

But now I need to respond to my young colleague of 1932 who at nineteen wondered whether his perfect God might not be perfectly evil, a speculation from which he eventually escaped by a tautology ("only a good God could produce good things"). Forty-five years later I, too, wonder whether the guarantor may not be evil—that is, the Devil.

On the subject of God and the Devil humans tend to be exceptionally stubborn with respect to their beliefs. The atheists I've known consider God-believers to be absurd. And agnostics, despite the modesty of their claim, are absolutely positive that God's existence or nonexistence cannot be known: no question about it. Similarly, many who follow Jung are fully convinced that good and evil always go together, and that there are no pure saints or devils; a conviction analogous to the discovery that social planners cannot be "objective," and that *certainly* every judgment has a subjective component.

But the more I think about evil, the more confusing the concept becomes. Thought suggests that were the guarantor perfectly good, we would not have a world as full of evil as this one is. Whereas if the guarantor were evil, it surely would use what game theorists call a "mixed strategy"—that is, making "good" moves among the "evil" ones. But can we define evil? The chapter on the ethics of the systems approach suggests two ways to define the good, and thought will generate two complementary ways of defining evil: the generation of unhappiness and the generation of inequity. So thought goes. But there is something about evil which thought cannot grasp. One hardly grasps the depth of evil in Iago by saying that he made Othello and Desdemona unhappy or wasn't very fair to them. The Japanese novelist Yukio Mishima in *Confessions of a Mask* wrote about a young man who is overcome at times by a fantasy in which a handsome youth is bloodied o'er; the tragedy does not lie in the fact that the fantasy made him unhappy or discriminated against good-looking youths.

Consequently I must postpone the discussion of evil until I've written about the enemies, *not* because the enemies are evil (they are not in this account), but because I can say more sensible things when thought is not the predominant influence.

Finally, I come to images of the guarantor, the fantastic variety of ways in which humanity has viewed God. I made no scholarly search for my list on page 101, but simply recalled some that I have come across. (Some of the views listed are more conceptual than imagined, of course.) If one were to consult Frazer's *Golden Bough*,° the list would become much greater. Of course, there is the temptation, inspired by hubris, to take many of these images as "primitive" and hence as having no relevance for our "advanced" civilization, until we recall the Nazi conviction that God is Aryan; I have no doubt that many Americans see Him as a supremely successful tycoon.

°James G. Frazer, *The Golden Bough*, abridged edition (New York: The Macmillan Co., 1963).

Some Images of God(dess)(s)

1. Monotheism
   a. God as everything: pantheism (e.g., Stoics and Spinoza)
   b. God as perfect (Plato, Augustine, Anselm, Descartes, Leibnitz, etc.) (here God loses personality—there is no personal God)
   c. God as Trickster (e.g., practical joker, as in Descartes' speculation)
   d. God in relation to humanity
      i. as one to be loved (worshiped, sacrificed to, etc.)
      ii. as one who loves
      iii. as listener (to be prayed to)
      iv. as trinity (Father, Son, Holy Spirit)
      v. as designer (e.g., Leibnitz)
      vi. as guarantor (e.g., Kant)
   e. God as Evil

2. Pantheism
   a. the gods as archetypes (e.g., in the Greek myths): *puer-puella*, father, Great Mother, messenger, etc.
   b. the gods of agriculture (e.g., the Aztec gods)

3. Neither of the above
   a. God as imaginary, nonexistent (atheism)
   b. God as unknowable, even regarding its existence (agnosticism)

The last three categories need not be discussed here, since they form the subject matter of the second and third parts of this book. In Chapter I, I tried to give a personal defense for my assumption of the role of a systems philosopher. Since I've introduced my nineteen-year-old self, I might add that I've been "keeping a journal" ever since, in the sense that a great part of what I write feels like a letter to myself. Whether publishing such letters is wise, is a matter for continuous reflection.

The Ego in Planning

The next section of the *Critique of Pure Reason* deals with the "deduction" of the categories, with what "right" we can claim them to be necessary for all experience and thus to be a constituent aspect of reality.

The major lesson I want to draw from this section concerns the concept and the image of the ego. One of the apparent consequences of British empiricism of the seventeenth and eighteenth centuries is that ego must be that which has experience; in other words, ability "to see" implies that "I see." From this rather plausible implication emerges an image of fantastic loneliness, because of the realization that I and I alone know what it means to have my experiences: "You cannot possibly experience directly my pain; you can only see my grimaces and feel sympathy, but you cannot sense the pain I am sensing." In the loneliness of this imagery there is a figure standing on an isolated landscape with no one and no shape as far as the eye can see. Indeed, the ultimate of this loneliness is to be found in solipsism, the argument that there is no (empirical) evidence whatsoever that there are any other sensing creatures in the world besides myself.

The tragedy continues as ego contemplates its future and its death. There is no guarantee of a "life beyond death," and indeed there seems to be overwhelming evidence that all the other egos with whom this ego has been acquainted simply disappear forever after death. Never again will one be able to converse with the departed. So the lonely ego looks forward to its death, when suddenly it will be ego no longer, but a blankness, a nothingness that will last forever. To be sure, the material body will become a part of nature in some way, but ego consciousness ceases. The sadness of this image of cessation seems even deeper than the sadness of the lonely one on the vast empty plain.

Now let's see what Kant had to say about this imagery. Kant's problem in this section of the *Critique* is to explain the unity of consciousness at a moment of time (his name is the "transcendental unity of apperception"). The mind is capable of sensing a diversity of things in consciousness—the chair one sits on, the color of the table, the scratch of the pen, the murmur of the refrigerator. Whence comes this unity? Not from the category of unity, because that functions to distinguish between one and many within the field of consciousness and does not unify the field. Kant's answer is that ego serves to unify consciousness; all of the varieties of things perceived by the mind are held together by "I see," "I feel," "I hear," etc.

But the implications of this discovery go far beyond Kant's theory of perception (and apperception), because now the "ego" is *not* the whole of consciousness and certainly not the center of being of the mind. Kant himself made use of this conclusion in the *Critique of Practical Reason*, where he speculates on the existence of a good will for each individual, which is clearly *not* the ego. Furthermore, he argues in this section of the *Critique of Pure Reason* that the ego cannot operate without a non-ego. The non-ego is the content, so to speak, of an "outside reality" which makes up consciousness.

Thus the ego has lost its loneliness with Kant; it can only exist if there are other realities.

Later psychology borrowed heavily from this Kantian idea (which, of course, was not brand-new with Kant). Freud distinguishes between the id, the ego, and the superego; Jung between the ego and the self.

If we turn now to the planner, we can see that a new dimension of ego has been added—namely, the plural ego, the "we" rather than the "I." This in itself is also a rather fantastic development, of both imagery and idea. The planner easily escapes loneliness, because his individuality is part of the collective "we," who must strive so hard to make the world a better place to live in. Furthermore, there is the "they," the helpless, who so desperately need to be served. What *we* must do is help *them* to understand, to eat better, to exploit less, and so on. Even the pronoun "you" has a different image from that of the lonely ego. The lonely ego speaks of a "you" who cannot sense its pain, may not even exist. The plural ego speaks of a "you" who needs to be taught; "they" become "you" when "we" are directly in contact with those who need to be served, or who can serve those who have the need. Then, of course, it must be remembered that "you" is the pronoun of love, though we planners may not know how to make use of this fact.

The question of immortality also takes another shape under the plural ego. The "we" stretches back in the past to all who have attempted to understand human destiny. There is nothing odd about saying that we—including Plato, Thomas Aquinas, and Kant—perceive the need for a better food policy for the world. No matter that these three, as individuals, are dead, and God only knows where their souls reside, if anywhere; they are still as much a part of the collective "we" as we living are. So are those to come—the endless generations who will surely concern themselves with human destiny. Of course, none of this says that individual planners may not get an ego kick out of their publications, public lectures, or workshop performances; the singular ego is always there and will display a life of its own.

Although the plural ego escapes the distress of loneliness and mortality, nonetheless it does have a suffering of its own: isolation. This is both the imagery and the paradox of the plural ego. The image is an isolated "we" completely surrounded by a "they"—the image of an island in a vast sea.

The paradox arises because of the special nature of the planners' "we." Later on, in talking about politics as an enemy of . the systems approach, I'll take the view that the political approach to human affairs also involves a plural ego. But this is the plural ego of community ("polis"), a sharing together of a common concern. The plural ego of the planner, on the other hand, is much more like Kant's singular ego which unites the consciousness of the individual mind. The plural ego of the planner unites a collective consciousness.

It is strange in a way that Jungians have devoted so much attention to the collective unconscious and practically none at all to the equally mysterious phenomenon of a collective conscious, a "we" that brings the multitude of aspects of the consciousness of humanity into a unity, sometimes called "holism." Some writers describe holism as the attempt—on the part of an individual—to understand as much of the "whole system" as he can. This is a case of the individual ego striving to enlarge its consciousness. But the original meaning of holism was that there is a sense in which the properties of the whole cannot be inferred from the properties of the parts. As applied to the plural ego, this means that the collective consciousness of the "we" has a grasp of reality which is greater than the "sum" of the grasps of the individual egos. "We" are not just a collection of individuals but are in fact an ego itself that is "more" than the contributions of each individual's consciousness.

What is paradoxical is that such an ego should feel isolation from the "they," who are not part of the collective plural ego. If the immense "they" that surrounds us is apart from us, then in what sense has our collective consciousness grasped the "whole system"? Paradoxes are not to be solved; since they depart from doctrine, they are the spirit of change.

Now I should note the differences in the meaning of the collective plural ego for the goal—the objectives—and the ideal-planner. The goal planner regards "them" as his clients who need his special services. There is nothing particularly lonely about the goal planner's ego; it shares tasks in a kind of partnership between the manager and the expert. The objective-planner, too, sees the need for partnership, because the manager has a good sense of reality and feasibility, both of which are essential for objective-planning. It's the ideal-planner who feels the alienation, but who also feels the need for the withering away of the "we-they" dichotomy, not by committing collective "we"-suicide, but rather by absorbing all of "them" in "us," through participatory planning, through public involvement, etc. Nevertheless the voice of the enemy, politics, can be heard: "We" need to get "them" more involved. How do "we" get "them" to attend more public meetings?

A Priori Science

The next section of the *Critique* is of fundamental importance for both Kant's epistemology of phenomenal events and the planner's epistemology of recommendations, because it deals with synthetic a priori knowledge. An analogy may help as far as it goes. Suppose a computer program has been designed to estimate the cost of construction of a highway. If the program designer could program a function called "reflection," the computer might ask itself how it knows its print-out is approximately correct. It might then realize that a part of the answer to this question is "because I assume the inputs were approximately correct." The other part is "because when I operate on the inputs (add, multiply, etc.), my operations are valid." The second part is the domain of synthetic a priori knowledge of the computer program. The point is that all raw inputs must be processed through the program's arithmetical operations. The result is a set of universal principles, holding for all inputs. The principles are "valid" because that's the way the program was designed, and *not* because the raw information confirmed them as true.

Kant saw that there were two radically different "tests" of a theory about natural events. To test Galileo's theory that the acceleration of a freely falling body is constant, one makes suitable observations which form a sort of "raw input." But one also assumes the transitivity and asymmetry of the process of events in time ("if a is before b, and b before c, then a is before c" and "if a is before b, b is not before a"), and these two principles are not confirmed or refuted by observations.

Kant was designing another kind of "science," the science of the conditions under which phenomenal science is made possible. It is a science consisting of universal laws.

Since later thought and experiment cast considerable doubt on the validity of these laws, there was a strong tendency to throw out all of Kant's a priori science. Singer, I think, offers the best way to redefine a priori science, as a kind of evolution of intellectual thought. There is a logical manner in which observation may force a revision of a priori science, or the basic Weltanschauung of science. Such revisions tend to be slow in happening and have some of the characteristics of revolutions in the social order. Singer's forte was careful conceptual analysis; Thomas Kuhn found a less precise but more popular version by introducing the concept "paradigm" to describe the evolutionary process. Of course, the important difference between Singer and Kuhn is that Singer was trying to find a suitable design for the human inquiring system, whereas Kuhn was describing how historical inquiries have worked. There is considerable evidence that the reluctance of a discipline to change its paradigm or Weltanschauung may be far from what an appropriate design would indicate. The "revolutionaries" and the "counterrevolutionaries" are both convinced they are right, but not through any process of systems thinking. Hence, for Singer a great deal of so-called scientific inquiry is badly designed, even in the changes of its paradigms.

If we turn now to the categories of planning, a similar set of principles emerges. I don't want to pursue each one in detail, because this would lead to a repetition of what has already been said, but the following is a partial list:

1. Every deliberate (planned) action on the part of humans ought to serve a specific class of individuals (who need not be human), called "clients" (and ought *not* to serve some other classes).
2. Clients are served by attempting to coproduce ethically defensible goals, objectives, and ideals.
3. There ought to be an integrating (comprehensive) theme of the clients' goals, objectives, and ideals.
4. For every deliberate action there are individuals (decision makers) who ought to coproduce the action (and individuals who ought not to coproduce the action), through the use of appropriate resources (components).
5. For every deliberate action there are coproducers of the goals, objectives, and ideals, which cannot be, or ought not to be, changed by the appropriate decision makers.
6. There exists a class of actions that ought to be planned by an appropriate individual or group.
7. Such appropriate plans ought to be implemented.
8. There exists (ought to exist) a guarantor that prevents the disaster of erroneous plans (or guarantees human progress).

(There are nine categories, but only eight postulates since I've condensed categories 4 and 5 into one principle.)

None of these principles has the status Kant gave to his principles of phenomenal science. Indeed, some of them appear semantically to be tautologies, and others are rather questionable. As we'll see in the next chapter, they may be regarded as the thesis of a dialectic, the antithesis of which contradicts some of them. Nevertheless, except for 8, they probably form the operating policy axioms for both objective-planners and ideal-planners.

The question remains whether these principles in some sense describe reality or, rather, reside in the imagination of the planner. For the goal planner, reality stops at the boundaries of the problem. For the objective-planner, it stops at the boundaries set by feasibility and to some extent by responsibility. For the ideal-planner, there are no "real" boundaries, since over time more and more of reality will be "swept in." Singer used to say that the ideal is a "limiting concept," ever approachable by approximations. But it is also the real: the real distance between two points is an ideal of physical science. The ideal-planner takes an analogous stance: the ideals of humanity are the most real aspect of our lives.

The differences between the philosophies of the objective-planner and the ideal-planner form a dialectic, to which I'll turn in the next chapter.

CHAPTER V

Dialectics

THE MAJOR THRUST of Kant's *Critique of Pure Reason* was, as its title suggests, to determine how reason works in human experience. The section that deals with this topic is called the "Transcendental Dialectic." It might be described as laying down the limits of reason—for example, as a precursor of the concept of "bounded rationality." But it is by no means Kant's last word on reason; in the offing is his *Critique of Pure Practical Reason*, which describes the role of reason in a world other than the phenomenal: the noumenal world of the good will. What Kant is striving to accomplish in the "Transcendental Dialectic" is to show that certain reasonable and apparently important questions about phenomena can never be answered, even approximately, by "phenomenal science" and, specifically, by physics.

We have now the question whether Kant's lesson applies equally well to the planner and his "science": are there important questions the planner can never respond to, even with approximate answers?

Let's begin with one of Kant's examples. From a reasonable, if not a rational, point of view, the question whether the world (of reality) had a beginning in time seems relevant, exciting to explore, at least as important as, say, life on Mars. The question is rooted in imagery. On the one hand, there is the imagery of Genesis, where a God systematically creates the reality of the world in "six days." If the curious mind asks how long God had been around before he got onto the idea of creating the world, the image asks us to imagine that in God's worldless existence there was no time: he created the days along with the rocks and the animals. The other image asks us to view a world stretching back through the endless caverns of reality: a time stretching "to infinity." Kant represents these two images in the following way:

THESIS	ANTITHESIS
The world had a beginning in time and is also limited in regard to space.	The world had no beginning in time, has no limit in space, but with regard to both is limitless.

Kant proceeds to "prove" the thesis by reason, and then the antithesis by reason. His point is that once you allow the process of reason to be applied beyond any possible phenomena, the result will be that reason eats itself up: it can as readily prove x as non-x. And the beginning of the world in time, and its endless recession in time, are both beyond any experience.

Now planners are not really interested in the beginnings of the physical world. But they are interested in system "boundaries": How much of reality needs to be incorporated in a social systems design study?

Again, two images can help set the stage. The one (the antithesis) is of a child who wishes to play with a new toy a loving uncle has given. But the parent says, "First, you must thank Uncle Bob," and then, "Before you play with this nice white kitten, you must wash your hands," and then, "Wait till after lunch, dear," and so on. The toy, the center of it all, never gets played with. The other (the thesis) image is of violence: a large man in a hurry pushing things, animate and inanimate, out of his path, the image of modern technology. The conceptual representation of this imagery is:

THESIS	ANTITHESIS
All (social) systems (at given moments of time) have real boundaries; it is not necessary to investigate beyond these boundaries in designing the system.	There are no real boundaries of social systems; those that are temporally assumed must be broadened endlessly.

(Rather than use Kant's word "proof," I've chosen "explanation" instead for each of the theses and antitheses, since the unfolding process does not "prove" anything but rather elaborates on meaning.)

EXPLANATION	EXPLANATION
The argument is already a familiar one, of the objective-planner. To plan "realistically," we must set the boundaries, in both time and space, and in the scope of the problem. Otherwise, we are forever bringing in a new facet, and our planning stretches out forever, never reaching the point of making recommendations, never getting near implementation.	The argument stems from ideal-planning. Recommendations and implementation may occur, because they may both be rich sources of learning. The human species is a strongly inventive species. The major task of planning is to learn enough about the ramifications of interventions (both technological and psychosocial) so that we are in control, and this means a constant vigilance through ever more comprehensive systems design.

In his second antinomy Kant considers the basic material of the world, whether, as some pre-Socratics argued, it is made up of simple parts that themselves cannot be subdivided, or whether, as other pre-Socratics, especially Anaxagoras, stated, every "thing" can always be subdivided. This antinomy translates more or less directly into the planner's world. Many objective-planners like to use the term "systems analysis" for the work they do; indeed, there is, just outside Vienna, an International Institute of Applied Systems Analysis (IIASA), where objective-planners from many parts of the world, including some Communist countries, come to study energy, computers, mathematical programming. "Analysis" implies the ability to break down a system conceptually into its basic parts, and then to put it back together, usually by means of a model. A ready image is carpentry.

Our ideal-planner, on the other hand, although he may use analysis, does not regard the "parts" as simple. If, for example, we break down a system into a set of tasks (marketing, production, administration, etc.) and each general task into a class of subtasks, we may end up with individual people. But each person is a fantastic "system," with an ego, consciousness, unconsciousness (or ego, superego, and id), and each of these is a system with components. In Jungian terms each archetype is a "component" of the individual's psyche. But each archetype is itself a system, because each represents some aspect of the whole world. As I argued earlier, "in every problem is to be found all problems," and this translates into "in every system is to be found all systems." The imagery, therefore, is not that of the endless onion, but that of implosion turning into explosion, and vice versa, the same imagery that cosmology uses for the universe.

THESIS	ANTITHESIS
Every system has ultimate components which are not systems, but componentless entities.	Every system has components which are also systems, and hence there is no end to the chain of subsystems.

EXPLANATION	EXPLANATION
Realistically we can only understand a system by analyzing it down to its elements. All systems planning is comparable, say, to computer programming, where there are basic, simple instructions on how to operate on the elements, or to symbolic logic which starts out with "primitives," unanalyzable elements of the system. If we keep seeking for "deeper" aspects, say, of the people involved, we'll never end our search, and hence the problem solving will never come to a conclusion; such a problem solver is irresponsible, since he expects endless funding with no results.	Social systems are comprised of people. If we break down a system, say, to individuals, each individual will be found to reflect a world, and that world will be a system. Similarly, if we reach for the "ultimate" meaning of a concept, we will inevitably be led to the system of all concepts; concepts are not built up from primitives therefore. The search for understanding—i.e., comprehensiveness—is endless, but this does not preclude recommendations and acting which are part of the learning process.

Kant's third antinomy deals with freedom and necessity. The thesis opts for freedom, the antithesis for necessity. But the debate we have been following between the objective-planner and the ideal-planner is not concerned with the human freedom of either the decision maker or the planner, primarily because the classical dialectic between freedom and necessity has been synthesized today into a model of human behavior where purposive action and determined action are no longer seen as contraries.

However, one critical aspect of the freedom of the professional planner remains. The objective-planner functions to serve a "contractor"—say, a private company, a government agency, a foundation, etc. He is free to develop his own methodology, including formulation of the problem. The ideal-planner, on the other hand, cannot expect that the intentions of the contractor will be broad enough to include ideal-planning, so that inevitably he will have to go beyond the intentions of the contractor.

THESIS	ANTITHESIS
The planner is limited in his freedom to design the social systems by the intentions of the contracting party; he should not go beyond the boundaries set by these intentions.	The planner is not limited by any conditions in setting the boundaries of the social system; he is free to set them according to his judgment.

EXPLANATION	EXPLANATION
Both legally and morally the planner must serve those who support his work. He may use persuasion and argument to change contractual intentions, but once the contractor's intentions are clear, his choices are either to accept the conditions of work or not to work for the contractor.	The planner's main client is humanity, and when a conflict occurs between the contractor's intentions and what the planner judges to be the betterment of humanity, the planner should strive to serve the latter rather than the former.

Since this antinomy is partially autobiographical, some illustrations from my own planning experience are in order. During the 1960s, when the National Aeronautics and Space Administration (NASA) was in the midst of its Apollo program to land a man on the moon, its administrator, James Webb, thought it would be a good idea to have scholars in management study the innovative methods NASA was using to manage its complex program. I became head of one such group at the University of California at Berkeley. Ours was an interdisciplinary group which assigned itself the general task of the design and management of research and development projects. This assignment led many of us into a formulation of a philosophy of social system design. Indeed, many of the ideas in this book originated in that period of my life. There is no question that we went far beyond the intentions of most NASA personnel who monitored our project, with the exception of Webb himself. We freely questioned and debated the purposes of the Apollo program, which, from a systems point of view, were of dubious import for the betterment of mankind. In fact, one monitoring group in NASA headquarters graded the social science projects NASA supported in terms of (1) relevance to NASA's mission and (2) interdisciplinarity; we received F for the first and A for the second.

Now in the explanation of the thesis the words "morally" and "legally" appear. None of our attempts were illegal, since we clearly stated what we proposed to do, and widely published our results; only the support of the administrator kept us funded. But the moral issue is less easy to evade. NASA was funded by Congress to accomplish a specific mission. It is very unlikely that our efforts contributed anything toward that accomplishment; and, indeed, if we were listened to, we probably undermined public appreciation.

The same remarks apply to the sequel of the first project, when a group of us turned our attention to the Earth Resource Technical Satellite (ERTS), that NASA launched in the late 1960s. ERTS could take pictures (including infrared) of a section of the earth's surface every eighteen days, and it more or less covered all the surface that was free of cloud cover. ERTS was regarded by many as a great boon to mankind, because the imagery could be interpreted by experts to reveal various resources: watersheds, forest fires, rock and mineral formations, plant growth, etc. Our "systems minds" naturally turned to the evil side of this good. Since ERTS information could be obtained by any country that applied for it, ERTS was also a military spy. Many in South America called it another "U.S. spy in the sky," because it potentially could detect mineral resources that could be exploited by United States firms. It could also tell banks how much of each crop was being grown, and therefore whether to lend to farmers at harvest time.

Now it was not NASA's intent to look into any of these issues, since its mission was to launch ERTS and manage the data flow. The end of the story was a parting of the ways, once NASA understood what we were doing.

Finally, in the geothermal example in Chapter IV, it was certainly not the intent of the funding agency to consider what geothermal development does to the people who live around it, although we made clear that we intended to concentrate on this aspect of the system. Another parting of the ways occurred.

I have purposefully phrased this antinomy in terms of professional planning, where there is a contractor who pays for the work. But there is a more general form, which also highlights the morality issue. The thesis states that he who would serve another through helping him to plan, should not go beyond the boundaries of the other's basic intentions; "basic" refers not to goals that serve as means, but to the ultimate ends. The antithesis states that the ideal-planner is not limited by the basic intentions of those he serves; he may believe he knows better what ends should be attained. If the "other" is humanity, then the ideal-planner has the arrogance to say that in some regard he knows better than humanity what ideals we should strive toward. In an attempt to soften the arrogance, the ideal-planner may assert° that the ideals are what humanity will tend to want as it develops as a species; that is, the ideal-planner has a grand anthropomorphic theory which depicts the value-evolution of the human species.

Whether or not this really softens the arrogance is debatable. The ideal-planner must now face each of the enemies. Morality charges him with trying to intervene in the lives of others who don't want his intervention. Religion charges him with taking on God's role. Aesthetics charges him with an attempt to ruin the lives of others with his conceptual schemes. And politics slyly offers its services if he would like to form a "World-Concern Club" by means of which some of his plans could be implemented.

The ideal-planner may acquire some comfort in reflecting that he has plenty of company, since in the long tradition of the systems approach, writer after writer was declaring the need to pursue values which were far beyond the boundaries of the basic intentions of their contemporaries.

Kant's fourth antinomy deals with the necessity of certain beings in the world. For the planner, the question of necessity can be posed in a logical manner: namely, the necessary conditions that must be satisfied if there is to be an improvement in the human condition. Can some of these be known?

THESIS	ANTITHESIS
There exist absolutely necessary conditions, some of which can be known, for there to be a betterment of the human condition.	The necessary conditions for the betterment of the human condition either cannot be known or do not exist.

EXPLANATION	EXPLANATION
Two examples of such necessary conditions are survival of the species and freedom from continuous severe pain. No policy that leads to the destruction of the human species could ever be regarded as a "betterment," any more than could a policy that produced in a large number of people a debilitating state of mind and body.	*All* supposed necessary conditions are subject to scrutiny, because in planning for the betterment of humanity there are no obvious principles. Survival of the species may not constitute a "betterment," because we may be a highly dangerous species relative to the rest of nature, and our "best" condition may be nonexistence. Also, at times it may be necessary that large sections of humanity suffer pain, if that is the correct route for the betterment of the human condition in the future.

° I did so in *Prediction and Optimal Decision* (Englewood Cliffs, New Jersey: Prentice Hall, 1961), p. 26.

The image of the thesis is "a place to stand," and of the antithesis an eternal dance.

This antinomy takes up one of the themes of this book: the role of common sense in systems planning. For the objective-planner, common sense is a constant aid, because it blocks out the necessity of examining pathways that are "obviously" undesirable. For example, one option an organization may have is self-destruction, but common sense says that most organizations will avoid this option with all their might. However, for the ideal-planner, all options must eventually be studied, else the learning process is inhibited.

But on the negative side we see again the alienation of the ideal-planner from his fellow men; their destruction or pain is always an open option in the vision of the ideal-planner. He's not a very decent fellow.

This completes the review of Kant's antinomies as they relate to planning, and especially to the differences between objective-planning and ideal-planning. The differences have been presented in a dialectical manner, and hence it is time to review the dialectical process, first historically and then in the context of planning.

First, Kant. Kant had no doubt that the conflict of cosmological ideas as presented in the four antinomies was a serious matter for the mind, and not just a clever puzzle. Nor can we—as do those who expound on "bounded rationality"—retreat to the position that these ideas are simply beyond our powers to deal with: "We cannot . . . escape the responsibility of at least a critical solution of the questions of reason, by complaints of the limited nature of our faculties, and the seemingly humble confession that it is beyond the power of our reason to decide [on these cosmological issues]." °

Kant does have a solution, which he calls "dialectical." I can illustrate his method by a variation of his own illustration. Imagine that I bring to a potluck dinner a dish and, uncovering it, invite you to smell its delicious fragrance. You, however, being more frank than polite, simply say, "It stinks!" We are logically in opposition and might then turn to a third party for judgment: Is it fragrant or does it stink? But the judge may sensibly reply, "None of the above": it is not fragrant, neither does it stink, because it has no smell at all.

Kant's way of putting it is as follows:

When we regard the two propositions—the world is infinite in quantity, and, the world is finite in quantity—as contradictory opposites, we are assuming that the world—the complete series of phenomena—is a thing in itself. . . . But if we dismiss this assumption, this transcendental illusion, and deny that it is a thing in itself, the

°Immanuel Kant, *Critique of Pure Reason*, "Antinomy of Pure Reason," Section IV.

contradictory opposition is metamorphosed into a merely dialectical one; and the world as not existing in itself—exists—neither as a whole which is infinite nor as a whole which is finite in itself.°

Later, in the history of logic, De Morgan † invented a label for Kant's dialectical idea, the "universe of discourse." Thus Descartes, in one version of his philosophy, argued that either I doubt or I do not doubt my existence. If I doubt it, I think, and therefore I am; if I do not doubt it, I am certain, and therefore also I think and therefore I am. But the "universe of discourse" within which doubting and certainty are contradictory ideas is the universe of thinking. According to this account, therefore, Descartes committed a perfect *petitio principii:* in assuming that doubt and certainty exhaust the universe, he assumed (implicitly) that I am a thinking being. Were I a rock, I would neither doubt nor be certain.

We see, then, that Kant's dialectic is logical in nature: it seeks to find another ground between two opposites which seemingly exhaust the universe. It's "none of the above" method is highly useful in the unfolding process.

In Hegel the dialectical process becomes central. Instead of being a tool of critique, as in Kant, it is the essence of the learning and evolutionary process of humanity, at both the psychological level *(Phenomenology of Spirit)* and the historical *(Philosophy of History)*. Contradiction (or, rather, contrariness) plays the role of driving the process.

The logical implications of this shift are broad and deep and, even to this day, rarely appreciated. Perhaps the best way to dramatize the change is to suggest that objective-planning, following disciplinary science, is episodic in its approach. The word "episode" originally meant a story that was apart from, or in addition to, the main stream of a narrative. It has now come to signify a way of breaking up the learning process into segments, so that the main stream is no longer visible.

In disciplinary science the episodes are thesis (or hypothesis) testings. The Ph.D. candidate is told that he must set forth a thesis which he is to "test." Once the test has been performed, the episode comes to an end in three copies filed in the campus library. Sometimes the episodes are connected around a larger episodic theme—for example, as in the case of Arrow's "impossibility theorem" mentioned earlier.

But in ideal-planning the planning process is based on a "world view," or Weltanschauung. This Weltanschauung is used to shape raw data into information. A good example is "opportunity cost," which, as mentioned

° *Ibid.*, Section VII.
† Augustus De Morgan, a nineteenth-century logician and mathematician.

earlier, represents the value of the best forgone opportunity when an action is taken. But to estimate this cost, the planner needs to have a conceptual vision of the decision maker's world, both realities and values.

Since the ideal-planner sees the narrative as essentially a learning process, his method consists of systematically questioning his Weltanschauung; no aspect of it is "sacred" or obvious. Now one of the best ways to question a Weltanschauung is to design a plausible and hopefully powerful opposite. Thereby the learning process is put to a critical test. The next chapter illustrates how this can work in that aspect of the Weltanschauung which describes humanity's basic values. As we'll see, there the two view of human betterment can be described by the words "happiness" and "virtue." When we come to the second, we'll find reason to question the logic of this chapter, because a new set of categories will emerge.

It is natural to wonder whether the enemies could be swept into a dialectical process, and it's certainly tempting for the ideal-planner to do so. But the enemies have good reason to believe that he'll fail. In that last sentence you'll find a clue to the strategy of the enemies: use reason to show why reason can't absorb them.

CHAPTER VI

Ethics of the
Systems Approach

Why "Ethics"?

WE HAVE seen from an examination of the tradition of the systems approach that the problem of human destiny—that is, of ethics—has been central in historical writings. However, today we find a most curious phenomenon in which books on systems analysis, planning, operations research, etc., rarely consider ethical issues. I know of one rather well-respected school of public policy which up until recently offered no courses in ethics and discouraged discussion of ethical issues in its seminars.

One reason frequently offered for such neglect is that in order to mature, public policy requires a background of careful analysis, based on hard and solid data, in the "tradition" of the "scientific method." But, so goes the argument, ethical issues are slippery and seem not to be based on any universally acceptable analysis and data. Yet in the sixteenth and seventeenth centuries, when the tradition of the scientific method was founded, ethical issues were central to all those who thought and wrote about human inquiry. Many a twentieth century intellectual has become an aberration in the evolution of human learning, by blocking off critical issues of knowledge because his methods are not adequate to address them reliably.

There are a number of tactics that can be used to keep out the monstrous ethical issues that clearly surround the systems analyst. One is to insist that he who pays the bill for the analysis must state his goals clearly. But this lets in too much: crime, exploitation, cruelty, neglect, etc. Another is to adopt a "disaster" ethic: never recommend a policy that has a "reasonable" chance of producing human disasters (starvation, radiation, disease, excessive air or water pollution, floods, etc.). This is a little better, but it assumes that human life, no matter how it is lived, is better than death or a diseased body. In other words, this suggestion makes a strong assumption about system separability: that the values associated with disaster can be separated from other ethical values.

I think one reason a professor may discourage the discussion of ethical issues among his students in class is that he himself has no satisfactory answer; as a person, he may hold strong ethical beliefs, but he cannot "objectively" profess them since his intellect recognizes that they are all subject to doubt. What he fails to realize is that ethics is not a body of theory substantiated by facts. Instead, it is a process of continuously—and I think eternally—discussing and debating and occasionally fighting over the issues. In short, ethics is a dialectical process in which all humanity, past, present and future, must take part. The compulsive will want to know whether the discussion "gets anywhere," or whether it is merely a battle of abstractions that rarely if ever has anything to do with human affairs in action. The response is that the debate must include action as one of its components: ethics has to flow through real actions as well as through real ideas. It dries up once it is locked in a debate between academics who have rarely seen or touched the vital ethical body of real human beings in their daily lives.

Hence as we proceed, we'll be constantly introducing, as part of the theme, the ways people interact with people in the ethical mode. The compulsive may still want to know whether all this gets us anywhere—that is, whether there is overall maturation, evolution, or progress; but we'll have to postpone his question for the time being.

A Historical Debate: Kant and Bentham

If I were to follow the policy of this book up to now, I should have to turn to the history of ethics in this chapter to show how the process has occurred among our predecessors in the debate. But fortunately, and surprisingly, there were two "synchronous" debates—one in the eighteenth century, one in the twentieth—which are so rich that they virtually contain the essence of the whole historical process. I call them "synchronous" because the parties in the debate apparently were not aware of each other's existence and yet wrote at the same time. The first debate is between Kant and Bentham, both of whom were deeply involved in considerations of human ethics during the 1780s, Kant in Königsberg, Bentham in London. The second debate is between Singer and Jung, both of whom spent their active lives on ethical matters, most especially in the 1930s and 1940s, but neither of whom seemed aware directly of the other's work, Singer in Philadelphia, Jung in Zurich.

Bentham

We can begin with Bentham. It was his intent to design a methodology for assessing the worth of a proposed piece of legislation. In this sense he was a founder of the class of "evaluation" or "assessment" techniques which have infiltrated into every aspect of government today: cost-benefit, technological assessment, social impact assessments, etc. What is required for so bold a venture is to discover the source of all human value. Bentham takes this task to be relatively simple: "Nature has placed mankind under the governance of two sovereign masters, *pain* and *pleasure*. It is for them alone to point out what we ought to do, as well as to determine what we shall do. On the one hand the standard of right and wrong, on the other the chain of causes and effects, are fastened to their throne. They govern us in all we do. . . . "°

This principle of human values is not new with Bentham; he borrowed it from David Hume, himself one in a long line of philosophers who believe that the only "realistic" approach to ethics is to be found in everyman's search for happiness. Not only is the principle realistic ("after all, once you get rid of rhetoric and abstract garbage, everyone is out for himself"), but it also can be given a more or less rigorous form. This point seems to have been recognized at least as far back as Epicurus (341-270 B.C.), who, as I remarked earlier, would have been very pleased had cybernetics been discovered in his day, because he was struggling to develop a stability model for the flow of pleasure and pain in the human body.

Bentham, who was certainly not the deepest of thinkers, almost immediate-

---

° Jeremy Bentham, *Introduction to the Principles of Morals and Legislation* (New York: Hafner, Macmillan, 1948), chap. I, p. 1.

ly takes an enormous step in his quantification of the pleasure base: "A measure of government . . . may be said to be conformable to . . . the principle of utility, when in like manner the tendency which it has to augment the happiness of the community is greater than any which it has to diminish it."° Community, he says, is a fictitious body made up of members. The quantification now emerges as the addition of the pleasures of the members minus the pains. The size of the community is determined by the number of "interested parties," a concept that, as we have seen, still remains frustratingly vague, for "interested parties" are, I suppose, the same as my category "client," and we have no solid methodology for determining the class of clients. Nor is there any clear explanation of why the individual who "realistically" takes care of his own interests should now operate under a "principle of utility" which declares that the community government should maximize the pleasures of all members.

Finally, Bentham's program becomes bogged down in the meaning of pleasure and pain, both of which are elusive concepts with apparently limited applicability. It's probably clear to most of us adults that sexual intercourse is pleasurable at times, and that a toothache is painful, but whether writing this book is pleasurable or painful I'd be at a loss to say. Furthermore, many writers have talked about the "paradoxes" of hedonism—for example, that planning for pleasurable events often reduces their pleasure. Hume seems to have sensed these difficulties and used the concept of "utility" instead. The measure of the utility of an object is the degree to which the object facilitates one in the pursuit of his goals. This definition does two convenient things. It removes the necessity of trying to assess the degree of pleasure one has in attaining a goal, and it enables us to measure utility along some recognizable scale, such as a combination of money and probability. Thus we escape the awkward task of "interpersonal utilities"—for example, comparing my enjoyment of a good meal with your enjoyment of a sail on the bay. There are technical difficulties with even this money-probability measure; but these have been thoroughly studied, and to some utilitarian planners, at least, satisfactory methods are emerging. Furthermore, we avoid invidious comparisons of the different goals people pursue. Hume dramatizes this point in one of his dialogues where a traveler recounts his visit to a strange land in which one of the leading citizens has a homosexual affair, is married to his sister, has murdered one of his best friends, and yet is one of the most highly respected of the citizens. When the traveler's friend interrupts to ask whether this tale is not total fantasy, the traveler replies that the land he "visited" is

° Ibid., p. 3.

none other than Greece and Rome in the classical period. Hume's point is that we can question only the utility of a goal in relation to other goals, and not the moral worth of the goal itself.

We shall see how Singer improves on Hume's and Bentham's ideas, but now we need to examine one of the really puzzling aspects of all utilitarian ethics—namely, where the center of value lies. If we say, as Bentham did, that pleasure is the driving force, what does it drive? Bentham says, "the individual." But who or what is the individual? Or, in Hume's case, who or what has goals?

I suppose that both Bentham and Hume would reply "the conscious ego," because, after all, it is the conscious ego that "has" experiences, and pleasure and pain are experiences. Whether conscious ego has a utility function is not so obvious. In any event, modern empiricists such as consumer surveyors and pollsters also assume that conscious ego is the value center which tells them what product or politician it most prefers.

However, we have already seen in the last chapter that conscious ego is not the whole of the intellectual mind; it is what unifies experience at a moment of time, but it is not clear why this property should make it a center of value for the individual mind. But Kant goes even farther and finds the center in a totally different part of the individual.

Before turning to Kant, I should discuss a far more sophisticated attempt to preserve Hume's idea, by trying to define the center in terms of the potential behavior of an individual. The theory states that what an individual wishes ("intends") in terms of goals can be ascertained by observing behavior and inferring potential behavior. The "individual" is a complex of potential behaviors individuated by space and time. The goal or goals an individual wants are those he would pursue if he had perfect knowledge and access to all potential goals (other stipulations, not detailed here, need to be added). The point is that even though the "individual" is a complex of inner attitudes, categories, or whatnot, his potential behavior is a resultant of all these.

But this suggestion, appealing as it is to empirical investigators, doesn't necessarily solve the problem. Suppose the "inner" self of the individual is a battle between a number of forces, as Jung suggests. And suppose that maturation (or, as Jung says, the process of individuation) is losing the battle. Then does it make sense to say that the "individual," who is really not an individual at all, truly wants what his potential behavior says he wants? "He doesn't know what's good for him" seems to make good sense for someone who has lost touch with his inner self.

Kant

Now let's see how Kant tried to frame the ethical issues of human life. It may help to turn back to Bentham's beginning and compare it with Kant's:

Nothing can possibly be conceived in the world, or even out of it, which can be called good without qualification, except a Good Will. . . . Power, riches, honor, even health, and the general well being and contentment with one's condition, which is called happiness, inspire pride, and often presumption, if there is not a Good Will to correct the influence of these on the mind, and with this to rectify the whole principle of acting, and adapt it to its end.°

So close together in time is the writing of the two passages by Bentham and Kant, that I can easily imagine such a synchronism as the two authors penning them at the same moments of time, with Bentham's unconscious responding so vehemently to Kant's statements as to drive him to state unequivocally that pleasure and pain are the only drivers of human beings, and with Kant equally driven to make his strong remarks about the weaknesses of human happiness as a guide to the good life.

What does Kant mean by a Good Will? Since it is absolutely good, it does not operate by conditionals. "If you want to be happy, or healthy, you ought to do such-and-such" is a conditional. But the Good Will has only one principle, which is categorical. A friend of mine was thinking of using the threat of electric shock in his experiments with human subjects. I advised him not to. "Why not?" he asked. "Because it would be immoral." This is the property of morality that Kant found appealing; there are no further arguments to be found other than an elaboration of meaning.

Kant's metaphysics led him to his formulation of morality. As we have seen, the *Critique of Pure Reason* dealt with the world of phenomena—that is, intelligible experience—but it left open the question of whether there are other worlds of things-in-themselves, which he called "noumena." If the Good Will is such a being, it can have no relationship to experiential concepts. Thus, "Thou shalt go to mass each Sunday, or thou shalt eat only kosher food" are both too directly tied to the specifics of experience. Hence the moral law must be as general (universal) as possible. The result is his categorical imperative, which I'll translate somewhat. If, on a street with heavy traffic, you cut in ahead of another car, its driver may roar, "What's the big idea?" If his

° Immanuel Kant, *Foundations of the Metaphysics of Morals*, 1787, sec. I. p. 191. Translation by Thomas K. Abbott, Kant's *Critique of Practical Reason and Other Writings* (London: Longman's, Green & Co., 1889), p. 9.

question makes good sense to you, then it's easy to understand Kant's imperative. You are to imagine that every action you will to occur has a "big idea"—
that is, has a point to it. You are also to imagine that your will has universal
legislative authority, so that you can will your "big idea" into a universal law,
applicable to all other wills. This feat of imagination places an extraordinary
burden on your will; you have become king of the world! If you can tolerate
the burden of having your big idea become a universal law, then your big
idea and the action are moral. If you cannot tolerate it, then the big idea and
the action are immoral. Thus if the big idea of cutting in on another driver is
to shorten the time of travel, then your universal law says that all drivers must
take any means available to shorten their trip home; I'll leave it to your
imagination to picture the resulting traffic scene.

As in the case of many philosophical systems, we can cut off Kant's
metaphysical base and appreciate his idea on its own. What he has done is to
elevate equity to the highest pinnacle of human values. Our morality is based,
not on maximizing benefit minus cost in a community, but rather on making
sure that no inequities occur, that everyone is treated fairly. Kant's way of
putting this idea is again in the form of a moral maxim: each of us is to will
his/her actions so as to treat humanity, either in ourselves or any other,
always as an end in itself, never as a means only. This follows, he thinks, from
the first maxim, because everyone is in principle a universal legislator, who
must on this account have equal importance with everyone else.

Kant's theory of morality is not egalitarian; that is, it does not necessarily
say that all shall share equally in the world's resources. Rather, he emphasizes
that moral equity implies that the will of every rational being is a universally
legislative will. The ideal is a "kingdom of ends," in which in matters of
moral duty everyone legislates universally, everyone is king.

If we are to accept Kant's moral theory as part of the systems approach,
then we arrive at another perspective of the categories of planning discussed
in the last chapter. In Kant's ideal, on matters of moral duty, the client, the
decision maker, and the planner are one. The purposes and the measure of
performance disappear (there is no "trade-off" for immoral acts). There are
no components or environment. Implementation occurs immediately, as each
individual wills the idea of his act to be a universal law. We could say that the
Kantian social objective is that the planner and the decision maker "wither
away" in the moral domain: there is no need, in the ideal, for laws or lawyers,
no need to regulate. Of course, a new set of categories emerges. In place of a
trade-off principle, there is repentance and forgiveness, for example. If I will
an immoral act, I cannot "pay" for it, but I can repent and pray for
forgiveness.

But now we run into a difficulty: What does the phrase "in matters of moral duty" mean? Surely the citizens of the kingdom of ends will not be deciding how strong the steel should be for a bridge, or the manner of operating on a cancer patient, or teaching mathematics. What is the boundary between the moral and the technical? Kant tried to help in this matter by distinguishing between different types of "imperatives." Hypothetical imperatives like "if x is to occur, then do y," may be technical and require the expert—for example, if x is building a bridge, curing a disease, or teaching a course. On the other hand, if x is a Benthamite imperative "be happy," then y may be a combination of expert and nonexpert knowledge. When the imperative has no conditional—that is, when it is categorical—then it is moral, and every will can decide. This by no means stops the questioning, as we shall see.

On the matter of categories we still have the question of the guarantor in Kant's moral theory.

But before considering the central role of the guarantor in Kant's philosophy, it is important to examine some of the philosophy's inherent difficulties. It's very interesting to see how appealing, and even glorious, both Bentham's and Kant's programs are when viewed in the large, and how troublesome they both become for thought when considered in their specifics. It seems very noble to say that the prime objective of all legislation should be the greatest happiness for the greatest number; but when we consider the happiness of a specific individual, we have great difficulty in determining *what* is being happy and *how* happiness takes place.

Similarly, what more noble ambition could mankind have than to create a kingdom of ends, where each individual wills his acts so as to create equity for all, each willing the universal laws that hold for all?

But, though we may be able to discern why certain "big ideas" can*not* be universalized, it is very puzzling to determine which can be. In the *Foundations* Kant gives examples of actions whose underlying "big ideas" cannot be universalized—for example, suicide and lying. This seems to imply that we could will two universals: never take your own life and always utter the truth (at least as you understand it). Neither universal seems very palatable. If I am almost completely certain that I have a cancer that will soon turn me into a vegetable for a prolonged period of time, why shouldn't I set my affairs in order and commit suicide? Such an act, indeed, seems fully to treat humanity both in myself and in others as an end, whereas restraining from suicide seems more like treating my temporary living self as a means for pure survival, not to mention those who will have to care for me. Kant's logical mind responded to this argument as follows: "We see at once that a system of nature of which it could be a law to destroy life by means of the very feeling whose special nature it is to impel to the improvement of life would contradict itself. . . ." But the question is whether the life of one who faces nonhuman living would not be "improved" by the act of suicide. The point is not to bicker with Kant regarding his examples, but to show the extreme subtlety in trying to find principles that can be willed to be universal.

As for always telling the truth as we see it, God help us! Deception is an integral part of human living and communication, where the truth often exists in the unconscious, and properly so. That most marvelous communication device called "silence" is a powerful way of *not* uttering the truth—or anything—in order to send a message. Of course, our pragmatist will point out that lying or silence have pragmatic truth, since they serve well in attaining specific goals. But then the pragmatic maxim says, "Always speak— or not speak—so that the right goals may be obtained," which is a very difficult maxim to understand.

It begins to appear that all universal moral maxims are not simple. To spell out the maxim concerning suicide or lying, we are forced rationally to consider again the whole system, its clients, its components, environment, etc. Consider another example, our human relationship to other living species. The simple maxim would be, "Thou shalt not will the act of killing." But this seems a quite unnatural maxim for a species to follow with respect to all other species, assuming that predator-prey and food chains are biologically natural. On the other hand, wanton slaying of masses of living beings, leading to the extinction of a species, also appears unnatural. The maxim that emerges is, "Act with respect to other species so that your act is natural." But this is *not* a simple maxim; among other things, human intelligence vastly obscures its meaning, because it blots out any instinctual knowledge we might have that would aid us—as it aids other species—in obeying the maxim.

Now we can return to the matter of expert knowledege with respect to Kant's categorical imperative. Suppose, as Henry Ford was designing the first assembly operation for the manufacture of automobiles, he had asked, "Should I, morally, make cheap autos?" He might very well have replied, "Yes, because I can easily will the law that all persons who desire it should have cheap automobile transportation; it is my contemporary auto makers who are immoral because they build cars only for the rich." A time traveler from 1977 would have been able to tell Henry that his "universal law" would eventually produce the smoggy cities of today. Hence, aren't experts really needed in Kant's world: systems planners who can trace out the consequences?

None of these difficulties with Kant's moral philosophy diminishes one bit its value and importance for planning. It is always relevant for the planner to ask whether it is possible to universalize a principle that is being used to evaluate a policy or action. In one cost-benefit study for a new London airport, the planner estimated the cost of the possible destruction of an old Norman church in terms of its extant fire insurance; the universal maxim becomes: "The monetary value of anything is the price that would be paid were it to be destroyed." This would put a lot of us who fail to carry insurance into the category of complete unimportance in relation to social changes. Another government C-B study used "expected future income flow" as a measure of human value, thereby condemning old-age programs to a very minus benefit-minus-cost. In all these cases the failure to be "universal" with respect to all humans leads to immoral policies which nevertheless satisfy a total cost-benefit criterion.

It is absolutely essential for the health of our species, I think, for us to use "moral assessment" as well as economic assessment. We may judge that we should adopt a policy where we also judge that the underlying principle cannot be universalized, just as we often judge that the policy may not be economically sound. But we should bring up to our collective consciousness the inherent immorality of our policies. Or should we? The voice uttering the "should" is the voice of systems rationality; the enemies probably find such utterances inappropriate.

We find difficulties similar to these if we turn to Kant's other version of the moral law, never to treat humanity as a means only. How are we to understand this principle? One likely guide is to say that if in our planning we treat people the same way we treat machines or rocks, then we are treating their humanity as a means only. But is this much too strong? On an individual level we Americans treat postmen, ticket takers, policemen, soldiers, "as means only," in the sense that were they automated, we'd not recognize the difference, except perhaps to worry about unemployment.

And what is the word "humanity" supposed to mean? Kant himself was aware of the danger that his maxim might be interpreted in a purely negative way, with its ominous "never." One way to handle the maxim might be to gather together your resources and retire to the wilderness to become a hermit. Then the only way to break the moral law would be to treat your own humanity as a means only. But, Kant says that it is not enough that the action avoids treating humanity as an end in itself; it must also *harmonize* with it. He goes on to say that "humanity" is something that has degrees of perfection, and that the maxim implies, not mere avoidance of treating humanity as a means only, but the obligation for advancing humanity on the scale of perfection. One can recognize how rich a meaning Kant was able to squeeze out of his rather sterile, logical categorical imperative. But here again we see the need for the expert on human development to guide us in the improvement of the human species.

This idea of harmony takes us back to the guarantor. But a few concluding remarks on the difficulties are in order. First, there is no question that the general idea of Kant's "humanity principle" is very rich, both as a planning guide and basic human policy. It was an eighteenth century dream of total human equity, regardless of race, age, status, whatever. Its ideal was to remove in human societies all hierarchies based on empirical criteria such as power and wealth.

Second, Kant himself recognized the difficulties of ultimately justifying the rationality of his moral law. The *Foundations* ends:

"Thus, while we don't comprehend the practical unconditional necessity of the moral law, nevertheless we do comprehend its *incomprehensibility*, and this is all that can reasonably be required of a philosophy that struggles to carry its principles up to the very limit of human reason."

I made this passage an epigraph for this book, because it says as well as any other writing how we rational types are to relate to the enemies.

The Guarantor

We have seen how, for Kant, there are two basic values of the human being, happiness and the moral law. One cannot act to achieve happiness and thereby be moral, for morality demands that the moral law be the sole motive. Does the reverse hold? Can one achieve happiness by acting morally? In practice the answer is, "Apparently not," since virtuous actions so often lead to unhappiness. But in principle there is no reason why acting morally can't cause happiness, for we can surely imagine a world, a kingdom of ends, where morality and happiness are in complete accord. Kant calls this vision the *summum bonum*.

But it is unattainable, for Kant. It can make sense, therefore, only if we humans can gradually approximate it. What are the necessary conditions for the reality of this constant struggle? They are Kant's famous trilogy: God, Freedom, and Immortality. Only a supreme being could guarantee the reality of the endless pursuit; only if the will is free, could the "pursuit" be possible; only if the soul (will) is immortal, could the pursuit exist for each will.

History, as we are about to see, did not leave matters as Kant describes them. To be sure, the immortality of the social system seems essential if, besides goals and ends, there are also ideals that can be approximated more and more closely but never attained. And to be sure, if this ideal-seeking is to make sense as a human pursuit, there needs to be freedom of choice at the individual level. And finally, as we have seen in Chapter IV, a systems approach that includes idealism as part of its rationality, must also assume a guarantor. But what is the modern version of the guarantor? To get an answer to this question, as well as to examine the modern dialectic of social versus individual values, we can turn to Singer and Jung.

Jung

To introduce Jung, suppose we go back to Kant on individuation. In order to account for the "Freedom" part of his trilogy, Kant says in his *Critique of Practical Reason:*

Now in order to resolve the apparent contradiction between freedom and the determinism of nature in one and the same action, we must recall what was said in the *Critique of Pure Reason,* or what follows therefrom, namely, that the necessity of nature, which cannot co-exist with the freedom of the subject, pertains only to the properties of the thing which is subject to time-conditions. In other words, the necessity of nature applies only to the subject as a phenomenon. . . . But the very same subject, who on the other side is conscious of himself as a thing-in-himself, also considers his existence *insofar as it is not subject to time conditions,* and thinks of himself as being determined by laws which he gives himself through reason. In this aspect of his existence, nothing comes temporally before the determination of his will. . . . °

Hence, in the noumenal world of the second *Critique,* time and its correlate, causality, do not exist. Furthermore, the Good Will even transcends anthropology as a behavioral science, as we have seen, and becomes the "archetype" of the pure moral law.

However, Kant leaves us with a deep puzzle vis-à-vis the psychological *in-*

° Kant, *Critique of Practical Reason,* trans. Thomas K. Abbot (London: Longman's, Greene & Co., 1889), p. 191.

dividual. As we have seen in the first *Critique*, he argued that things may be individuated in one of two ways—by a space-time framework or by minute description. Both methods have been used by science from its very beginnings. The planets are individuated by their orbits in the heavens—that is, by space and time. Men are often individuated by their fingerprints—that is, by minute description.

But now we come to the world of the Good Will. What individuates one Will from another? Not space and time, as we have seen. Nor minute description either, because all the categories of rich experience have nothing to do with the Good Will. What then? Although Kant may have been aware of this problem, and somehow thought of a Good Will as being related to a specific space-time individuated human, no really satisfactory story is forthcoming. But Jung can help, because he was inventing a new theory of psychological individuation as he went along. The individual is the self, but the self is a unique form. The point is a very subtle one, but suppose we try it this way. That two leaves in the forest cannot be exactly alike is almost certainly true. But as Kant pointed out, *in principle* they could be: there is no logical or physical reason for the impossibility of two leaves being the same. Furthermore, even though two leaves are not exactly alike, they may be much more alike than they are like other things; there are degrees of likeness, so to speak. But in the case of the unique individual, we must say that *in principle* no one is exactly like anyone else, and there are no degrees of likeness: he isn't more like this individual than like that individual. We see the similarity in this last point between uniqueness and morality. In morality there are no degrees of goodness, no trade-offs of good for evil; in uniqueness there are no degrees either, no comparisons. Grammatically we can't say, "You're pretty unique," but, most important, psychologically we can't either.

But remember all along we are trying to speak to a mind that will want to know what this uniqueness really is. And the answer is not readily at hand, because we lack a logic of uniqueness. Nevertheless, Jung presents a number of very helpful as well as radical ideas. First, individuation is a *process* for Jung, and in this regard he differs from Kant and all the rest of science. At a given moment of time, a body is individuated for Kant and for all physics, even including modern quantum mechanics, where statistical distributions of the position of a particle do not in the least negate the static nature of its individuation. But what does Jung mean by a process of individuation? Does he mean we move toward uniqueness? But, then, are there degrees of uniqueness after all?

Thus, as so often happens with one's reactions to Jung, we have both an insight and a deep puzzlement. The insight is the idea that psychological individuation is a process, and not a completion. Another way to put the matter is to say that individuation by space and time is *essentially* dependent on the object's relationship to other objects, just as is individuation by minute description, while the kind of individuation Jung seems to have in mind seems not to have this essential property. Although relationships are important, especially relationships to other psyches, the individuation itself is not essentially built out of such relationships.

Further to deepen the insight and confound the perspective is Jung's elevation of the process of individuation to the pinnacle of the Good, so that the process is alike to Plato's soul contemplating the pure idea, and to Kant's Good Will motivated by the moral law within.

In the Platonic myths not all souls reach the blessed state; indeed, it seems apparent that the great mass of them do not. And here is Jung on the same topic:

> These proceedings [of therapy] rest on the assumption that a man is capable of attaining wholeness, in other words, that he has it in him to be healthy. I mention this assumption because there are without doubt individuals who are not at bottom altogether viable and who rapidly perish if, for any reason, they come face to face with their wholeness. Even if this does not happen, they merely lead a miserable existence for the rest of their days as fragments or partial personalities, shored up by social or psychic parasitism. Such people are, very much to the misfortune of others, more often than not inveterate humbugs who cover up their deadly emptiness under a fine outward show. It would be a hopeless undertaking to try to treat them with the method here discussed. The only thing that "helps" here is to keep up the show, for the truth would be unendurable or useless.°

What is the process of individuation? Jung sees the inner psyche as a vast land, for most of us unexplored at the conscious level. For present purposes it is enough to say that it is the land of types and archetypes. In *Psychological Types*,† Jung felt he had found four basic human functions (thinking, intuition, feeling, and sensation) and two opposing basic attitudes (introversion, extroversion). Usually one of the functions becomes highly developed, while its "opposite" is underdeveloped and frequently operates through the unconscious. Hence one voyage of exploration of the self is the understanding of your functions, how they operate, and how the undeveloped side can be strengthened. Jung's description of the types is fairly logical in form, although a curious logician might wonder whether the functions are exhaustive and exclusive. Certainly the attitudes are not; Ackoff and I discover four basic attitudes rather than two: energy is drawn from outside, directed outside (objec-

---

° C. G. Jung, *Two Essays on Analytic Psychology* (New York: Pantheon Books, Bollingen Series, 1953), p. 109.

† Jung, *Psychological Types* (New York: Pantheon Books, 1959). First published in 1923.

tive externalizer); drawn from outside, directed inside (objective internalizer); drawn from inside, directed outside (subjective externalizer); drawn from inside, directed inside (subjective internalizer). Ackoff has made use of this expanded classification in his studies of alcoholism.° I suspect that the functions are similarly nonexhaustive. They are certainly not exclusive; feeling cannot function unless all the other functions are there, for example.

But the archetypes are another matter, where intuition rather than thought predominates. One identifies archetypes through the history of human cultures, but the method of identifying an archetype is open. In a collection of essays, *Four Archetypes*, Jung reveals the state of confusion regarding the methodology. He begins by asserting, "I am an empiricist, not a philosopher; I cannot let myself presuppose that my peculiar temperament, my own attitude to intellectual problems, is universally valid."† He then goes on to mention Kant's categories as changing the whole concept of empirical research, which has led, he thinks, to the realization that thinking, understanding, and reasoning are *psychic* functions and are based on the fact that each of us has a preconscious psyche. After giving some credits to his predecessors, Jung says, "If I have had any share in these discoveries, it consists in my having shown [!] that archetypes are not disseminated only by tradition, language and migration, but that they rearise spontaneously, at any time, at any place, and without any outside influence."‡ Furthermore, archetypes (unlike Kant's categories) are not determined in regard to content and only in a peculiar way with regard to form (his analogy is the axial system of a crystal).

All of this is extremely puzzling for a critical philosopher. Are we to suppose that Jung's strong assertions about the universality of archetypes are *not* universally valid? If he is an empiricist, what does he observe that confirms the existence of archetypes? If the analogy is correct, is the method of the archetypal psychologist analogous to the method of the crystallographer? I've come to the conclusion that this type of passage, which appears elsewhere, was "Jung's joke." In his later writings he didn't really care about methodology; the appeal of archetypal psychology was enough.

I've seen no definitive list of the archetypes. They include the archetypes of the mother, the father (old man: senex), boy and girl (puer and puella), rebirth, and the trickster. Freudians have their own list and seldom use the term archetype. And, of course, there are at our disposal a plethora of other views of the inner psyche.

° R. L. Ackoff and F. Emery, *On Purposive Systems* (Chicago: Aldine, 1972).
† C. G. Jung, *Four Archetypes* (Princeton: Princeton University Press, 1970).
‡ Ibid., pp. 3–4.

From my point of view here, I am interested less in the details of archetypal psychology (to which I'll return in the chapter on religion) than in its implications for the systems approach. The process of individuation includes the search for types and archetypes, or some other mapping of the inner self.

The moral principle that emerges in Jung is: "Thou shalt undergo the process of individuation." We arrive at a translation of Kant's principle of treating every man as "an end withal" into: "Thou shalt never interfere with the process of individuation of thyself or another." Jung seems never to state the principle in this form, but he comes close to it:

Here one may ask, perhaps, why it is so desirable that a man should be individuated. Not only is it desirable, it is absolutely indispensable because through his contamination with others, he falls into situations and commits actions which bring him into disharmony with himself. From all states of unconscious contamination and non-differentiation there is begotten a compulsion to be and to act in a way contrary to one's own nature. Accordingly a man can neither be at one with himself nor accept responsibility for himself. He feels himself to be in a degrading, unfree, unethical condition. But the disharmony with himself is precisely the neurotic and intolerable condition from which he seeks to be delivered, and deliverance from this condition will come only when he can be and act as he feels is comfortable with his true self. People have a feeling for these things, dim and uncertain at first, but growing ever stronger and clearer with progressive development.

When a man can say of his states and actions, "As I am, so I act," he can be at one with himself, even though it be difficult, and he can accept responsibility for himself even though he struggle against it. We must recognize that nothing is more difficult to bear with than oneself. ("You sought the heaviest burden, and found yourself," says Nietzsche.) Yet even this most difficult of achievements becomes possible if we can distinguish ourselves from the unconscious contents. The introvert discovers these contents in himself, the extrovert finds them projected upon human objects. In both cases the unconscious contents are the cause of blinding illusions which falsify ourselves and our relations to our fellowmen, making both unreal. For these reasons individuation is indispensable for certain people, not only as a therapeutic necessity, but as a high ideal, an idea of the best we can do. Nor should I omit to remark that it is at the same time the primitive Christian ideal of the Kingdom of Heaven "which is within you." The idea at the bottom of this ideal is that the right action comes from right thinking, and that there is no cure and no improving of the world that does not begin with the individual himself. To put the matter drastically: the man who is pauper or parasite will never solve the social question."*

We see in this passage that if we define individual morality as the obligation to undergo the process of individuation, and social morality (planning) as the obligation to satisfy people's needs and wants, then Jung

* C. G. Jung, *Two Essays*, p. 223.

makes individual morality a necessary condition that must be satisfied before social morality can exist. Here we have one answer to the relationship between morality and (social) prudentiality. But there must be a certain amount of uneasiness with this answer.

The uneasiness arises out of the need, for Jung, to create an environment for the process of individuation—for example, the sessions where the analyst and his "patient" interact. Of course, no specific environment is required, and Jung does state that many people have gone through the process of individuation without any clearly recognizable professional help. But there can be no question that many others desperately require such aids, or else they run into a deep danger of following pathways that run out in a dry and rocky wilderness whence there is no return. Thus it apparently follows that there are some, and perhaps a very large number of souls, who can become blessed only if the social environment provides assistance. In this regard Kant seems to be on safer ground, for there is no indication in Kant that a particular social organization is needed to help humans be motivated by the Good Will. But even for Kant the matter is not at all clear. It is reported that he criticized on moral grounds a poor man's stealing bread for his starving family; somehow, obeying the moral law "Thou shalt not steal" does seem a bit easier for the affluent than for the deprived.

Hence, we owe it to ourselves to see whether the opposite of Jung's thesis is not more correct; individual morality presupposes the solution of social morality. That is, we ask whether there is some social institution that would help bring about everything Kant wanted to have happen in his Kingdom of Ends, or Jung in his Kingdom of Heaven. Otherwise expressed, the question is this: Can we extend social ethics—that is, social prudentiality—far enough so that it will provide us with all we need for a code of individual morality? If we can, then perhaps the need for the uniqueness of the individual will also disappear.

Singer

Our spokesman now is Edgar A. Singer. We note first of all that Singer's program (of defining all morality within what I am calling "social morality") needs to reintroduce purpose. For Kant (but not necessarily for Jung), the moral law is not valid because it serves some purpose; it is valid in and of itself. In other words, Kant's morality is ateleological, while Singer's is teleological. Singer characterizes ateleological goods as follows:

And so, to make a beginning—a convenient rather than a forced one—any definition of *the good* must do one of two things: it must either imply or not imply *reference to an end and a means*. So much in the way of classification logic alone may effect, but only the historian can say which of these possibilities the thought of the past has accepted, or whether its opinion lies divided between the two. One will, in fact, find the latter to have been the case; and moreover find the alternative ways of defining to have been called from an early day the "teleological" and the "ateleological" respectively. For reasons that will appear as we advance, we may let the historian provide us first with examples of "ateleological goods."

These ateleological goods are the easiest of all to find, for they cost no thought to formulate and still less to follow; together they make up the world's treasure of maxims. "Let justice be done though the heavens fall," the Roman saying had it, and no wording could have been better conceived to bring out the virtue to which all maxims pretend—that of setting forth practices universally good; not good as means to one end and not to another, nor yet ends for which now one means and now another is good, but practices certain to be good "whatever happens." Primitive taboos, sacred customs, decalogues, unwritten laws of heaven, categorical imperatives are all of this character; they all purport to be universal and necessary rules of conduct issued in the name of virtue or of piety or of both. The authority accorded them by the mind accepting them never differs greatly from that acknowledged by Antigone in her hour of trial: all that man may devise "must yield unto the changeless, unwritten word of God; for this is not of today or yesterday, but lives forever; and no man knows when first it came to be." As for the theory of contentment that goes with this conception of purposeless goodness, Antigone again best suggests the essence of it: *not* to live by the unwritten word is to suffer an inner discontent so incurable that a life lived in the torment of it would not be worth the living.°

But for Singer, the question of whether we should pursue an ateleological ethics is quite simply answered in today's world, because ateleological goods have no place:

Of the many simplicities and sincerities of the past there is none the modern mind feels itself more confidently to have outlived than such as seek contentment in a life of obedience to purposeless laws, laws for which no more can be said than that "no man knows when first they came to be" or why or wherefore. To more experienced thought the whole history of the part played by such laws (written or unwritten) in the lives of men is likely to be viewed as presenting a problem of interest to the anthropologist and psychologist, but to none other. In so far as these scientists have found explanation for the phenomena involved, the origin of the law and of the fear to break it are given a common reason: the law represents a general principle of practice that once served the common purpose of those who felt bound to observe it. Their bondage, enforced by social sanctions slow to change, long outlived the purpose that bound them, with consequences anything but happy to those whose morality must in

---

° Edgar A. Singer, Jr., *On the Contented Life* (New York: Henry Holt & Co., 1936), p. 125.

the end have become an inexplicable slavery. Evidently this explanation will hold as true of the moral bondage of today as of any that ever withheld the past from intelligent self-emancipation. So far as one can observe, the faith that still abides in inviolable principles is a source of anything but content, even to those who live by it.°

For Singer, if we are to search in a rational manner for the good, it must be found in our purposes—that is, our goals or ends. One might conclude immediately that Singer is on his way to relativism, that very dull philosophy which answers all questions with "it depends." If the good is to be found in our purposes, then doesn't it follow that one man's goal is inevitably another's evil, and there is no absolute good?

But Singer does not end up in relativism at all; instead he arrives at a modern form of absolutism. He does so by borrowing an idea directly from Kant—namely, the notion of an "ideal," a notion that has formed the heart of our discussion of systems planning. An "end," Singer tells us, is a goal that in principle can be attained—for example, the goal of eating a meal, or reading a book, or defeating an enemy. An ideal in principle is unattainable but in principle can be approximated within any prescribed limit. We have seen (p. 47) that the concept of ideal is no empty abstraction, and that Singer pointed to an example of his notion of ideals in modern science. According to Singer, the *answer* to any question anyone can meaningfully pose is always an ideal; the statements we make in response to questions about the natural world are always approximations. Singer's philosophy is an idealistic realism: the real is always an ideal.

Singer used the whole community of ideal-searching scientists as a model for his theory of the good. But he is much too close to modern culture to equate the good with the true—that is, to say that our moral obligation as humans is solely to approximate ever more closely the answers to questions. There must be a more fundamental ideal that explains why truth approximation is a good. If we can find such an ideal, then we have an absolute good, not a relative one. But it is an absolute good that we can only know imperfectly, even though it exists absolutely. Singer is very much like Kant in that he uses his introverted thinking to do the job for him. Were he more an extrovert he might pose his question as follows: Is there anthropological evidence that man is an ideal-seeker, and if so, what ideals does he seek? Such a question might have led him on a search over cultures and ages for the basic patterns of ideal-seeking, as Jung searched for evidence of archetypes. Instead, he saves himself the cost of this trip, at least temporarily, by some thought. As we shall see, in the end he still has to attempt the hero's voyage with a different mission in mind. His thought is this:

°Ibid., p. 127.

Everyone will have heard a certain slangy sentiment with which the man of our day is given to toasting the fellow of whose projects he approves: "More power to his arm!" This toast will have been raised to a thousand undertakings, different enough and even contradictory; yet the wish of him who proposes it will always be the same. Well, but there is always one fellow of whose projects a man is bound to approve, one man to whom each of us is ready at every moment to raise this toast: from the beginning of life to the end thereof every mortal man will constantly want for himself increasing power of arm. Is there not then this unchanging wish that runs like an unbroken thread through all life's moments, on which are strung the varicolored beads of desire? And yet there is such treachery in words one must not accede in haste. Here, for example, it is certain that there is an ever-repeated wish, a wish that always expresses itself in the same form of words, but is it certain that these same words always mean the same thing? Indeed, do they ever twice denote the same thing? If their prayer were twice granted, would the two increments of power accorded the petitioner add up to one increment by which his power was enhanced? Of one who has been granted a wish to become a more powerful chess player and thereafter his wish to become a more powerful flute player, what would one say in the end; has he been increased in power, or multiplied in powers? With no more than this to guide us the latter no doubt is all we should feel justified in affirming; but if we were asked, not which of the two we had prayed for but for which of the two we should pray, could we hesitate? Not if there is any soundness to the "ancient wisdom of childhood," learned from a thousand fairy godmothers who have left no godchild untested on this very point. Their lesson is always the same: "With only one wish to be had, choose rather the power to get whatever you may come to want than the pleasure of having any dearest thing in the world." Our modern at any rate takes this ancient wisdom to have touched the bottom of things; he takes the deepest wish in any man, the common wish of all men, to be no other than the wish for more power—the wish to grow more powerful.*

The word "power" in this passage is rather unfortunate, because the meaning of the term has been changing radically in the last few years. To a nineteenth century mind (and a part of Singer was nineteenth century) there could be nothing wrong with each individual's having more power, because it meant that he had an increased ability to cope with life and its environment, and, in particular, to aid his fellow man. The same remark can be made about "control." When Singer writes on the idea of progress, he concludes that "the measure of men's cooperation with man in the conquest [i.e., control] of nature measures progress."† But "conquest" or "control" of nature did not mean exploitation of nature to the nineteenth century mind. However, for today's youth, "power" and "control" both have strong negative connotations and are in a sense antithetical to the emerging morality of the individual.

Thus to appreciate Singer, we will have to be tolerant of his language as

---

* Ibid., p. 145.

† E. A. Singer, *Modern Thinkers and Present Problems* (New York: Henry Holt and Co., 1923), p. 279.

well as of his introverted thinking. As far as the latter is concerned, we can see the trick it has played on us. If we are teleological creatures, as Jung and Singer both believed, then we seek goals; if we seek goals, then all of us must also want the power to attain them, and this therefore is our common ideal. Thinking tells us so. It tells us that if anyone wants x, he also wants the power to attain x.

Now one question that it is always appropriate to ask an introverted thinker when he is being very introverted and thoughtful, is whether his pronouncements are tautologies; he, above all, will recognize the fairness of this question, because he is intensely interested in tautologies. Leibniz, for example, believed that God thinks only in tautologies—that is, that tautological thinking is perfect knowledge. So we ask Singer whether the sentence "If A wants x, A also wants the power to attain x" is a tautology, and I suspect that his answer must be yes. Indeed, the evidence we use to establish the fact that a person "wants x" is the fact that he seeks the power to attain x, so that "wanting x" operationally means "seeking the power to attain x." But the critical point is not the semantics of a tautology, but what the tautology creates. So Kant's "discovery" of the categorical imperative by pure thought is somewhat absurd. But something beautiful and powerful came out of it— namely, his Kingdom of Ends. So, too, Singer's bit of "deducing" the moral law, "Thou shalt seek power," is also somewhat absurd, but out of it comes one of the deepest and most significant accounts of social morality that has even been written.

Singer's story of social morality is divided into two parts, which can be labeled "positive" and "negative," provided we, like good Jungians or Hegelians, recognize the positive side of the negtive as well as the negative side of the positive.

The positive side draws heavily on the nineteenth century optimists, Bentham, Mill, etc., but vastly enriches their concepts of social utility. The general idea, which emerges from Singer's basic tautology, is to develop an "enabling" value theory—that is, to categorize those activities that increase an individual's chances of gaining what he wants. These are rather easy to enumerate: (1) a richness of means at his disposal—that is, "plenty"; (2) an awareness of the appropriate means to select—that is, "knowledge"; and (3) a desire for goals that are consistent with the goals of others—that is, "cooperation." This trilogy of ideals neatly summarizes all that is contained in Singer's concept of power. A member of a community that progressed toward such a combination of ideals would find himself rich in opportunities, skillful in the selection of the right ones, and not only free of interference by others, but enjoying their help and his own helpfulness.

But the simple listing of these ideals is not enough, because the important point is the dynamics of their pursuit, which is most complicated. One clear story that history, especially recent history, tells us is that societies that become reasonably successful at creating plenty, at the same time become dangerously noncooperative. Indeed, it seems likely that a strong technological society tends to produce indifference to others, and especially to those who are deprived. But if we could better understand what brings about a cooperative society—for example, a scientific community or an artists' colony, then we might better understand how plenty and cooperation can coexist.

Perhaps the best illustration of Singer's idea of progress is to be found in the myth of the Chinese Revolution. I call it "myth" because the story satisfies the dictionary's requirements that there be a "superhuman being" and an account "without a determinable basis of fact or natural explanation." Of course, it may not be a myth for some Chinese or later historians. The myth begins with Chairman Mao and his sayings, especially his "superhuman" faith in the hundreds of millions of people. There is a withering away of ego desire and a strengthening of community sharing. In Singer's terms, the beginning emphasis in the Chinese Revolution is on cooperation rather than on industrial technology (science and plenty), as it was in the United States. But the interesting point is the different definition of cooperation. In Singer's case, "A cooperates with B" means that when A successfully pursues his (A's) goals, such pursuit increases B's chances of success vis-à-vis B's goals. But in the Chinese myth, "A's goals" are indistinguishable from the community goals; A "cooperates" as his ego desire withers away or becomes merged in the community goals. Once this magic transformation takes place, then a plethora of noncooperative behaviors disappear: crime (stealing and murder), drug traffic, malnutrition, etc. Furthermore, the vexing problem of centralized versus local planning is resolved: where a high degree of technology is required (e.g., in surgery or in allocation of rice crops), the planning tends to be centralized. Where less technology is required (e.g., in adequately feeding people in a village), then local planning takes place. There is a minimum of local versus central tension as ego desire withers away. Thus, according to the Chinese myth, many Americans translated "life, liberty, and the pursuit of happiness" into "life, liberty, and property rights" and thus came to resent Big Government and its interventions. The myth says that people can become "free" by banishing the demands of ego desire, by escaping "human bondage."

In any event, even accepting the myth as history, it seems clear to me that Singer's ethical theory does not yet admit of any "measure of performance," so that we lack any plausible way to determine whether progress is taking place or ever has taken place. The affluent part of the world has undertaken an awesome adventure in technological growth that may set the human species back beyond the primitive. If so, we surely do not have "developed" countries. It would be like calling the man who holds the bomb in a crowded theater the "developed" man, while those who are cowering in fear are "underdeveloped" or "developing."

But for the moment I want to put aside this puzzling aspect of Singer's theory of progress in order to turn to another puzzle. The question that will be raised by any reasonable man who is aware of his own self-interest, is this: Why should I pursue these ideals to any extent beyond what serves me best? Specifically, why should I seek the betterment of the lives of future generations?

Singer's answer is that the ideal of life is to seek not *comfort* but *contentment*. "Contentment" comes from the Latin *contentus*, "to be contained," and hence connotes a state of mind or spirit which is stable and not subject to collapse. Singer's word for the ideal-seeker is the "hero," who is the blessed: "If to persevere in a progressive life is a necessary condition to contentment, then to win contentment one needs all the qualities of the hero."°

A similar idea of the hero appears in Jung. Here again there will be some confusion of terminology, because the archetype of the hero in Jung is only one among many, and the heroic is often taken as a description of one stage of development, rather than as a description of all development, as in Singer. But Jungians on occasion do refer to the whole process in this manner: "Not for nothing is the individuation process said to be an analogy of the 'quest of the hero.' "†

One senses a parallelism of discovery in Jung and Singer, each independently investigating the same mystery. The quality of mind that, for Jung, makes a person seek his own individuation is the same quality that, for Singer, makes him a "hero." Of course, the descriptions are different or, rather, complementary. The key concept in Singer is "renewal," the renewal that brings on a mood of dissatisfaction with oneself and one's surroundings. It is the very same psychic force that drives one through the "stages" of individuation. Indeed, the same image, the spiral, is used to describe the process. Compare, for example, these two accounts by disciples of Singer and Jung:

° E. A. Singer, *In Search of a Way of Life* (New York: Columbia University Press, 1945), p. 34.

† J. Jacobi, *The Way of Individuation*, trans. R. F. C. Hull (London: Hodder and Stoughton, 1965), p. 47.

The point of view we have tried to develop in this essay is that the time has come to recognize the circularity, or spiral form of science, and the complete interdependence of the sciences. It is perfectly proper to consider one phase of nature as though it were known, while we develop another phase, as long as we do not make this a permanent state of affairs.°

The individuation process, as the way of development and maturation of the psyche, does not follow a straight line, nor does it always lead onwards and upwards. The course it follows is rather "stadial," consisting of progress and regress, flux and stagnation in alternating sequence. Only when we glance back over a long stretch of the way can we notice the development. If we wish to mark out the way somehow or other, it can equally well be considered a "spiral," the same problems and motifs occurring again and again on different levels.†

For both pathfinders, Jung and Singer, there is the need to explain the psychic energy that drives the process of individuation or the heroic life. And the answers are alike. Here is Singer's:

. . . man is not inherently heroic, or if he be, yet he is not easily stirred to display his heroism in action. Seeing which, we cannot but reflect that if there were any source from which man could draw new heroism, new power to carry on the fight for power, how invaluable to his contentment would be the discovery of this source! But if, indeed, the only one to whom man can turn for help is man, and if all a man can do for himself and all his neighbor can do for him is exhausted in the scientific and moral equipment already organized into the texture of a progressive community, he cannot turn at the moment of acting to any living being for additional help. Such help as the living are able to give has already been given. What remains? Beside the living, what other humanity is there to turn to, except the dead?‡

And the help that the "dead" may provide the hero is, for Singer, through art, through the creation of a heroic mood, which is his "fourth ideal":

Among the states of being commonly, and, as I think, properly classed as moods is one we call the *heroic*. Under its sway we see things neither in rosy red nor somber black, face things neither with emotionally drunken courage nor emotionally stricken fear. The hero looks on the chances that lie before him with all the clarity of vision his intelligence can command; he faces the known risk with neither fear nor fury in his heart; he accepts the dangerous game for but one reason; realising that some objective dear to himself and his kind is only to be won by someone taking the inevitable risk of trying for it, he offers himself as that one, or quietly accepts at the hands of fate the role for which fate has cast him. Such heroism as this has no biological past. It is not a biologist's category; the hero did not come into being until the artist, the tragic artist, created him. And since he, with the mood to which he gives his name, is essentially a work of art, is it not into such as he that the artist makes us when he moves us out of

---

° C. West Churchman, *Theory of Experimental Inference* (New York: The Macmillan Co., 1948), p. 216.

† J. Jacobi, *Way of Individuation*, p. 34.

‡ Singer, *In Search of a Way of Life*, p. 34.

ourselves? When he moves us out of our ordinary humdrum selves into a newness of being strange to us?°

Jung's concept of renewal is based on the "collective psyche," which, in spirit, is exactly what Singer meant as well:

Access to the collective psyche produces a renewal of life in the individual, whether the sensation resulting from it be agreeable or disagreeable. One would like to hang on to that renewal, in some cases because the vital feelings find themselves thereby fortified, in others because it promises the mind a rich harvest of new knowledge. In both cases, those who are unwilling to renounce the treasures buried in the collective psyche will try to retain, by any means possible, the new elements whose advent has added something to their primary reason for living. The best means would seem to be identification with the collective psyche, for the dissolution of the personal positively invites one to plunge into that "ocean of divinity" and, losing all memory, to merge oneself with it. This mystical phenomenon, which is a propensity of all mankind, is as innate in every one of us as the "desire for the mother," the longing to return to the source from whence we came.

As I have shown elsewhere, there lies at the root of the regressive nostalgia which Freud regards as "infantile fixation" or incestuous desire, an essential value to which the myths, for example, bear witness. It is precisely the best and the strongest among men, the heroes, who give way to their regressive nostalgia and purposely expose themselves to the danger of being devoured by the monstrous primal cause. But if a man is a hero, he is a hero because, in the final reckoning, he did not let the monster devour him, but subdued it—not once but many times. It is in the achievement of victory over the collective psyche that the true value lies; and this is the meaning of the conquest of the treasure, of the invincible weapon, the magic talisman—in short, of all those desirable goods that the myths tell of. Anyone who identifies himself with the collective psyche, or, in symbolic language, lets himself be devoured by the monster and becomes absorbed in her, also attains to the treasure defended by the dragon, but he does so in spite of himself and to his own great loss.†

I think I have said enough to establish a close relationship between Singer and Jung with respect to progress and the process of individuation, even though both were working independently and knew little or nothing of the other's efforts. But now something needs to be said about the difference between the two, which is also striking. Jung's basic exhortation is toward the psyche as a reality and toward the individual psyche, while Singer's is toward the collective "mankind" and toward the most general psyche. Jung's hero seeks the completeness of the Self, Singer's the completeness of all Selves.‡

° Ibid., p. 54.

† Jung, *Two Essays*, p. 280.

‡ The distinction is subtle but important. In Jung the Self is a collective but is not the "sum" of all individual selves, while for Singer it is: nothing more can be added to the concept of Self than what is contained in all "selves."

Jung devoted most of his life's work to the scholarly examination of the sources history provides of the myriad pathways of individuation, while Singer devoted most of his life's work to the philosophical study of science and society. Singer has made social morality a necessary condition for individual morality; individual morality only gains its meaning in the context of a service to mankind. Jung does the opposite: only when the individual has attained a degree of maturity will he adequately respond to social problems. But I suspect that the children of such parents would find their differences to be ones of life-style rather than basic. It is certainly natural that an introverted thinker would in his later years regard service to mankind as the most relevant aspect of the world, for thereby he can introvertedly explore his extroverted side. The young Jung of the early experiments strikes me as being extroverted thinking, and if this guess is accurate, one can account for his second stage of life as a search for the inner life.

It may be helpful to assess the journey thus far. Bentham said our fundamental drive is toward pleasure, away from pain. But he introduced a bit of mystery by telling us that the drive is toward maximum pleasure of the maximum number. The mystery is this: Why should any of us be motivated by such a drive? He might have replied: "Because if you're not so motivated, your fellow humans will punish you, and you'll become 'a wretch concerted all in self' and shall 'descend to the vile depths from which you sprung, unwept, unhonored, unsung.'" But all that is the daydreaming of the visionary.

The mystery deepens as we read Kant. Here is something called a "Good Will," which wills actions whose principles can be universalized, even though the psychological self may suffer deeply. It is a timeless Will in the sense that the universal principle applies to all times equally. If an act treats an ancestor as means only (e.g., by ridiculing his life to create present laughter), then the act is immoral; if one wills to build a strip mine and thereby destroys an environment that future generations might enjoy, then the act is immoral.

The same timeless quality appears in Singer's heroic mood. All mankind of all ages, dead, alive, to be born, share in the endless quest for ideals, and even when an age feels the enormous well-being of its present state, it "should" feel moved by a moral dissatisfaction. Why? Why should the endless quest go on?

And in Jung's case at least the past is level with the present, since the past exists in the present psyche in the form of archetypes. The role of the future is not so clear, though there is the prescription to continue the exploration of the inner self, however happy one may be. Why?

The mystery has a great tradition. In Hindu philosophy, we are urged to give up our desires and replace them by a desireless state to be gained through meditation; though at times the Western mind becomes confused, because the "desireless state" as described seems to be something very desirable. In Plato, the good is to be sought; it is not pleasure, though there is a hint, highly developed in Christianity, that seeking the good wins rewards in the afterlife. The eighteenth century rationalists tried to axiomatize the mystery, and nineteenth century philosophers like Sidgwick tried to make a mixed stew of Benthamism and Kantianism.

But the mystery is also to be found in the history of revolutionary action, where the rewards to the revolutionaries themselves are highly dubious. Marx seems to have tried to explain the mystery of revolution by a kind of determinism—that is, that humanity as a species is determined to pass from feudalism, through the bourgeois stage, to the dictatorship of the proletariat. But why?

And in this book we have found the same mystery in the ideal-planner. As we'll see in the next chapter, he may be overwhelmed by the image of the possible future of humanity going to its living hell, disease-ridden, malnourished, energyless. But why should such an image disturb him? There may be psychological causes why it *does* disturb him, either archetypal or in his own past history. But why should it?

Could we find a teleological explanation of the mystery? Hobbes thought we could and explained it by showing how our egoistic drives have led us to the need to be gregarious and subsequently to form a commonwealth. But one would surely have to stretch matters beyond belief to show how such drives could account for a deep concern for past and future generations or for a deeper exploration of the self.

A more likely, though highly speculative, teleological explanation is to be found in the biology of the species. Perhaps, as human intelligence evolved, a concurrent evolution of broad-sweeping concerns also took place, to counter the tendency of intelligence to invent dangerous techniques for satisfying human desires.

Another, also speculative, explanation is that this mysterious "heroic mood" is neither teleological nor ateleological: it is a form of psychic energy which does not seek goals, objectives, or ideals, nor does it obey ateleological laws. Its roots lie, not in rational morality, but in a "spirit" of morality. This is a suggestion to which I'll return when I review morality as an enemy of the systems approach.

One final note on the mystery. Despite Kant's claim that the Good Will is universal (all of us can will our actions), or the eighteenth century claim for universal postulates of morality, the heroic mood is clearly not universal, at least not at the conscious level: a large number of people care neither for the past nor for the future generations.

If the morality of the herioc mood is not universal, then what? We are back to the "we-they" image. The hero dearly wishes to be at one with humanity, just one of the boys/girls, but can't help observing that a vast number of people are different from him/her in their moral concerns. But he may take some comfort in the reflection that his vision, though not universal, is essential for the survival and the betterment of humanity, and that the vast majority of humans, taken collectively over the ages, agree that if betterment is possible, it should take place.

We have come to the confrontation of the systems approach with human affairs, to the question whether other approaches are "better." But before we explore the land of the enemies, we need to give the hero—the ideal-planner—one more opportunity to make a plea for rationality.

CHAPTER VII

Retrospect and Prospect

> All the interests of my reason, speculative as well as practical, combine in the three following questions:
> 1. What can I know?
> 2. What can I do?
> 3. What can I hope?
>
> Kant, *Critique of Pure Reason*

THE TIME has come to look both backward and forward. And the account need not be long.

The story began with a somewhat disgruntled hero, who perceived of the world as populated with stupid people, everywhere committing the environmental fallacy. The fallacy was a case not merely of the "mind's falling into error,"* but rather of the mind leading all of us into incredible dangers as it first builds crisis and then attacks crisis.

Like all heroes, this one looked about for resources, for aids that would help in the dangerous battle, and he found plenty of support—in both the past and the present. It won't hurt to summarize the story thus far. If the intellect is to engage in the heroic adventure of securing improvement in the human condition, it cannot rely on "approaches," like politics and morality, which attempt to tackle problems head-on, within the narrow scope. Attempts to address problems in such a manner simply lead to other problems, to an amplification of difficulty and away from real improvement. Thus the key to success in the hero's attempt seems to be comprehensiveness. Never allow the temptation to be clear, or to use reliable data, or to "come up to the standards of excellence," divert you from the relevant, even though the relevant may be elusive, weakly supported by data, and requiring loose methods.

*See H. B. Smith, *How the Mind Falls into Error* (New York: Harper and Brothers, 1923).

Thus the academic world of Western twentieth century society is a fearsome enemy of the systems approach, using as it does a politics to concentrate the scholars' attention on matters that are scholastically respectable but disreputable from a systems-planning point of view.

But all this diatribe sounds like politics itself. Isn't the systems approach just an excuse for anti-intellectualism, a device for justifying third-rate articles and books that have nothing intellectually worthwhile to say except that every excellent scholar's work is irrelevant?

The study of the tradition of the systems approach was, in part, an attempt to show that the excellence in minutiae that scholars often hold dear today has never been the sole criterion of excellence: some of the greatest minds of the past have advocated a comprehensive approach to human destiny. But there was a definite change in the methodology of the scholarship that the systems approach uses to study its tradition. "Excellence" lies not in divining the conscious intent of an author, but in the way we, as his intellectual progeny, can interpret his remarks in the modern context: we converse with our ancestor across the centuries to learn what he/she has to suggest about our present and our future. Recently I read in a Sunday supplement an account of Jefferson's draft of the American Declaration of Independence. The author pointed out that Jefferson used the intent and the vocabulary of the Enlightenment, which the nineteenth century (e.g., Lincoln in the Gettysburg Address) "romanticized," and which we today convert into our own form of universal democracy. But systems approach scholarship recognizes that each of these changes in interpretation *is* a part of a legitimate process of understanding the Declaration—that is, understanding what it says to us today and not merely what at one time it said to Jefferson. By assuming he had gained solid ground for observing what Jefferson "really meant," that Sunday supplement author can only be regarded as representing an aspect of the decline of good scholarship. A century from now this kind of critique will probably be regarded as another example of the phlegmatic 1970s.

The tradition supplies one unfolding perspective of what "comprehensiveness" means. The "logic" provided the next. It helps little to admonish would-be heroes to be more comprehensive, or merely to supply them with the pitfalls of narrow planning. They need some practical and theoretical guides for the work ahead of them. Here there are many possibilities, and I've chosen but two. The first was an attempt to show how systems planning differs from the classical laboratory and its idea of objectivity. The point was supposed to be helpful for social scientists who have mistakenly come to believe that the standard of excellence in social research must be the same as the standard of excellence of physical science research.

Take, for example, the foolish attempts to apply experimental design to human beings engaged in such difficult decision tasks as education, health, purchasing, investment, or just plain running an organization like a family. The point about experimental design is that changes in the system, with the exception of random fluctuations, are all controlled by the experimenter. The amount of control demanded to conduct an adequately performed experiment is formidable; I know, because in my younger days I tried to design and run experiments in physical chemistry. It took a long time and a lot of learning, about people and physical chemistry, to succeed. And I became convinced that most researchers in the physical sciences really didn't want to attain complete control; they were satisfied with enough control, because if there were any doubts they could always obtain more observations (an advantage of lots of funding). When it comes to human beings, the required control is not only formidable but downright immoral. There ought to be a law against experimental design on people beyond the "obvious" need to study toxic substances and the like; even (or maybe, especially) here a lot of moral debate is called for in order to make adequate judgments.

But my point was that, in giving up the standards of experimental design, we do *not* have to give up the standards of excellence in research. We do have to relinquish the notion that there is "one best way" to conduct our research, and that this depends on the one best way of formulating the problem or hypothesis. "Objectivity" is a characteristic not of the data, but rather of the design of the inquiring system as a whole: does it try to be open to all those aspects it deems relevant? Here again we see the same principle of comprehensiveness at work. The narrow approach to objectivity tries to identify specific characteristics. For example, in the classical laboratory strategy, a necessary conditon for data to be objective is that two competent observers, working independently, arrive at essentially the same results (within statistical limits). In contrast, the question the comprehensive inquiring system asks when it gets widely diverse information, is what strategy to follow. Bringing different observers more closely together is one strategy. Another is to use the divergences to suggest another area to investigate. A third is to decide that the divergences show the irrelevance of the information. A researcher is not "objective" if he sticks to but one of these strategies.

The use of Kant's *Critique of Pure Reason* to describe the logic has one big advantage, because it is plausible to say that the essence of the systems approach is the design of an inquiring system that is most capable of unfolding the relevant issues concerning the human condition. Kant, in his search for the role of reason in the process of acquiring knowledge, had to seek out the many facets of the human inquiring system, and his orderly procedure provides a guide to those of us who wish to seek out the facets of the planning inquiring system.

Of course, there is one aspect of knowledge acquisition which Kant largely ignores—namely, what is given by experience—because to him the possible answers seemed irrelevant with respect to the role of reason, except that a "something" is given that can be subsumed under the category of the real. (In the "Schematism" he refers to the intensity of the sensation.) The question of the "given" also does not receive a clear answer in this book, because it is in effect the same question that motivates the whole book. If, in effect, we humans can learn from experience how to improve the human condition, then whatever experience contributes to our ability to learn can be regarded as the "content" of learning—that is, as the "given."

It is strange how planners tend to bemoan the lack of good data, as though it were potentially available—if only the data gatherers would do their job properly. It is true that the data gatherers (census bureau, economic tabulators, etc.) are often separated from the policy planners, and this inevitably leads to confusion. But the real point is how should we design an adequate process of acquiring information? It was this question that Chapter IV addressed—that is, the "objectivity" of information. It's clear from that discussion, I hope, that we don't know how to design a "good" data bank, and that the quality of data does not depend on the size and the availability of computers.

Next, the unfolding led us to the basic ethical issues. Naturally these had been with us all along but needed some explicit unfolding. The dialectic I chose is not necessarily the only one, but it does satisfy the essential quality of dialectic—namely, that it be dramatic. It is possible to view today's changing social world as an experiment in ways in which every individual is precious and is at the same time free from starvation, nakedness, tyranny, and all other forms of oppression. Some nations try the route of freedom and bear the brunt of blind greed. Others try the route of communalism (or communism) and bear the brunt of aesthetic boredom or privileged bureaucracies. Others try nationalism and bear the brunt of war. Perhaps mainland China is the synthesis, but no doubt every nation sees itself as in process of forming a synthesis.

So far the retrospect. The prospects before us are the enemies. But once again I have to ask *why* they are enemies. After all, the promise of the systems approach (ideal-planning) is to be comprehensive. If the enemies are real (they are) and important (they are), then shouldn't the systems approach include them in its vision of the human condition?

The response, in part, depends on which enemy we're talking about.

Politics is the "closest" enemy, because it uses reason as one of its most powerful tools. But there is one important psychopolitical law that says that the closer we are, the greater the distance between us really matters—a law that applies as much to lovers as it does to politics. The political approach also often wants to better the human condition. Its question is, How do things change? And the answer is, by forming polis around specific issues. The systems approach will try to swallow this enemy by saying that there needs to be a guiding principle in the selection of issues around which polis is to be formed. And therein lies the difference. Plato no doubt had no objection to the workers forming polis around issues of productivity, or the military around issues of the tactics and strategies of combat, but the philosopher-kings were the ones who put all these issues into some coherent form. He never glimpsed the Marxian point that the workers' issues are paramount—namely, the issue of how to overthrow the nonproductive aristocracy. Who should absorb whom?

The other enemies are much farther apart. Indeed, they regard togetherness and apartness to be irrelevant, because they reside in a world where these categories are more or less meaningless, since it is a world in which "meaning" does not depend on concepts. But "comprehensiveness" seems to be basically a concept, doesn't it?

Perhaps not. Perhaps we can say that comprehensiveness means both an idea and an action. The idea determines strategies for dealing with one's enemies, but the strategies must be turned into action in order to fulfill the meaning.

I am thereby led to one of the most fascinating problems of human life: How to relate to one's enemies? The topic, important though it is, seems not to have created a cohesive genre of literature. It's discussed widely in novels and plays; it often appears in ethical and religious writings; it is discussed in a quite different way in books on management (Machiavelli's *Prince* being an outstanding example).

Suppose, without allowing logic to interfere too much—as it would, for example, by using its tedious exhaustive-exclusive question—we list some strategies for dealing with one's enemies:

1. fight
2. avoid
3. appease
4. surrender
5. convert
6. love
7. be

Each has a number of subcategories. One may fight the enemy by killing or subduing him so that he surrenders; one may engage in "cold wars"; or "if you can't beat 'em, join 'em." One may avoid him by running away, surrounding oneself with impregnable defenses, etc. "Appease" means giving the enemy what he demands so that he no longer seriously threatens: blackmail, sacrifice to the gods, tribute, etc. "Surrender" means that you relinquish all your goals, and let the enemy's goals determine your fate. None of these is acceptable to our hero, for none can be regarded as "comprehending" the enemy; that is, each isolates the enemy from ourselves or else relinquishes our ambitions.

But the last three are attempts at comprehensiveness. Number 5 says in effect that the systems approach is the final enlightenment. Once humans have fought out their battles and have "raised to consciousness" their underlying feelings, then the human race will gradually approach the ideal of a state of affairs where ideal-planning is everyone's chief concern. In other words, the anomaly mentioned on pages 143–44, where the hero is alienated from his fellow humans, will gradually disappear.

It is certainly true that ideal-planners have been fascinated by the "withering away" image of the state, of human indifference to other humans, of human bondage to the passions, of human ignorance. There is usually precious little evidence for any such withering, so that the origin of the image may lie in the aesthetics of human life—namely, in hope. But if so, then the origin is basically nonconceptual, since hope, as opposed to belief, is not based on evidence or theory; as Saint Paul put it, if you have good reasons for expecting a certain kind of future, then you can't have hope for it. Hope operates in the absence of knowledge.

The next strategy, "love," is thoroughly confusing as to its meaning, but whatever plausible meaning it has seems antithetical to the ambitions of our hero. The Greeks had more than one word for what we call "love." The one that the Bible uses most frequently meant something like an affection so deep that it is indistinguishable from one's affection for oneself. Of course, this runs into certain difficulties: is someone supposed to "love thy enemy as oneself" when in fact he hates himself? Christian theologians have written extensively on the meaning of love. Paul, in Corinthians 13, makes it central to the meaning of life. A modern translation of one of the versus would read: "Even though our forecasts are perfect, and our technology and productivity are so high that each of us lives in an environment of plenty, unspoiled by pollution or disease, and have not love, we are nothing." Gerald Heard, in his *Social Substance of Religion,* says that the essence of love in the early Christian communities was ecstasy and joy: "But as Love was a general self-forgetting ecstasy, so is its consequent Joy no quiet self-contented cheerfulness, but a rapture that whoever experiences it knows that he is possessed: body and spirit are no longer distinct, nor I and you." °

The last quotation carries the strategy of love to the extreme and far beyond the mood of our hero. If he is to love the political human in this manner, then his own vision and the political vision somehow merge and become indistinguishable—an intolerable demand on his intellect. Nor does the milder version, of a caring for another so as to preserve his being, help at all, for it implies that the enemies are to survive perpetually. It implics a fundamental pessimism regarding the destiny of humanity; the nonrational approaches are all to be sustained, forever, by the love of the rational human.

Having said this much about the strategy of love, the strategy of "be" must seem even more intolerable. The last part of this book is an exploration of this strategy, which is really not so strange after all. The "enemy" is within us, *is* our being. The hero's vision always fails, because he perceives a world that never can become "reality." If he stops there, just with the perception of eternal failure, then his powers of survival are not strong enough for surviving, and he must yield and surrender, or in today's vernacular of planning, he must "burn out." But if he realizes that at one and the same time he is both a visionary *and* the enemy of his visions, then "failure" becomes objectified: it is, objectively, a feature of reality, just as is his vision. The road to survival is to be your enemy.

Does this make sense? It is *not* a "conclusion," because the unfolding it introduces is, for me, enormously invigorating and confusing.

Finally, in my view of the past and the future, I must ask one of my favorite questions: Is the holistic prescription, "Thou shalt be comprehensive in thy planning," a tautology? Certainly at first glance it seems to be semantically tautological. If "comprehensive" means "taking into account all the matters that are relevant—that is, that make a difference in the outcomes"—then the prescription simply reads: "You ought to consider all those aspects that you ought to consider." Indeed, the tautological prescription goes even farther—"Consider all those aspects and *only* those aspects you ought to consider"—thereby ruling out such things as prolonged massaging of irrelevant data.

The tautology, therefore, may be pragmatically meaningful, because it alerts the young planner to be aware of the fact that there may be externalities, hidden variables, incredibly broad consequences far beyond the

° Gerald Heard, *Social Substance of Religion* (London: George Allen & Urwin, Ltd. 1931), p. 222.

obvious boundaries of the system, and so forth, just as it cautions him to beware of trying to use tables of valueless data even when they are laid out neatly by region and time.

But the rationality of the systems approach demands a foundation that is *not* a tautology. Furthermore, the most basic demand of logic requires that the systesm approach define a class of approaches to human conduct and hence, in terms of such a class, display the arguments demonstrating that the systems approach is "best." I should point out that the search for such an optimal in the class of approaches is vastly different from the search for the optimal within a systems approach: it takes us out of our galaxy into the universe. Within the systems approach we can talk about suboptimality, or the theme that there is no "one best way," or even the bounds of rationality. These are all discussions within the club, based on some version of rationality. But now we are to explore a fantastically different question: Is there a class of different ("nonrational") approaches to human affairs, and can one distinguish between good and bad within such a class?

The question seems damnedly confusing to the rational mind, because it must ask its inevitable question: How should the judgment of good and bad be made? By a rational approach or by a nonrational one? Indeed, how should the members of the class be defined: by using rational standards of clarity, or by using nonrational methods of nonconceptual imagery?

We see again the tragicomedy of rationality pushed beyond the boundaries of its domain. Reflection is one of the strongest instruments of rationality and is also its enemy. When reflection is allowed full sway, then can we really say that the rational approach is the best way of using the human intellect to improve the human condition?

For the next part I've chosen a mixed strategy. The "enemy approaches" are never clearly defined, though concepts are frequently used to describe some aspects of them. At times the language becomes antithetical to rationality, as when I say that the systems approach is absurd. At times it becomes thoroughly rational, as when I discuss the meaning of "forming polis."

The final chapters are a beginning attempt to say something about an inquiring system that does not feel impelled to choose the best in a class of approaches to the problem of human destiny and yet does not at the same time fall into the trap of relativity.

PART TWO

ENEMIES OF THE SYSTEMS APPROACH

CHAPTER VIII

Politics

FOR a rational mind, the last chapter must be taken to have failed to make its case. Either the case for rationality and holism is a tautology, because it argues that the good should be enacted on the basis that what should be enacted is the rational and the rational is good, or else it is a nontautology without an acceptable proof—that is, a proof acceptable to the rational mind.

It seems that the rational mind has bound itself into a domain of its own. It wants humans to accept some version of holism in their actions. But why? Why should humans obey the prescriptions of rationality? And there is another "Why?" Why are the rational types urging more rationality on others? What is there about these people that makes them continuously fight battles to overcome perceived stupidity? In the last chapter we saw that there is really no rational defense of the first "Why?" In this chapter we turn to the second.

The justification of the second "Why?" is the Socratic "Know thyself." The rational planner cannot exclude himself from the whole system, else his holism is unholy. But how can he obey the prescription? As we have seen, he has tried hard enough—by an account of his past and his tradition, logic, and ethics. But all of that was a description of the inner man, so to speak; an outsider might still wonder how he got that way.

When I was young, my mother told me I would discover the cure for cancer; mothers should never do such things, because for a long, long time I thought I would. Eventually I became a planner-holist. Would it have been "better" to find the cure for cancer? As a holist, I think not, because God knows what the holistic effects of a "cancer cure" might be for human lives. But any person with a little common sense and human sensitivity "knows" that finding the cure for cancer would be a "good thing." The holist is an

155

oddball, not a common man. Since he is therefore crazy, we need to find the cause of his insanity.

To break out of himself, as best he can, he clearly needs to understand what he is not. I say "clearly" only in deference to his own logic. Of course, Saint Thomas Aquinas tells us that any thing is *not* an infinite number of things, so that the search for what one is not may take forever. But the point is that the "nots" of the holist are everywhere in his everyday life, among his friends, family, bosses, politicians—everywhere are people who are not rational, not holistic. His rational thought is that if he can understand who these people are and why they are not rational, he may understand something deeper about himself.

I've called these "others," these not-holists, "enemies." Enemies are hostile, out to stop you, to eliminate you and your ideas; they are also to be loved, even as yourself.

As we saw in Chapter I, I've identified four enemies: politics, morality, religion, and aesthetics. The logical part of the rational mind immediately asks if these are mutually exclusive and exhaustive. The unfolding argument says that they are neither, that each unfolds into the others in intricate ways, and that all together hold the mystery of other approaches to human affairs. But it may be a help to mention one logical aspect of the four, because politics is the most extroverted enemy, as it relies on people's relationships to people around a common issue.

Now there is ready to hand a commonsense view concerning the meaning of the political approach to human affairs: the world should be run by people who have the power to run it. Sometimes one group of people become powerful, but then through revolution or evolution, power begins to spread so that lots of people, especially adults and often males, have a power of sorts. When this happens, the so-called leaders have to pay attention to their constituencies and particularly to forces who may remove them from leadership. The "best" decision is the one that keeps the individual politically powerful. In a democracy, all who want to can play the political game, though some may be eliminated (e.g., those in jail) by political powers who get restrictive laws passed. In the international arena, various nations will adopt tactics and strategies to maintain or increase their powers. This point fully explains, and justifies, the enormous defense budgets of the United States of America and the Union of Soviet Socialist Republics, which are thoroughly irrational to our holist, given the poverty, pollution, and general low quality of life in both nations.

But this commonsense version of politics is not the one that interests me at present, because it describes the politics of greed. The notion that those who have the power *should* rule is morally shocking: that is, the enemy called "morality" regards such a policy as evil.

Here I'd like to discuss a much more general meaning of politics, by trying to describe one very human feeling we all share, to be part of a community. But since I am talking about the "political approach," which means the approach to decision making, the "community" is a community centered on an issue about change or no change.

In *The Human Condition*, Hannah Arendt describes a long tradition, the *vita activa*, which Aristotle dealt with at some length, and which came out of the Greek understanding of *polis* (city-state), the actions of citizens in a nondictatorial society.° I've taken this idea and called it "making polis" around an issue, although Arendt is not responsible for the homespun manner in which I have used the term. Examples of making polis abound in our age. A family becomes polis if there is a common concern— for example, getting a child through school. Nations become polis in time of war. In the last three decades the United States has become polis about brinkmanship, sputnik, civil dissent, and energy. Groups have become polis over pollution, antidevelopment, gay rights, etc. In the process of forming polis, there frequently arises a counterpolis to oppose the first.

Several aspects of polis making need mentioning. First of all, it is a process, in which the polis tries to do something about a specific issue. If it "succeeds," the polis is likely to dissolve, and its members will go on to other issues. If it does not "succeed," it may last a long time or burn itself out. It has no self-consciousness about what the ideal-planner calls "overall progress," or even about his "measure of performance." Hence the quotation marks around the word "success," which depends on the feeling of the polis; "success" is evidenced by expressions of joy, celebrations, parties, cheerful announcements, etc., even by monetary rewards.

Also a definite, often hard attitude toward information occurs in the life of polis. This may best be described by using Karl Mannheim's notion of ideology:

> The concept "ideology" reflects . . . that ruling groups can in their thinking become so intensely interest-bound to a situation that they are simply no longer able to see certain facts which would undermine their sense of domination. There is implicit in the word "ideology" the insight that in certain situations the collective unconscious of certain groups obscures the real condition of society both to itself and to others and thereby stabilizes it.†

° Hannah Arendt. *The Human Condition* (Chicago: University of Chicago Press, 1958).

† Karl Mannheim, *Ideology and Utopia* (New York: Harcourt Brace & Co., 1954), p. 40.

In the earlier example of geothermal development (pp. 81–82) the group who were so strongly for development simply ignored the "facts" concerning other like developments and the fate of the residents who did not benefit but lost disastrously. Ideology exists in each polis, whether or not it is "ruling"; in one sense a member of a strong polis may feel like a ruler, since he feels so deeply involved in its life.

Before discussing further examples, consider the tragicomedy of the systems hero as he encounters polis at work. He wants to tell the conservationist that conservation by itself means very little: whether we conserve or use depends on aspects of the larger system. But the conservationist's joy comes from saving a redwood forest from destruction, and *not* from planning the whole future of a state or nation. The issue dissipates when it's put in the larger context. For one thing, it may indeed be sensible—in the broader context—to cut down redwood trees. To a keen conservationist, the real enemy is in the counterpolis, the guy who says, "Once you've seen one redwood, you've seen them all." He cannot even hear the voice that tells him to put conservation in the proper context.

The fantastic multitude of forms polis can take gives us an idea of the ingenuity of mankind. I'd like to discuss some examples.

The post-World War II period opened an enormous number of opportunities for the peoples of the world to form nations by declaring their independence. Now to the systems approach, nationalism seems a disastrous step, permitting debilitating wars, preventing proper development, accounting for enormous starvation and malnutrition. As that old, very sensible philosopher Epictetus observed long ago, one might as well be proud that one comes from, say, Mill Valley, California, as that one comes from the United States. The only important point is that one comes from the world. Why then don't humans understand this, abolish nations, and form themselves into a world community before they all murder each other? The answer is given over and over in the national songs: "My country, 'tis of thee," "God save our gracious Queen," etc. "Breathes there the man with soul so dead who never to himself hath said, 'This is my own, my native land'?" So strong is national polis that humans die for it, feel lost when "wandering on a foreign strand," and are willing to punish with death, if need be, those who threaten it.

Another example of polis at work says, in effect, that disciplinary science is basically political. This will also sound shocking to my academic colleagues who pride themselves on being apolitical. After all, no longer can some strong ruler force them, as Galileo was forced, to recant a well-established theory. But they themselves form polis around this pride: the truth is what matters. And the truth can be endlessly pursued. Thus the disciplines have been able to form polises which have endured over long periods of time. And apparently truth allows itself to be split into separate pieces. To show how strong and sturdy the polis of a discipline has become, one should look at the manner in which national research funds are allocated in the United States. Any member of a discipline may submit a proposal to one of the funding agencies (National Science Foundation, National Institutes of Health, etc.). The proposal is first screened by the administrative staff for obscurities, obvious failures in methodology, etc., and is then reviewed by a team made up of members of the disciplines, "obviously" the only people competent to evaluate it. As a rule, this evaluation based on the competence of the researcher, his method of conducting the research, and the "significance" of his hypothesis carries the day, and the funds go to those who are evaluated the highest. Of course the total funds available are set by Congress or the Office of Management and Budget, but the distribution is determined by the members of the discipline, who also decide who should be promoted in the research laboratory or university.

The results of this appalling way of running the basic research industry are pretty much what one might expect: a great deal of research is conducted on questions that have no relevance to anyone except members of the discipline. Furthermore, excellence in research does not include courage. In one health institute where I served on the council, there were very few proposals to conduct research on infectious hepatitis, even though the disease is one of considerable public concern. The reason given was that it is almost impossible to design a "good" proposal in this area where so little is known, and he who did get funded would probably not produce anything significant for five years, thus missing out on promotions.

My analogy is a firm where only marketing managers decide on marketing strategies and promotions, only financial managers decide on investments and promotions, etc., with an overall budget being assigned to each group by top management. Or a ship where only the steersmen decide where to go, only the engineers decide how fast the engines should work, only the cargomen what should be carried. The interesting point is that despite the inadequacy of this method of funding the disciplines, the disciplines have been able to persuade Congress and the Executive Branch that this is the correct policy. I sometimes cannot believe how strong polis can be, obscuring as it often does the reasons that things are done the way they are.

I should mention that the social sciences have had a more difficult task in forming polis and using it for funding. Part of this difficulty has arisen because the polis itself is weak. For example, in mathematics I understand that most people at the top recognize the difference between a trivial and a nontrivial problem. But social science disciplinarians cannot agree on this issue. To me, most of the basic research in social science seems trivial and naïve; to others, it seems far more important than any applied research. Nor have computer and statistical methods helped, for while one can factor analyze huge quantities of data, the "So what?" question continues to be embarrassing.

Another aspect of the polis of the disciplines is that the disciplinarian cannot understand "interdisciplinary" research. The strength of a discipline lies in its ability to judge "excellence." The strength of interdisciplinary research is its ability to combine a number of relevant considerations, including the ethical; but it has only a weak basis for defining excellence in research terms alone, because, for planning, "excellence" cannot be defined in research terms only.

Even when an effort is made to initiate an interdisciplinary program, it is amazing how quickly polis is created, and the interdisciplinary character changed into a discipline. When we designed the first graduate operations research programs at Case Institute of Technology, we thought of OR as an interdisciplinary effort, which could use any intellectual resource useful in its planning. It took much less than a decade to transform OR into a hard discipline, whose core was model building. I may have even aided and abetted this process, because as editor of *Management Science* I could only get my referees to agree to publish model-building articles; the rest were "pure junk." Since some of us still hoped to maintain an interdisciplinary approach, we had to change the label to avoid confusion. That's why we latched onto "system." But today we run the danger of being identified with "systems analysis," which tends to be disciplinarian in its approach.

So far my examples have been negative, in the sense that the ideal-planner finds each of them to have serious systems flaws. The final example, on the other hand, is positive though puzzling: it is "community," an idea so difficult to define and yet so common. It arises from a combination of the enemies, often all four of them. A community is a polis, because its members share the concerns of all. In many villages and tribes throughout the world, citizenship means the right to be protected from starvation and the obligation to protect others. In fact, it may be that the erosion of this polis of the villages is one of the main causes of malnutrition. Community is also aesthetic, in that it helps its members understand and appreciate the quality of their lives. It is also religious, not only because its members are bound together by a common belief or way of worship, but because they are devoted to their environment, the mountains, say, or the ocean. And morality becomes the community's weapon when it is threatened, for example, by development from outside.

But community is puzzling to the systems planner. In the first place, his logical mind wants to know whether community "exists." I remember once listening to the psychologist Floyd Alport give a talk in which he was quite emphatic about there being no such thing as "group mind"—I believe because he thought that no one had ever seen the creature. But then there is nothing to stop a researcher from studying, say, the behavior of the General Motors Corporation as an entity, without going into its insides to observe the people: the corporation has knowledge, habits, intentions, etc. Of course, there is the question whether the study of the behavior of a collective mind is useful; but the same question can be raised about individual minds, which are, after all, collectives themselves.

But does the behavior of a collective mind mean the same thing as "community"? I don't have a good answer to this question, because there are so many mysterious manifestations of community that I can't explain by behavioral evidence. How, for example, do people know when the party is over and they should go home? They learn this knack very quickly, and those who don't are easily recognized and rarely invited. A behaviorist might want to explain the phenomenon by "gesture language," according to which people know the party's over because the host yawned twice. But this doesn't satisfy me; I've often known the party was over without seeing the host. How do people know when to give a standing ovation? Or to flock to a movie? Why do some towns clearly have a togetherness, and others not?

Or consider that strange mixture of community and anticommunity called "urban automobile traffic." I don't think the number of automobile accidents is unbelievably high; I think it's unbelievably low, given trackless roads where swerving can always occur. Some strong sense of community must be there to guard us. But there is also a strong sense of anticommunity, as each driver recognizes that he "owns" the space of his car and therefore has certain rights—for example, the right to cut into a space between two cars.

The question remains: Can we rational types explain the manifestations of community and polis in general? Asking the question unfolds a confrontation between politics and the systems approach. Politics is the most rational of the enemies, because it often considers it important to justify itself as a way of running human affairs, whereas the other enemies tend to believe they are their own justification. If politics can justify itself, then why isn't it one version—maybe the only version—of systems planning?

I should start the conversation with politics by pointing out that I am interested in the ideal-planner's counterpart: the person who is dedicated to helping the human race ease its burdens through the design of a political process. He also has a logic. There is a client and a purpose, but no measure of performance, and there is no ideal, except as an occasional guide. The decision maker is the key figure, who must be understood thoroughly if the political process is to work. Many things block decision making, and the problem is to understand where the moves can be made and where they cannot be. The components and the environment remain the same. There is comparatively little interest in the planner except as an agent of change. Implementation is a key concept, since the basic idea is to form polis in order to change. Finally, there is no guarantor, and there is really no need for one. We go from problem to problem; the process is the thing. If on a quiet evening we wonder what it's all about, whether the pathway leads to heaven, hell, or nothingness, such wonderings are largely irrelevant to how we will proceed the next morning.

Of course, our ideal-planner seeks for an ethics in this whole process. The political approach recognizes that all kinds of alternatives are blocked out, some by logic, some by nature, some by custom, some by law, and some by the ethics and morals people live by. So the ethics is "situational"; don't try to move people beyond what they regard as ethically acceptable. The ideal-planner finds this thoroughly frustrating and asks whether the political approach would work for criminals, or dictators, or corporations without a social conscience.

Before the argument gets too hot, we should see how the political approach justifies itself. One justification lies in the nature of people. People, according to this theory, are never motivated by large images, by holistic perspectives. The more that's included in the consideration of a problem, the less likely are people to form polis around the issue. The key to forming polis is to concentrate on a specific issue, not on a large overwhelming one. Lindblom and Brayebrooke° suggested the term "incrementalism" for this approach; indeed, they went farther and called it "disjointed incrementalism" to emphasize the absence of some grand theme overriding social change.

My favorite example of this kind of planning is the medical school at Berkeley. For years faculty committees had studied the question whether Berkeley should have a medical school. Big problems were addressed: how to fund the building, how to design a hospital, how to support two hundred students, and so on. Then an incrementalist suggested that Berkeley start a tiny medical school with only twelve students; that the East Bay doctors be asked to use their clinics to give the students clinical experience. No big building, no big hospital. The decision was made in April, and the first twelve students were admitted in August. Instant polis was formed. Never have so

° D. Brayebrooke and C. E. Lindblom, A Strategy of Decision (New York: Free Press of Glencoe, 1963).

many faculty devoted so many hours to so few students. Of course the "systems minds" on the faculty pointed out the huge cost in hidden dollars that this medical option entailed. But their voices went unheeded by the polis, which included the top administrators of the campus. I was chairman of the evaluation committee during the first two years. I decided that my committee's role was *not* to conduct a systemic evaluation, but rather to maintain polis at its high pitch. Hence we made ourselves into detectives, searching for clues indicating the decline of polis. And there were many. The promised freedom of choice of the students never happened because they had to be trained to pass their "MCAT" examinations. The East Bay doctors were never given their promised recognition by the campus. And so on. Personally I found the experience thoroughly rewarding, because I'd made up my mind to find out how incrementalism works. The rational, systems approach side of me graded the entire effort a failure, but the other side, my polis-joining side, found it thoroughly exhilarating. I certainly had to admit that a very strong polis was formed, and that polis is real.

Well, if it is real, it is part of the whole system. And therefore we systems planners should be able to include polis formation in our planning. A good example is the implementation experiments described on page 95. The subjects quickly formed polis and excluded the information supplied by the stooge. When we tried the friendly stooge, then polis was not formed, or rather, polis was formed around him. And, indeed, some of the most "successful" planners recognize that the most important aspect of their job is to break down the alienation between the researcher and the manager. This was the intent of the phrase "mutual understanding" which Schainblatt and I used in one of the earliest papers on the implementation of management science.[*] I must say the academics put a strange twist on our meaning, by inferring that we meant that the qualities of the manager needed to be studied, e.g., his personality type, attitudes, etc. This may be useful, but it hardly grasps the meaning of forming polis with the manager.

But can politics be made a part of the systems approach? It may be time for a fable. Once upon a time a prince was born. He had a loving fairy godmother who, in order to protect him when he became a man, gave him the ability to transform himself into a very large mouth so that he could swallow *any* enemy he met in the forest. So we are to picture the systems approach swallowing its enemy, the political approach, by incorporating into its general scheme the all too human urge to form polis and making that urge a central aspect of the category of implementation.

[*] C. West Churchman and A. H. Schainblatt, "The Researcher and the Manager," *Management Science*, series B, vol. II, no. 4 (February, 1965), p. B–69.

But the fable has a twist. Those who advocate the political approach point out that systems planning is one of the instruments of politics. When we tried to sell OR in the early days, we called it "scientific planning." We could easily be accused of gathering managers into the fold under the banner of "science." Who would want to be an unscientific manager when a scientific way of managing is available? Since then various techniques have been invented, usually with a quantitative flavor, which at least appear to be "scientific": Critical Path, PERT, PPBS, and C-B analysis. The last attempts to estimate the total costs and benefits of a proposed program. The ideal-systems-planner hastens to point out that none of these is necessarily scientific. But how is he to know whether his own methods are being used for purely political purposes? After all, he, the idealist, is first of all human and therefore political.

The twist in the fable is that the kindly godmother also bestowed the same ability on another prince whose father became the deadly enemy of the first prince's father. One day, the two princes met in the forest. . . .

One final unfolding question: Could the debate between the systems approach and the political approach be made into a dialectic, and if it could, would a synthesis emerge? I think the answer would be a definite affirmative on the part of the systems approach, because then the entire dialectic would become an expanded systems approach, and nothing is more satisfying to the heart of the ideal-planner than expansion. But I can't imagine that the political approach would agree. For it, debate and fights emerge as polis and counterpolis. It does form a counterpolis to the systems approach,° which it regards as either absurd or dangerous. But it does not form this counterpolis to arrive at a synthesis, and it is not likely to consider the fight a "dialectic."

So I leave the matter in the form of a paradox. If the systems approach attempts to swallow the enemy by setting forth the rules of their battle—for example, in terms of a dialectic—the political enemy will retaliate by forming a counterpolis of people who will eschew the results of systems thinking, make sure it is not funded or promoted, and generally carry on political processes that will thwart systems planning.

What did happen in the forest, anyway?

° See Ida Hoos, *Systems Analysis in Public Policy: A Critique* (Berkeley: University of California Press, 1972).

CHAPTER IX

Morality

1. This has been for me the most difficult chapter to write, because it has never developed a coherent theme. I felt I was chasing something that had acquired the art of hiding. Or, I was being chased. The words of *The Hound of Heaven* began echoing in my ears:

> I fled Him, down the nights and down the days;
> I fled Him, down the arches of the years;
> I fled Him, down the labyrinthine ways
> Of my own mind; and in the midst of tears
> I hid from Him, and under running laughter.
> Up vistaed hopes I sped;
> And shot, precipitated
> Adown Titanic glooms of chasmed fears,
> From those strong Feet that followed, followed after.
> But with unhurrying chase,
> And unperturbed pace,
> Deliberate speed, majestic instancy,
> They beat—and a Voice beat
> More instant than the Feet—
> "All things betray thee, who betrayest Me."

Finally I decided to let the chapter stay as fragments, as "notes on morality." Since Nietzsche is one of my guides, I've borrowed—not his style—but the format of *Beyond Good and Evil*.

2. I have already discussed ethics and morality in this book. What is new here is the suggestion that there is deep in the human spirit a moral force that cannot be conceptualized and is certainly not expressed in ethical or moral theories. This moral force is expressed in various forms of dissent: revolutions, strikes, civil disobedience, etc. It also has a positive side: the joy of the moral spirit.

This moral force is also the origin of the hero, discussed in Chapter VI, the mystery of what drives a social progressive beyond a satisfactory state, or an individual to the next stage in the process of individuation. Singer believed that the explanation of the hero's drive lies in a "mood," which Singer defined as a complex of emotions. But here morality is taken to reside in a collective psyche rather than in an individual state of mind.

3.   At one point in my search I read Maria von Franz's "Unus Mundus." ° She described a pervasive psychic force in the universe: the suggestion that all matter is basically psychic. I was led to the image of morality as one aspect of this force, a morality that erupts through individual behavior. When morality appears at the conscious level, it leaves "residues"; and it is the residues that moral theorists like Kant have formalized. Of course, some clues may emerge about the force itself by studying the residues, but a "categorical imperative" by itself does not describe the force. Kant seems to be aware of this when he talks of "harmony" and "humanity." But nowhere does he really explain what these are. Nor, of course, do "force" and "residue" really explain matters.

4.   The above may suggest to Jungians that morality is archetypal. But it can reasonably be asked whether morality as an enemy is really typal rather than archetypal. If one uses Jung's *Psychological Types* as a guide, then the question of whether morality comes essentially from the feeling function is very puzzling. In the first place, I should think my vague image of morality suggests that if it has its origins in a function, it would be introverted feeling. But Jung's description of introverted feeling doesn't fit at all; he regards such feeling as characteristic of some women who show an exterior calm, although inside is a seething turmoil. But the morality I'm talking about often shouts, and it can be male or female. Furthermore, Jung thinks of feeling as "rational," by which I gather from his definition of rationality,† that it operates through a long historical tradition of development. But morality seems often to break with tradition, to object to evolution, and to choose revolution instead.

5.   Now just suppose that Singer's idealism really began manifesting itself. Poverty withers away. People learn to control their desires, so that their normal actions and policies are cooperative rather than conflicting. People understand people much better, as well as themselves. Society and the environment are designed so that each can find the fulfillment of his lifetime. Everyone has "more power," and all share in the faith in an endless progress.

° M. von Franz, "Unus Mundus," in J. Wheelwright, ed., *The Reality of the Psyche* (New York: G. P. Putnam's Sons, 1968).

† C. G. Jung, *Psychological Types*, pp. 583–84.

All feel, nonetheless, a dissatisfaction, a need to move on. Horrible! Why? At the end of *In Search of a Way of Life*, Singer says, "for all this way [progress] may hold of what to those still able to retain the faculty of faith seems cold, austere, grim even, I do not see why it should. . . ." Well, perhaps not grim, but devoid of laughter and tears, which are the core of our living. Perhaps unfair. Singer meant that laughter and tears would be a part of his "progressive community," expressed in its art. But the progressive community itself was not funny, nor was it to be wept over. The systems approach is absurd. And one can feel sadness that so many have so seriously devoted their lives to it. Above all, it is antimoral. It wants to tell people how a part of their lives should be led. So it's bossy. And if it succeeds in implementing, it imposes its will on others; it becomes a case of "people telling people what they must do," and the spirit of morality is outraged.

6. When morality and politics join forces, there is often violence. Morality-politics is the spiritual basis of revolution, which shapes violence into one of its chief instruments. Since morality always operates so as to create countermorality, the countermorality also joins with politics to make its own violence. Thus, the British executed the leaders of the Irish Revolution of the 1910s, the American authorities violently reacted to the Pullman strike of the 1890s, slave revolts were usually followed by killings, and so on. Or, when the students erupted at Berkeley in 1964 and "sat in" the administration building, people in Orange County called the governor of California to "get them out by any method." Clever manipulators can design a convergence of morality and politics, as did the Nazis in their purge of the Jews: first arouse moral indignation at Jewish behavior, especially their economic behavior; then organize people against them to the extent that the work of the concentration camps proceeds unimpeded.

Our systems hero cannot even approximately understand war. If there weren't so many people killed or injured by it, he might regard it as a human theater of the absurd.

7. I remember once when Tom Cowan, of the Rutgers University Law School, paid me a visit at Berkeley and sat in on the "Churchman seminar," a perennial unlisted gathering of my students. We were struggling through Kant's *Foundations of the Metaphysics of Morals*. Tom asked them why they were reading Kant. Most of them were caught off guard and couldn't reply. "You ought to be reading Nietzsche," said Tom. I was caught off guard. I'd never thought one could read Nietzsche sensibly without first reading Kant. Of course Nietzsche was having fun with the stuffed-shirt morality of his day, which still hangs on. But Kant, and not Bentham, was surely his main target. Nietzsche thought that the "greatest pleasure for the

greatest number" was ridiculous, and not worth more than a jibe now and then. Bentham's original version amounts to saying that humanity ought to amass the moments of pleasure; it's like saying that the progress of science is measured by amassing facts, no matter what they're about. However, Kant's is another matter; his doctrine is not ridiculous. To attack his basic theme of harmony and fairness, one needs to question that all too human feeling that humans should be fair to other humans and to all living species. As we are seeing, all the enemies question this quite rational idea. The motivation of seeking equity often threatens to kill polis, because the polis may be built on race, sex, wealth, prestige, or poverty. Similarly, to ask a devout person to be "fair" about his devotion often amounts to saying that all religious worship is pretty much the same, a concession that ruins the spirit of the devotion. (How dare Catholics say that unbaptized souls will reside in Limbo forever? They dare because the spirit of Catholicism requires it.) And as for aesthetics, the quality of an experience may well be in its *not* being shared, or only shared with one other being; aesthetics eschews the crude dictum that humans should learn to share their deepest feelings. To regard "mutual communication" as an ideal of humanity is to be an aesthetic moron. So, we are to talk about a morality that is *not* based on equity, and (to our systems hero) *that's* a very serious matter.

Here's an example from Nietzsche: "You say that a good cause justifies even a war? I tell you: it is the good war which justifies any cause." ° A Kantian would point out that willing a war is immoral, because war cannot be universalized and always treats people as means only. So what is a "good war"? But Nietzsche is always turning the point around, so that we see the other side. He might have suggested: "So act that the principle of the action is unique, and not applicable to any one else at any time or place." What he does say is: " 'Compassion for all' would amount to rigor and tyranny for *you*, my dear friend."†

8.   Singer believed that art creates in us a mood of dissatisfaction, which moves us on in the endless story of progress. And in *Beyond Good and Evil*,‡ Nietzsche observes that compassion for another does *not* mean an attempt to remove his suffering; "you want, if possible (and there is no more insane 'if possible') to do away with suffering." Don't we know, he asks, that the heightening of man's powers has been created by the discipline of suffering? Is "dis-

---

° Friedrich Nietzsche, *Thus Spake Zarathustra*, trans. M. Cowan (Chicago: Henry Regnery Co., Gateway Editions, 1957), p. 49.

† Friedrich Nietzsche, *Beyond Good and Evil*, trans. M. Cowan (Chicago: Henry Regnery Co., Gateway Editions, 1955), sec. 8.2.

‡ Ibid., p. 150 ff.

satisfaction" the "discipline of suffering"—and is this how we reconcile Singer and Nietzsche? It seems incorrect to say that a man of comfortable circumstances who is willing to go to the villages to help nourish the starving is "suffering," although once there he may suffer from dysentery. Jung may be better off, because I suspect that most of us who embark on the process of individuation do suffer some mental anguish. But it may be that the explanation of Singer's heroic mood lies deep in the morality of suffering. However, the prescription "Thou shalt suffer" has neither teleological nor ateleological justification. It is "none of the above." Finally, is there really such a prescription? Thomas Edison is quoted as saying, "I never did a day's work in my life—it was all fun."

9.   In *Thus Spake Zarathustra*° is the suggestion "Distrust any man who talks much about fairness—his sort is devoid not merely of honey." But Kant (and I) talk a lot about equity—e.g., equity with respect to the client. One could easily write a PhD thesis on this quotation from Nietzsche. Chapter 1: on the distinction between talking and doing. Chapter 2: past and recent literature on equity (who's talked?). Chapter 3: the inequity of talking about equity ("we" and "they"). Chapter 4: a statistical study comparing the equitable acts of those who have talked about equity vs. those who have not. And so on. What is important is the image of the man, deeply frowning, who is so concerned about the amount of inequity in the world. Don't trust him.

10.   But why is morality an enemy of the systems approach? Why not say that although its meaning is forever elusive, we can approximate it? After all, *Beyond Good and Evil* is an exploration "beyond" the very inadequate notions of good and evil of Nietzsche's day. As Marianna Cowan says in her introduction to her translation of this book, "beyond" may mean what it does in English, a place beyond this one; but it also means "aside from" or "without reference to." Thus the book is also about the irrelevance of good and evil, or about the need to take a giant step away from today's notions. However, Nietzsche does talk about superior or super men, so that there is a direction to be followed. Toward what? Toward a "better" approximation? It's incredible what nonsense is allowed to stand in the texts on planning on the grounds that, although admittedly inaccurate, it is an "approximation." Thus we are told that the current theory of risk and uncertainty is an approximation of the real meaning of uncertainty. It may be an approximation of some aspect of uncertainty, but it takes a lot of nerve to claim that it approximates the awe of humanity as it faces its future. A reasonable supposition is that when someone like Kant tries to say something about

° Ibid., p. 115.

morality, he emphasizes one aspect of it and hence vastly distorts its meaning, so that what comes out is *not* an approximation but a further distortion. It's still the same old story: the enemy is one who can use reason to raise reasonable objections to the claims of reason.

11.   Throughout this book I've made little or no mention of the masculine and the feminine, and for good personal reasons. When I first came across Jung's anima and animus, I was much impressed, and, yes indeed, I could recognize the anima and the animus in myself. Then my analyst, Joe Henderson, informed me that men do not have an animus, just as women don't have an anima. My logical mind naturally asked for the definition of "men" in the sentence, "Men don't have an animus." If "man" means someone who likes to talk, dominate, etc., then tautologically a man "has" an animus. On the other hand, if "man" means someone with a sufficiently long and thick penis, then the assertion is nontautological but empirically invalid; most "men," under this definition, exhibit both feminine and masculine behavior characteristics.

Now to me the big trouble with many "language philosophers" is that they assume that if a distinction between two concepts is possible, it is therefore necessary. Whereas to my logical, systemic mind, if a distinction is possible, it may be wise to drop it because the distinction goes nowhere, has no value. I'm simply amazed that one can say, "It is very important to recognize the distinction between x and y," and then give no sensible reason for the importance. So I began to feel that in my own life, including the philosophical side of my living, the distinction between masculine and feminine was not helpful, even though lots of people make it and seem to believe in it. I can readily see its political importance in women's struggle for recognition and equity, and I can see that politically there need be no effort at all in "defining" a woman as opposed to a man. There may come a time in the woman's rights revolution when people ask whether some male gays are women, or some female lesbians are men, but that question is of no political relevance now.

But as I was finishing this book, and writing in the last chapter about organizations, the word "morale" came to mind. My constant companion, the *Oxford English Dictionary*, told me that morale comes from the feminine of the French *moral*. That set me to reflecting once more on the feminine, and in particular the feminine of the enemies as well as of the systems approach. Nothing much comes to mind on the feminine of politics. I think there's probably a lot to be said about the feminine in religion—that is, the worship of goddesses, large and small, as different from the worship of Gods. As for aesthetics, I feel that it's largely feminine, but that's primarily because I'm married to a woman with a deep aesthetic appreciation.

But the feminine of morality—that is, morale—is another matter. The *OED* tells me that it means "confidence, hope, zeal, submission to discipline (especially among troops)." This is certainly another side of the morality I've been talking about, which has been dissent, revolution, war, "beyond good and evil." This is the morality of patriotism, following the leader enthusiastically, being obedient and even zealous in one's loyalty. It's an important side of morality that I've more or less neglected in the rest of this chapter. But why feminine? What brought Frenchmen to use the feminine to describe the zeal of troops? It surely had something to do with the feminine in morality.

12.   In discussing the problem of evil, I'm going to let my logical mind make a distinction, to describe, so to speak, the two faces of evil. In the first place, for each approach to the conduct of human affairs, there are evil forces that try to thwart it. In the second place, each approach creates its own evil.

In the first chapter we had a glimpse of the first type of evil for the systems approach, as our hero becomes angry at those who repeatedly commit the environmental fallacy. But it is worthy of note that the implication of this anger is probably not blame and revenge, but rather education. The systems approach is not interested in identifying evil people and in blaming or punishing them. It is fairly sure that the so-called criminal justice system throughout the world is alarmingly counterproductive and unjust; that is, it seriously fails on both ethical grounds, the Benthamite and the Kantian. A bit of blame or even punishment may show up in the systems approach educational policy, but only if it can be justified in terms of more general goals. This type of evil is more the evil of the whole system; the approaches of each of the enemies are therefore evil insofar as they create their irrationalities. Thus morality often responds to its perception of evil by fighting, killing, incarcerating, and destroying everything about. Politics, too, will do likewise against forces that threaten to kill polis—for example, nations, communities, families, etc. And religion has fought many senseless wars, the Thirty Years War being perhaps the most extreme example. Aesthetics blindly fights the tragedy created by those who destroy the quality of life. In all such cases the ethical good of the social system may be seriously violated.

But of course education can very easily lead to an evil of the second kind, an evil that the systems approach itself creates. According to the *OED's* account of the word "evil," "it usually referred to the root of up, over; on this view the primary sense would be either 'exceeding due measure,' or 'overstepping proper limits.'" And the evil the systems approach creates does have this root meaning. To the goal planner, the ideal-planner clearly oversteps proper limits. For one thing, as we saw in Chapter V, the ideal-planner may go well beyond the intentions of those who support his work. To propose that population be controlled by whatever forces can be created, certainly seems to exceed due measure. All the writers cited in Chapter II stood somewhere and, from that vantage point, described the human condition and prescribed its destiny. Was the place where they stood beyond "proper limits"?

This is not the end of the matter, of course. The ideal-planner can recite the Confiteor as well as any: "through my fault, through my fault, through my most grievous fault." He can adopt the modesty(?) of Saint John: "I am the voice of one crying in the wilderness." Or, more simply, "I am just an ordinary citizen, and like anyone else, I have my opinions which others can listen to or not as they please." Such recanting, however, inevitably generates an inner voice that says, "But if you don't listen to me, civilization as we appreciate it is doomed." And, finally, there is the clever(?) device of this book, which says we must recognize and honor our enemies, and even be our enemies, lest we fail the test of comprehensiveness, and in so doing we return inside the proper limits. Or do we? In becoming political, don't we sacrifice our ideals?

Politics also has the two versions of evil, the first being the threat on the life of polis, and the second the need to threaten another polis in order to survive: we humans may have started a process of national defense that we humans can't stop, and that will in due course destroy all polises.

Morality usually stirs up countermorality which threatens to destroy morality. Strikes, civil disobedience, riots, revolutions, all create the moral mood in a sector of the population which seeks to destroy the strikers, the disobedient, the rioters, and the revolutionaries.

Aesthetics, in its protection of the quality of life, may act to destroy the quality of life of another; aesthetics drives some to increase wilderness areas and parks, thereby destroying the quality of life for residents who rely on trees to make their living.

Thus the evil that lies in all humans comes from the fact that humans are "approachers," and as they approach the conduct of human affairs, they cannot help but destroy the essence of their own approach.

13.   The last is a serious section, which deals with the tragedy of human life, of the lover who loves so strongly that he destroys the loved one. But humans, who recognize this quality of their lives, have created comedy to respond to it. Comedy will come in again when aesthetics is the chief topic. I brought it on stage at this point as an antidote to tragedy. Here's a way to look at the matter. Humans over the ages have sought ways of differentiating humanity from other species: we write our history, we have a refined logic, we reason in a highly differentiated way. Perhaps the best contribution to this rather futile exercise is to say that humans are the most ridiculous species.

CHAPTER X

Religion

THIS was the easiest chapter to write, I think, because this book itself is written in a religious mode; under the inspiration to worship the Divine, which thought has labeled "The Whole System."

In this discussion I am primarily interested in the manner in which the "religious approach" has been the directing influence in human affairs. Often this influence has expressed itself in terms of beliefs about a god or the gods, beliefs that have been turned into dogma or theology by the thinking mind. But here I am interested in something more than intellectual belief; my interest is in a combination of feeling and archetypal influence.

The religious approach to human affairs occurs *first* when we humans decide in terms of something we regard as superior, grander, more magnificent, than we feel ourselves to be. We act because we believe (feel) that this superior being has ordered us to act, or simply because it is appropriate to act so as to conform to the superior being's intentions or existence, or because our actions are forms of worship. The superior being may be many things, and I shall consider only a sample: a personalized deity, "Nature," community, and everything-nothing.

The religious approach to human affairs occurs *second* when we humans decide in terms of the small, minuscule, unique, which is not inferior to us, and is indeed superior because of its smallness. An apt comparison occurs in technology, between those who worship large technologies like automobile manufacture, military weapons systems, Apollo programs, etc., and those who worship small, "appropriate" technologies like solar heating of homes, mini-autos, small shops, etc.

In this chapter I use the appropriate religious words, "worship" rather than "evaluate," or "awesome fear" rather than "cost." And I do not undertake the inappropriate task of defining religious terms.

But of course I can't keep thought from either defining or theorizing about religion. Thought concludes that religion is not theology, which is a rational science. It also concludes that religion establishes a worshiper-worshiped relationship in which the decision center is moved away from the human being to something superiorly grander or something superiorly small. Finally, thought theorizes that human beings are influenced by the religious, which underlies many of our social policies.

Perhaps a comparison is apt here. The Aztecs developed a fantastic array of gods who, unless they were appeased, would do horrible things like drying up all the crops; thus the Aztec year saw many festivals and rituals designed to keep the gods quiet. The gods liked blood, and many of the rituals involved human sacrifices. All this seems primitive, because in our maturation we humans today have gone far beyond such practices. Except that in American culture we have replaced the capricious deities of the Aztecs by a deity just as capricious, called "The Economy." There is no doubt that It exists; no proof is necessary. (For men It is clearly neuter, though many women find It to be disgustingly masculine.) The Economy needs to be appeased in various ways, or else it will collapse and out of revenge do drastic things to all of us. We no longer find human blood sacrifice aesthetic and have replaced it by another form of sacrifice called "unemployment." In order to keep The Economy from collapsing, we must sacrifice millions of human employment opportunities. During the depression of the 1930s carloads of foodstuffs were destroyed, despite the fact that many people were hungry. People didn't realize that such destruction was necessary for the sake of the worship of The Economy. Furthermore, just as the Aztecs had a class of priests, so do we; they are appropriately called "economists," who understand the moods and the needs of The Economy, as well as the rituals and the prayers (called "economic theory") that will keep The Economy from collapsing. I imagine that many an Aztec priest at the end of a heart-rending day must have felt a strong mood of depression; so too our priests are wont to call their function the "gloomy" science. It is really not a very comic religion.

Of course none of the above is fair to those who struggle honestly and sincerely to give advice to our administrators and legislators on economic policies. But "fairness" is a thinking-rational approach which none of the enemies take seriously. One way to love thy enemy is to appreciate how he enables you to see yourself as you never could with your own imagery and thought. The hero of this essay is like the economist, or perhaps worse, because he believes not only in The Economy but also in The Whole System, which he worships ardently. When he becomes his own worst enemy, he may then see himself as an ardent worshiper. We planners often warn each other about our "hidden assumptions." Why are they hidden? Perhaps because planning is often an act of religious worship, and the most inappropriate thing you can do in the act of worshiping your God is to doubt His existence. It's much worse than interrupting two lovers in the act of love making to ask whether meaningful sex is possible.

Of course imagery and imagination play a strong role in the religious approach, as can be seen, for example, in the paintings humans have made of the religious feeling. It is often assumed that art works through the aesthetic, but I imagine that it is more enlightening to say that art is usually religious, especially when the artist is "driven" to paint, compose, sculpt, or write; the creative acts of artists are ways of worshiping the grand or the small.

When art is lacking in religious worship, the religious act turns dull. This is one reason why so many of us react unfavorably to the worship of The Economy. The best the priests can do is display dreadfully unaesthetic tables of economic data. They could at least have a drawing of a weeping God above a declining Dow-Jones industrial average.

One of the most attractive images of religion is the personal god, either masculine or feminine, who plays the role of parent of mankind, to be prayed to, even to be conversed with, in every aspect of our lives. "Dear God!" "Jesus Christ!" even "Good Grief!" are all ways of talking with the deity. Humans have been thoroughly inventive in finding ways of communicating with gods and goddesses, in poetry, song, drama, prayer, with no thought of definition, no puzzlement about existence, just feeling the joy-fear of His or Her presence. As a thinker devoted to making matters clear and explicit in much of my life, I have found this quotation most inspiring:

God Himself, the Father and Fashioner of all that is, older than the Sun or the Sky, greater than Time and Eternity and all the Flow of Being, is unnameable by any Lawgiver, unutterable by any Voice, not to be seen by any Eye. But we, being unable to apprehend His Essence, use the help of sounds and names and pictures, of beaten gold and ivory and silver, of plants and rivers, mountain peaks and torrents, yearning for the knowledge of Him, and in our weakness, naming all that is beautiful in this world after His Nature, just as happens to earthly Lovers. To them the most beautiful sight will be the actual lineaments of the Beloved, but for remembrance' sake they will be happy in the sight of a lyre, a little spear, a chair perhaps or a running ground, or anything in the world that wakens the memory of the Beloved. Why should I further examine and pass judgment about images? Let man know what is Divine. Let them know, that is all. If a Greek is stirred to remembrance of God by the Art of Phidias, an Egyptian by paying worship to animals, another by a river, another by Fire, I have no anger for their divergences. Only let them know, let them love, let them remember.[*]

It is awesome to recall how astronomy of the past centuries has threatened to destroy sacred religious imagery by the doctrine that the earth is not the

[*]Maximus of Tyre, *Discertatio*, VIII.

center even of its own solar system, and that millions of other solar systems exist in a galaxy that is only one of millions of galaxies. For many people God needs a locus if He/She is to be a personal god. Where in the world could God be? This reflection about the scientists' ruining of religion's imagery has always explained to me the strong reaction that people had to the "new science," which assumed so arrogantly that the revelation of truth was always right, for the new scientists believed that truth is a good-in-itself (i.e., a god). But from the systems point of view, a truth that is unaesthetic and antireligious cannot be all good. If the truth hurts, should it be revealed? The science of Galileo's day was becoming a god who could ignore the feelings of humans and later would transform himself into dangerous technological weapons—a cold and heartless god. (Of course, there was a political reason for the attack on Galileo, because he was also destroying polis; the enemies often act as a consortium.)

Nowadays, of course, that most fascinating religious sect called "science fiction writers" has provided all sorts of places where God can reside. Perhaps He's in some parallel universe, where our souls go when we die. Once we leave this universe, we can no longer change things here, though we may be aware of the loved ones we left behind. And we can pray to our God in the other universe: He hears us, and He responds. All that is possible until "science" proves it's fictional, and imagination is called upon to find another possibility.

An alternative is to give up the personal god, as did Spinoza, and imagine that God is all reality. In this case, called "pantheism," imagination and thought can smile at each other, although Spinoza's God hid most of Himself from us, revealing only two of his infinite number of attributes. In this view of God the cosmologists become the priest class, and to worship God is to try to understand how His universe works.

It can be seen, then, that there are many religions, most of them without churches in the ordinary sense, but all of them with churches in the extraordinary sense. For believers in The Economy, the churches are "data banks" where the priest comes with his offering, a model or a theory. For the cosmologists the churches are observatories.

Now let us turn to the religions of life. What does it mean to worship life? Let's consider a recent example. A few years ago the Congress of the United States passed the Endangered Species Act, which permitted the U.S. Fish and Wildlife Service to name endangered and threatened species and to take steps to prevent human interventions that might destroy a species. For example, a rather unattractive little fish (unattractive to humans, that is) called the "snail dart" was found in a stream that would soon be flooded once a large dam was completed. No one could prove that the snail dart existed elsewhere. The result was that this insignificant, ugly fish stopped a large dam from being completed: the small won out over the large.

The Endangered Species Act protects all species except microorganisms, even though some species are dangerous to humans, and others, like the coyote, threaten herds. Indeed, the coyote is an example of the economic systems approach and its enemies, because still standing is a congressional statute from the 1930s that calls for the eradication of this species. The U.S. Wildlife Service conducts research programs aimed at killing the coyote in grazing regions—for example, by placing in strategic places poisoned meat which gradually kills the animal by eliminating its white blood corpuscles. But of course the coyote, like the cockroach and the house fly as well as the mosquito, is far too clever as a species to be eliminated. Another example of the small winning out over the large: the insect versus massive DDT programs. The story of David and Goliath is a symbol of the mystery of how smallness can overcome largeness.

Of course the Endangered Species Act is endangered. For one thing it has no real economic base; for example, it would be impossible, given our present knowledge, to establish a positive benefit-minus-cost for the preservation of the snail dart. Furthermore, the act is anti-systems thinking, because in the larger "system of nature," independent of humanity, species do die off at a fairly regular rate, so that we are intervening unnaturally by protecting all species. Our protection of the whooping crane may be a case in point: although we humans were certainly the cause of its decline, it may have reached the point where it "wanted" to become extinct. Sometimes our efforts become absurd. One proposal is to persuade certain young whooping cranes that they are in fact sand cranes, so that they will go with their adoptive parents to another winter habitat besides the one (Aransas) where now all whooping cranes go. In one recent migration helicopters were sent to scare the cranes away from a polluted pond where they clearly intended to land; they landed anyway, perhaps thoroughly puzzled by this most peculiar species called humans.

Finally, there is the matter of the morality of the act. On the one hand, it does force government to tell people what they must do: "Look, kids, Uncle Sam says all species are to be protected, so you must quit using this nice lake for your boating and hunting during the migratory season, or using this insecticide, or building this dam." The public, apparently, is not to be involved in forming these conservation policies, even though the policies directly affect their lives. In one fairly populous section of Oklahoma, the Wildlife Service has created a 37,000-acre, fenced-in refuge, with a managed buffalo and elk herd and beautiful protected grasslands. The people who live in that region perceive a shortage of recreational areas, perceive that they are excluded from this Eden, and, no doubt, also perceive that it was paid for out of their taxes. There is thus a good deal of moral indignation. The service argues that this protected piece of land is our generation's gift to future generations, and thereby makes its moral point. We learned one significant lesson from our forebears of the nineteenth century who slew wantonly the buffalo, the egret, geese, bear, etc.: "For the sake of those to come, thou shalt not kill wildlife wantonly." The word "wanton" means "without reason"—or, as we systems people would say, "without heed for systems management." Here morality and religion merge, as we worship that immense Being, future generations.

Suppose now we turn to the very small. In his fascinating book *Lives of the Cell*, Lewis Thomas suggests that the reason for human existence is that our bodies provide an excellent host for certain types of bacterium. We, of course, being overwhelmed by our importance, hide the fact that our importance lies in providing a habitat for the very small. A recent news item states that the cat has a gland in its head that secretes an odor when the animal rubs its head against your leg; the speculation is that thereby the cat lays claim to ownership. It doesn't think you own it; it thinks it owns you, which explains a lot about feline behavior. The Sermon on the Mount tells us, "Blessed are the meek, for they shall inherit the earth"—a forecast that up to now has seemed singularly inept. But it may be an evolutionary forecast: those humans will survive who do *not* see themselves at the pinnacle of nature's hierarchy—that is, who understand the proper role of humans in nature.

In the New Testament, Christ is constantly contrasting the large and the small. "Consider the lilies of the field, how they grow; they toil not, neither do they spin: And yet I say unto you, That even Solomon in all his glory was not arrayed like one of these."° This is the theme that Wordsworth adopted at the end of his *Ode: On Intimations of Immortality*:

> Thanks to the human heart by which we live,
> Thanks to its tenderness, its joys, and fears,
> To me the meanest flower that grows can give
> Thoughts that do often lie too deep for tears.

Several years ago a group of my students were conducting research on a town in California in an effort to see how community spirit might be re-created; the rich lived in walled enclaves; the developers wanted to put high-rises on the beach, and artists and old folks didn't want them to; hippies were

°Matthew 6:28–29.

sleeping in caves on the hill; and the police department was quite jittery. The researchers designed a "Volunteer Post" in the downtown area, where people could come and talk about problems, plans, or old times versus new times. When I visited the researchers, they complained that one mentally ill young man had been "pestering" them for several days, so that they hadn't been able to get on with the bigger task of helping the community. I read them those verses of Matthew where the King on Judgment Day tells those on his right hand that when he was hungry, they fed him, or naked, clothed him, and so on. Those on the right hand ask, "When did we see thee hungry and feed thee . . . or naked and clothe thee . . ." "And the King will answer them: 'Truly, I say to you, as you did it to one of the least of these my brethren, you did it to me.'"° From a systems point of view, this may seem quite unreasonable, because surely as we develop social policies and programs, we need to consider the total impact. Teachers in crowded schools can't afford to spend a lot of time with one child, because such behavior would be "unfair" to the rest of the kids. How can we "justify" concentrating attention on "one of the least of these"?

But, to repeat, the enemies are not fair, and they do not regard justification to be an important human act. But they are reasonable, because they can successfully pose to reason questions about its foundations. To illustrate this point, let's go back and watch Aristotle composing his lecture notes on logic. He thought he could find a common schema of reasoning, which he called "syllogisms." Thus, once we grant that all humans are animals and all animals are mortal, we are compelled to grant that all humans are mortal; or so he thought. But now suppose we're talking not about humans in general, but rather about Joe Smith, "one of the least of these." Is Joe Smith, like humans, a class of objects, a class with only one member? Logicians have debated the point ever since Aristotle. But the religious response is, "certainly not." Joe Smith is not a number or a set of properties; he is a unique soul. If he is unique, then schema like the syllogism don't apply. Nor do social policies or programs. Government administrators would like to argue that the law says that all adult people with an income less than five thousand dollars per annum are to be given food stamps; Joe Smith has an income less than five thousand dollars; therefore Joe Smith is to be given food stamps. But the soul of Joe Smith is unique and cannot be described as putting Joe Smith into an income class. His soul doesn't "have" an income, and it doesn't belong to any class.

Although I taught logic to college freshmen for a number of years, I don't

°Matthew 25: 34–40.

know why I taught it the way I did (except that so many others were doing the same thing—*not* a very good systems reason). It's neither interesting nor significant to say that if all *a* is *b* and all *b* is *c*, then all *a* is *c*, and to use "Venn diagrams" to "show" the innocent student that it's so. In fact, bright students who are reasonably sophisticated in geometry are being "taught" that if one little circle is inside a bigger circle, and the bigger circle is inside a still bigger circle, then the first little circle is inside the third circle. This is being "taught" to freshmen who are simultaneously taking analytic geometry and calculus. No wonder the bright freshmen think there must be a gimmick that would catch them up in the final examination!

The really exciting issue is not what follows from "all *a* is *b*" but rather how we determine that something is "in *b*" in the first place. The history of science is replete with exciting debates about class membership. For decades astronomers argued about whether those "cloudy" areas outside our galaxy were galaxies or clouds, "island universes" like our own or immense gaseous things. Then they were convinced that a few of them were galaxies; then that millions of them were. Nutritionists still debate about what it means to say that someone is "malnourished." Business administration professors still are unsure when a company is "solvent." Wildlife professionals have a hard time determining whether a species is "threatened" or "endangered." Political scientists would dearly like to have a secure way of classifying a social disturbance as "civil dissent" or "revolution." A course dealing with methods of classification would certainly seem a lot more relevant than learning Boolean algebra or the syllogism.

The same remarks apply to numerical measurement. The formalists define measurement as the "assignment of numbers to objects," and they play around with the formal implications of such assignments. But the exciting question is how we should assign numbers. How do we know the velocity of optical light within 0.1 kilometer per second? Singer was the only philosopher, as far as I know, who appreciated the prime importance of calibration in measurement. And the process by which calibration is attained is usually quite complicated and certainly "theory-laden." But calibration underlies all classification and assignment of numbers to objects. If we humans could not calibrate, at least approximately, then the class logic and arithmetic would be utterly useless as aids in decision making.

But beneath all calibration is the question, Can this being be classified at all? The question is reasonable.° There was an enormous presumption on Galileo's part to lay down as an objective of science: to measure objects and to

---

°It also appears in the next chapter, on the aesthetic; the enemies often have common themes.

make measurable that which up to now has defied measurement. Why should this be a legitimate objective of science? The answer certainly does not come from logic, either deductive or inductive. The question is really one of psychology and religion, of the soul and its sacredness. To say that the soul belongs to a class is to elevate the class in significance above the soul. "Oh, no," the classifier may respond, "I make no value judgment when I decide that your soul is mortal or you are fundamentally white, male, over forty, etc." But of course he does make value judgments, because policy makers use classes as the basis of their policies, so that to them any individual is no more than the conjunction of a set of classes. More important, to feel oneself belonging to a class is often to have a religious experience of the grand kind: "to be a woman," "a man," "young," "old," "poor," "rich," and so on. In each case there is the sacred relation to something larger, superior, magnificent. I've already talked about patriotism as a political approach; but it is also a religious approach: to belong, as a citizen, to a nation is to belong to something grand. And treason is not merely illegal; it is religiously evil. But all the examples of the enemies reveal the four of them as facets of the same thing.

There are also awesome class belongings—"to be alive," "to be one with nature," even "to be dead"; or fearsome class belongings—"to have cancer," "to be destitute," or "to be convicted," or even "to be rich or powerful."

All of these are examples of the religious experience of belonging to a class, where the class is superior to the soul. Even logic must admit that the opposite is also possible or, indeed real: the religious experience of the small, the uniqueness of the soul in the sense that it "belongs" to no class. Why should the class of beings that are not classifiable be empty? And what of the paradox of a class of unclassifiable beings? Some logicians, however, might be tempted to point out that this whole matter was "solved" even as early as *Principia Mathematica*, which contains a logic of *the x* (*the* queen of England, *the* West Churchman who wrote this book). One can certainly question whether the *PM* logic captures the *the*-ness of the religious experience or even the commonsense meaning of uniqueness which abhors class membership of any kind.

I should note again an attitude of the systems approach vis à vis its enemies. The systems approach, in its eternal search for comprehensiveness, must seek to understand or "absorb" the enemy, who is forever posing reasonable issues which apparently show that the systems approach is *not* comprehensive. Hence, the systems approach must strive, for example, to understand uniqueness, even to the extent of designing a logic of the unique; but such a striving is probably not a religious experience, and hence not a matter of concern for the religious approach to human affairs, which is not bothered by comprehensiveness.

I once set out to design such a logic. It seems reasonable to argue that if an assertion is made about a unique individual—for example, an assertion that it belongs to a class—the very assertion calls for the need to change it, because its very uniqueness denies the assertion. So, as a beginning, we have assertion a, which must be followed by the instruction "change a into $-a$," where the operator "hyphen" does not necessarily mean "non-" but something like "changed." An example of this fluid logic is the last sentence of the preceding paragraph. As I was writing that the religious experience is not bothered by comprehensiveness, I realized that to strive for comprehensiveness, as represented by the god(dess) called "The Whole System," is a unique religious experience. So the instruction is "Change a."

But then my cautious reflective mind was overwhelmed by the vision of an endless series of instructions to change: once "Change a" is obeyed, it creates an instruction to change "Change a," and so forth. Since no further "insights" have occurred, I've let the matter rest for the time being.

Nonetheless, the challenge of uniqueness is rather overwhelming, because it suggests to the rational mind of the systems approacher that there may be another universe of decision making of which he is completely unaware. This suggestion gains weight if we turn to another aspect of uniqueness: the community.* The *Random House Dictionary* defines a community as a "social group sharing common characteristics or interests and perceived or perceiving itself as distinct in some respect from the larger society within which it exists." † Our hero is tempted to try classification again: Where is the community located? Is it primarily urban or rural? What is the family income distribution? etc. All of these questions could readily be answered in regard to Mill Valley, California, where I live, but none of the answers would reflect the fact that this community is extremely low key. In the nine years we've lived here, I once delivered a package to a neighbor, I once complained to a newcomer about the location of the house he was about to build, I once went to a neighborhood New Year's Eve party (never repeated), and I wave to people walking and jogging on the road. Only one neighboring family knows me by my first name. These data do not imply that we have no community. But our community has the quality that privacy is a high value.

It's almost as though "community" defies statistics, the latter being a word that originally meant data about the state; whatever is reported about the

---

* See also pp. 160–61, where the same theme is treated by the aesthetic.
† *Random House Dictionary* (New York: Random House, 1967).

number of "something or other" in a community tells us remarkably little about the community itself. Can this be so? After all, I just enumerated my encounters with people in my community, and this surely is a statistic. But the community's spirit in our case is privacy, and the feeling of privacy is not captured at all by counting encounters.

Does community exist over and above, or independent of, the individuals who belong to it? In my lifetime in social systems planning I've found that some people take the existence of community to be the most obvious beginning point of all social planning, whereas others cannot see it at all. Much can be learned about this dichotomy from the early history of the Christian Church. The early Christians were not concerned about the theory (theology) underlying their faith. The "datum" that was most vivid to them was the Spirit. Saint Paul asks, "Received ye the Spirit by the works of the law or by the hearing of faith?" °

In his *Social Substance of Religion*, Gerald Heard is inspired to describe the spirit of the beloved community: "There seems no doubt that the force was that immense love generated by the group itself, which, when it really satisfies, balances and reciprocates with the constituent, and so can break down the barriers of his individualism, making him one with himself and with it."† This passage was no doubt inspired by the young Paul:

> For as in one body we have many members, and all members have not the same function; so we, being many, are yet one body in Christ, and everyone members one of another. . . . Rejoice with those who rejoice, weep with those who weep, live in harmony with one another, do not be haughty, but give yourself to humble tasks. Be not wise in your own conceits.‡

In the next chapter on aesthetics we will also turn to "love" as an aspect of the Spirit.

When a group has attained love, it is love which is best known: the statistics of the group's life, its income distribution, sex distribution, age distribution, are *not* its facts.

Heard, as well as many others, regrets the fact that the beloved community of early Christianity eroded and changed into asceticism, fear (not love) of God, fear about the salvation of the soul, fear about the survival of the Church. Heard claims the cause of this change was the increase in the size of the communities, both the membership of the communities and the number of communities. The older Paul aided and abetted this transformation.

° Galatians 3:2.
† Gerald Heard, *Social Substance of Religion*, p. 212.
‡ Romans 12: 4-5, 15-16.

But, in the theme of this book, there is a more fundamental cause, the intellect. As Descartes tells us, the intellect works always through doubt. And there is the scene: doubt facing love.

Of course the community made of love is only one form of community, or perhaps the community of love can take a number of forms. There may be a guru, so that the love flows toward and away from one person. Or there may be agriculture, so that the love is a sharing in the pursuit of a common resource. Or it may be a family who shares together the glory of the ties of kinship.

In Chapter XIII I'll talk of murder and suicide of organizations, but here I'll mention the death of the Spirit of the community. We have few, if any, laws dealing with community murder, and thus it goes on all the time, unpunished and probably without a twinge of conscience on the part of the murderers. Developers come into a peaceful community, build something big—a mine, a recreational area, an industrial park—and murder the community. At least in physical murder there is a body and perhaps some blood to remind the murderer of his deed. But if he/she does not perceive the Spirit, then he/she cannot perceive the murder. I've already mentioned *Death of a Valley* (on p. 62); the photographs perceived the community and gave a visual account of its murder. I doubt whether the government administrators and engineers were even vaguely aware that they had committed murder.

I've also mentioned our research team which studied experimental schools; our group was "murdered" because we hadn't produced enough numbers! Hardly a justifiable murder. But there was no use saying to our monitors that they performed the execution of the spirit. They'd only laugh at the absurdity.

A Tale of Love

In a corner of George's Forest lived two lovers, as happy as they could be, day by day. One quiet evening they sat together watching the beautiful sunset, listening to the birds, smelling the sweetness of the flowers and themselves, holding hands that gradually went into a dance of caress, hither and there over the lovely skins. The dance becomes more intense as the kiss and embrace join in, and the lovely sounds that are the song of love fill the air.

Then the two lie back, snuggling next to each other, smiling, at complete peace.

"Wasn't it perfect-perfect-perfect?" murmurs the one. There is a pregnant pause. "Wasn't it? What's the matter?"

"Oh, it was perfect, all right. But what was it that made it so perfect? Was it because we came together? Or that we enjoyed the dance of the sensations? What is the quality of love that makes it so perfect?" A pause. A pregnant silence. Then. "Why are you crying? What have I said now?"

Postscript Chapter X

On the Immensity of Nothing

This section of this chapter considers the worship of nothingness, which entails, of course, the worship of everything. In such an excursion, every thing and everything, no thing and nothing are allowed to play together.

I'll begin with autobiography, though I imagine that the experience is very common around age 15 years, so I'll call it the adolescent image of the small and the large in nature. It comes when the young person has learned through chemistry about the tininess of matter as science has traced back through molecules to particles spinning around in regular and also somewhat erratic ways, and at the same time has learned about the immensity of the universe, which also displays somewhat regular and erratic behavior of the heavenly bodies. What more natural and marvelous of imagination than to imagine that this so-called immensity of the universe is itself quite tiny, an organic molecule, let us say of some gigantic living body composed of similar molecules constituting other "universes." And at the other end, the so-called inpenetrable particle is in fact a minuscule universe, its parts beyond any existing technique of dissection. There are difficulties with all this imagination that the adult mind must face. But to me the fascinating point was that there was always room for both a smaller universe and a larger one! The pathway to the smaller and smaller universes in no way led to nothingness, but rather to smallerness. In terms of size, 10^{-x} can be made as small as we please, and 10^x as large as we want. Nothing and everything are eternally elusive in this imagery. Something the size of 10^{-100} in. would regard something the size of 10^{-96} in. to be quite large, and something the size of 10^{-110} in. quite small.

What is nothing? It's above all a religious image, as is everything. Some believe at death "there is nothing." But this is far more fantastic than "there is something," as eastern philosophers long ago pointed out.

But western philosophers have had their hand in the matter as well, albeit somewhat unconsciously. It is no accident that this chapter spends so much of its discussion on the religion of logic. As I've mentioned before, when I was a freshman I kept a journal which dealt mainly with religious matters. By the time I had reached graduate school, it concerned itself more and more with symbolic logic, until, when I stopped the separate journal, it was altogether logic. It never occurred to me to put the two together. If I'd asked myself what the connection should be, I'd probably have responded that I could understand the logic of religion (e.g., in such matters as the proof of God's existence). I probably would not have said anything about the religion of logic.

And yet implicit in the foundations of logic is a fantastic religious pattern. Consider, for example, the logical rule that the conjunction of two classes (what belongs to both) must belong to each of the classes ("all yellow cats are both yellow and cats"). But what if the two classes have no members in common? The language of logic abhors general principles with exceptions, quite the contrary of most natural languages. Consequently, logicians would still like to say that the conjunction of two classes belongs to both classes even though they share no members. Hence, since they share nothing, then the "null class" is included in every class. The same logical process occurs at the other end of the spectrum of classes, the universal class of all classes. To keep the rules exceptionless, every class must be included in the universal class.

But if we allow a slight shift in wording, the language becomes mystical and perhaps Zen-like:

> in every thing there is nothing
> nothing belongs to every thing
> every thing belongs to everything
> everything contains nothingness,

and, if we permit "is" to replace "belongs to," or "belongs in" we have

> nothing is everything
> every thing is everything,

the second being reminiscent of the earlier principle "in every system are all systems."

It might be said of this section of a chapter on religion, that nothing much has been said about nothingness, but perhaps everything that can be said about it is nothing (much).

Final Notes

There was a time when I seriously considered becoming a Catholic monk. I was a young man who worshipped intellectual study, deeply and unreservedly. Furthermore, I'd had enough of family life, with the severe burdens one member can impose on all the others. The Catholic Benedictines seemed ideal, because of their dedication to scholarship. But then I went to visit one of their monasteries, and experienced the early-rising, and the first exercises of devotion. Kneeling and praying on cold slabs at 6:00 A.M. destroyed the substance of my spirit of admiration. It was then that I decided that the ritual of religion would always be unique and spontaneous for me, never formed out of some external rules of conduct.

And, finally, as I was writing this chapter, I had a dream of a fantastic dancer, leaping in beautiful, but often erratic curves. Suddenly I was given the vision to perceive his inner body, and there in every limb, muscle, flesh, was to be seen a tiny dancer, making up in his or her leapings and erratic curves, the whole of the dance of the dancer.

CHAPTER XI

Aesthetics

IN classical philosophy it was common to divide the philosopher's task into considerations of the meaning and significance of the Good, the True and the Beautiful. If these were to be the cornerstones of the real system in which humanity lives, then they somehow needed to be interrelated. In chapters III, IV, V, and VI, we have seen how the Good and the True interrelate. Once the ethics of equity is introduced, the basic logic underlying the inquiry of planning has to be changed, so that consideration of the Good influences our approach to the True. Similarly, the categories the planner uses to study social systems have a great deal to say about the structure of the Good; that is, the True influences our ideas about the Good.

But, curiously enough, the Beautiful seems to be absent from most of the writings dealing with the whole system. The Beautiful is implicit, I think, in the imagery of the *I Ching*, which often has a dramatic tone—of peace, or hope, or horror—all of which are qualities of the Beautiful-Ugly, which I'll call "aesthetics." One might have expected Plato to show how the aesthetic is incorporated into his *Republic*, which clearly builds on the True and the Good, but he does not. Nor does Aristotle claim that the highest function of the human being—contemplation—is also the most beautiful, although it clearly expresses the highest form of good and the highest form of truth. Kant's *Critique of Pure Reason* deals with the True as it is revealed to us in experience, and his *Critique of Practical Reason* with the Good as it is expressed by the actions of the Good Will. But the first *Critique* has no category of experience labeled "beautiful" or "ugly," and the second *Critique* does not speak of the beautiful or ugly quality of the Good Will or the absence of it. Aesthetics is added on only at the end, as an aspect of judgment in the *Critique of Judgment*.

The same phenomenon can be observed in philosophy curricula (where, however, one may also observe the attempt to segregate the Good from the True). Aesthetics is relegated to courses which rarely refer to the other cornerstones of the edifice and are often taught in dry and unaesthetic ways. To be sure, the hard Truth seekers, like the positivists, are often embarrassed when their mathematical colleagues wax eloquent about the beauty of a proof, or their physics friends speak of the elegance of a finding. There being no satisfactory way of operationally defining beauty and elegance, the positivists drop both in the ashcan called "psychology": scientific method operates through observation and logic, but scientists themselves, being all too human, lapse at times into "psychology," which is not logic. This rather crass way of dismissing the spirit of scientific inquiry in favor of its logic must also be regarded as unaesthetic.

When philosophers have turned to aesthetics, they have often regarded the problem of its meaning to be centered in the arts—pure or applied. What is it that makes Beethoven's Ninth Symphony a great work of art? And what shall we say to a critic who holds that the scherzo vastly overdoes its interruptions, that the adagio is oversweetened iced tea, and that the finale is German bombardment carried to Germanic extreme? Artists themselves tend to be frustratingly uncommunicative: if you don't see that this is a marvelous sculpture, a painting with zing, a far-out dance, then nobody can tell you so, and your failure to appreciate is sad but irrelevant.

Nevertheless, serious aestheticians struggle to find a clue to the mystery of what makes great art. Perhaps it lies in form. That's it! So beaux-arts lay down the "fundamental" form of all aesthetic buildings—a decree that lasts a few decades and is followed by functionalism, modularism, and now maybe a reincarnated beaux-arts. So it's all a fad, and God only knows what the next one will be. But few would deny the splendor of the Acropolis.

The trouble, of course, came at the beginning, when aesthetics was cut off from her sisters, the Good and the True. Things took a turn for the worse when we could no longer ask whether a building was "good" except in the sense of being "beautiful"; this is why functionalism tried to turn things around and ask whether a building is (any) good first, and to worry about the aesthetics later, if at all. And as for asking whether a building is true, what nonsense! What could a "true building" possibly mean?

And yet from a systems point of view it must mean a great deal. The part of the human system which produces knowledge is not separable from the rest. "Knowledge" doesn't just occur in books and lectures; it is a living part of our everyday lives. From the moment of waking to the moment of sleeping and on through sleep, we are using knowledge, learning, forgetting, adjusting, judging. The objects about us that help us learn are a part of our knowledge system, whether they are propositions, cooking instruments, friends—or buildings. So a building may be "true," in the sense that it helps us learn how to do the things we want to do.

All this sounds familiar to the ears of our systems planner. He can readily understand that aesthetics is a human value, and that it should not be separated from other values. Architecture is about the good, the true, and the beautiful in our edifices and landscapes, and physics is about the good, the true, and the beautiful in nature. Only some perversity of the disciplines made people say that we must carefully distinguish between the way a forest—as an ecological system—changes, from the aesthetics of the forest.

Where is the enemy? The systems point of view shows us that we should *not* search for the meaning of the aesthetic in the arts alone, and perhaps not in them at all, because often in art the connection of the aesthetic to its brothers, the Good and the True, is obscured. Thus, it may very well be that past writings on aesthetics were motivated by the wrong problem—namely, identification of the properties of great art—and thereby ignored the central systemic problem: How is aesthetics related to the other attributes that make up a human life?

The time has come (again) to speculate. Suppose we begin by listing some of the qualities of human experience that plausibly seem to fall under the rubric of the aesthetic. As a beginning: peaceful, attractive, exciting, anticipatory, luring; and threatening, repulsive, boring, anxious, frightening. We could go to "higher" levels and talk of comedy-tragedy, love-hate, attraction-indifference-repulsion. All this might lure the systems logician to set up the basic categories of the aesthetic. But before he too eagerly jumps into this job, we have to caution him. First of all, what has these qualities? The answer I gave was "experience." I could also have said "the field of consciousness" or "awareness."

Two things seem noticeable. First, all experience, including dreams, has an aesthetic quality. In fact, my logical mind is tempted to say that aesthetics *is* that which gives the quality—rather than the content—of experience, and that experience without quality is dead—just as experience without thought is unintelligible.

But suppose now that that which has all these qualities declares that the act of trying to define them is unaesthetic—that is, it spoils the aesthetic quality. How shall the systems approach respond? Why, simply by saying that such a declaration is unreasonable: why should the act of defining, which, after all, clarifies our experience, be regarded as unaesthetic?

Now the enemy employs his usual tactic—namely, he gives a reasonable response to this systems question. We can again appreciate the fundamental difficulty of a rational life: it cannot reasonably deny the need to consider reasonable questions, and the power of the reasonable is that it can throw up questions that threaten reason itself.

So the enemy now poses this reasonable thesis: the prime quality of experience is uniqueness. That which carries the aesthetic qualities is unique in the sense that it cannot be classified, categorized, defined, programmed, codified, subsumed, deduced, induced, named, numbered, or any of the other fantastic variety of techniques reason has used to describe and account for the individual.

The thesis is plausible (reasonable) because reason must recognize the need to try to justify the exhaustiveness of its method. If the logician says that his method classifies things of the world by their properties and their nonproperties, he must recognize that classification is a process that admits of nonclassification.

It is incredible what this enemy's plausible thesis destroys in our rational methods: priority allocation and hierarchy, the hallmarks of a large part of planning, all are aesthetically inappropriate.

The rest of this chapter is a series of commentaries on the foregoing. The force of the aesthetic image of uniqueness, and the pervasive, noncognitive quality that aesthetics generates in our experience, make a "theory of aesthetics" not merely a contradiction in terms but an anathema. But the unfolding can take place by examples.

We return to Paul once more and his three pillars of wisdom: faith, hope, and love. Faith is not a stranger to the systems approach. One way to view the nine categories is to see that as they unfold, they become more and more interdependent and necessary for each other's meaning. Thus, as the category "purpose" unfolds into "goal," "objective," and "ideal," the category of the guarantor becomes more and more essential. Hence, faith is a process in systems planning, a process in which there is a gradual realization of the necessity of the guarantor. The systems philospher realizes that the foundation of this faith forever remains incomprehensible, in the sense that he cannot comprehend it, but this does not prevent his regarding the comprehension as an ideal to be approximated endlessly.

But hope is another matter. It is tempting to define hope psychologically, as strong belief in and desire for a future without any perceivable evidence for its occurrence. Thus, shipwrecked passengers in a boat in a vast and little traveled sea hope for rescue, which they desire but realize they have no grounds for expecting.

But something crucial is missing, because a man could engage in a risky gamble or adventure on the grounds that his gain, if he is successful, would be very great. I recall that a friend of mine offered one hundred thousand dollars to anyone who could guess the seven-digit telephone number written on a slip of paper in his pocket; for the privilege of betting, you paid him one dollar. Even experts in probability theory cheerfully tried the bet, even though the "expected value" value of the bet was far less than one dollar. But the bettors were not heroes, and it is not appropriate to say that most of them "hoped" to win—at least not in Paul's sense.

The word I want is "radiance." The Latin word *claritas* can be translated into "clearness," meaning "precise," as in Descartes or later in symbolic logic. But it can also mean "light" or "brilliance." Thus, one way to talk about aesthetics is to say that it is the variety of expressions of radiance, including the dark. But it is not merely "black and white," for radiance includes the colors, and sounds, and aromas, and touches.

Back to "hope." It means belief in the desirable without perceived evidence, but it also means radiant belief. I don't know what this means, but I can imagine it easily enough. When I say, "I hope that humanity will succeed in using its intellect to improve the human condition," and someone says, "How can you hope anything of the kind, given the way humans exploit humans?"—then there is no argument: he is trying to destroy the radiance, to put out the light, and I must do my best to preserve the radiance despite his cynicism.

And, of course, radiance includes humor, because hope is a motley, which includes its own absurdity. Hope is always both serious and ridiculous. Only there is no lesson to be learned, no rational conclusion to be drawn, from saying, "Hope is absurd." The rational mind wants to say, "Hope is ridiculous and *therefore* . . ." It's like someone saying, "What's the point of *Hamlet* after all?"

Careless thought will try to put the lights out. It's ungrateful if it does, because radiance is marvelously adaptable to thought. The beautiful radiance and glory of human thought! Don't think about it! Let the radiance within you shine in that most marvelous gift of God, the incredible gift of human thought!

As for love, perhaps I've said enough already, except to add that love is a radiance, of course. And now I don't mean *claritas* alone. I mean the myriad ways in which humans can love each other, including the sexual. Here is more of Gerald Heard on the subject (see p. 183): "Love leads to joy, and as inevitably, joy leads to peace. Erethism, orgasm, and catharsis represent on the physical plane the three stages which on the psychic bear the names 'Love,' 'Joy,' 'Peace.' And there can never be complete Love without erethism, or complete orgasm without Joy, or complete Peace without catharsis. This is the psycho-physical interdependence of the mind-body unit."°

The facets of radiance are many. For example, try your hand at defining that common human experience called "happiness." It doesn't help much to give it a name of Greek origin like "eudemonia," though it may seem slightly more sophisticated to talk of the flow of eudemonia rather than the flow of happiness.

Try imagination. In early chapters I talked about the images that either go with or underlie the categories of planning. But I didn't talk about the aesthetics of such imagery, and indeed I suspect that many of my images lacked radiance. At this stage one might want to say that the meaning of a concept like "purpose" or "client" depends, not on the operational definition, but on the degree to which we can create a radiant image of the concept. If all our images of clients are "masses of people," "children under six years," "number of people having incomes less than $3,000 per annum," then we don't "understand" the concept of client, because the imagery is pale gray and uniform. All this recalls my complaint about environmental impact reports (p. 62); the imagery of *Death of a Valley* is radiant, while in the imagery of an EIR the light has failed.

And, finally, I come to that function of my psyche which I regard as the most radiant and therefore the closest to the aesthetic, intuition. Everyone knows it well; no one knows it at all. I know that Spinoza put it at the pinnacle of education, on top of the mountain built of hearsay, rules, and deductive reasoning. He didn't know what it meant, did he? Except that it was the strongest beam of light that revealed the truth unclouded by doubt. For Kant intuition is a kind of "grasping," as in his "sensuous intuition." If I were to interpret Kant in the present discourse, I'd say that intuition is that which gives experience its quality; that is, I'd identify aesthetics and intuition. But that may be too strong. Jung, strangely enough for me, says that intuition is the "function of unconscious perception," I guess because he found it so difficult to describe in consciousness-related terms.

Previously I've talked about alternative "approaches" to the conduct of human affairs. To me, it's relatively clear how politics and morality are "enemy approaches." Politics conducts the business of daily human existence by gathering people around specific issues and attempting thereby to create social action. Morality stirs the moods of humans into dissent and counterdissent. While religion is rather obscure as an "approach" unless it uses politics as its aid, still it is an approach because a great many of the things we do arise out

°Gerald Heard, *Social Substance of Religion*, p. 223.

of devotion—to a God, to wealth, to caring, to whatever. But aesthetics is another matter still; it may not even be appropriate to call it an "approach," because there are no rules, no consistencies. And if intuition is close to aesthetics, then "surprise" may be the better expression: to run your life through surprises.

PART THREE

SIGNIFICANCE

CHAPTER XII

The Negative

"I have met the enemy, and he is us!"

I'VE LABELED this last part "significance" (sign pointing) rather than "conclusion," for while the tale told in this book has no ending, it does point in a direction. It is a signpost along the endless journey of the planner.

It helps, I hope, to review the story of Part Two. We should recall the account of the word "enemy" (pp. 24–26), which goes "friend" into "nonfriend" into "opposite of friend." The question (of the strategy of conversion) thus becomes whether this process can be reversed.

Politics is first seen as a strategy for the planner, who realizes that implementation is crucial in his life. Politics suggests that in order to create change in the social order, one needs to gather together a community (polis), and that community making requires a specific problem that carries with it an aura of crisis (war, brinkmanship, sputnik, Cuban missile crisis, third world, energy, etc.). This suggestion has great appeal to the planner. His basic intellectual principle is holism, but he sees no reason why one cannot start with a concentration on one aspect of the human condition; he knows full well that one aspect inevitably unfolds into all aspects if one keeps raising significant questions. (Again, we see the concept of "sign": a continual pointing to broader issues.)

So we shall make our nonfriend, politics, into a friend who is helping us by giving us directions about how to proceed on our way. Indeed, we planners can go farther and suggest the need for "political variables," which would describe, with some degree of precision, what crisis and its related community means, so that we can examine a class of problems and choose the "optimal" problem.

But now our nonfriend, instead of turning into a friend, turns into the opposite. Any attempt to model politics, or to transform a problem into a larger problem, destroys the polis, and along with it any hope of implementation. At this point our systems planner feels entirely alienated, because if this meaning of politics is valid, then his vision is destroyed. Mankind would always have to act blindly, trying to solve crises and never knowing what lies beyond, what possible destruction such blind problem solving might leave in its wake. Such an enemy, surely, is *not* us.

Enter morality. Besides ego satisfaction, it says, there is another ethical value, call it fairness, equity, treating humanity as an end withal. A perfectly reasonable suggestion. Yes, we should not use cost-benefit as our sole criterion; Western economics has emphasized aggrandizement of wealth, to the neglect of the distribution of wealth. So we shall make our nonfriendly enemy into a friend. We're not sure how to do this, of course. Some will want to use the variance of the income distribution as a comeasure of performance with the average or median. Problems of trade-off between these comeasures are messy naturally. But our nonfriendly enemy points out that in matters of equity there is no trade-off. To exploit another by robbery, suppression, or murder is a sin that cannot be traded off by subsequent benefits to himself or his family.

But now our nonfriend turns "opposite-of-friend" by declaring that any attempt to rationalize morality—including Kant's categorical imperative—ruins the spirit of morality. Even the strategy of creating a dialectic between an ethic based on utility and an ethic based on moral law fails because it leaves out the essence of morality, its collective existence across all human lives or, perhaps, all lives. All that rationality does is to work with the residues of morality, much as one might try to discern the reality of a man by examining his feces.

Horrible! Are we to be left, not only blind, but driven by a blind collective feeling, which is not only whimsical but often downright dangerous as it creates dissent, strikes, wars, and revolutions? Such an enemy is clearly *not* us.

Now religion. In perfectly reasonable but nonfriendly terms, it points out that humans are not the only designers of change in the world, and, indeed, may not be the important designers, or may be the wrong designers. Of course. When we think of it and recall our tradition, we see at once that planning requires an understanding of all the designers of change. Indeed, we see that we are finite and liable to serious error, so that we need to understand what guarantees that our endless journey is not a sardonic joke.

But now religion shows its true face. It is not simply a matter of absorbing a rational guarantor into the world system. Rather, reason plays the role of rationalizing the true nonrational nature of humans, who are basically worshipers—blind adorers of the immense and the small. Even the man who is "out for himself" worships the immensities called "wealth" and "power." But the immense and the small cannot be "defined," and every attempt to do so obscures their true images and the way in which they influence our lives. Even "reason," which our systems approacher worships, is elusive and undefinable, as this book shows. So the conclusion is that the hero's persistent urge to improve the human condition is simply the hero's mode of worship; he is disturbed out of a mood of satisfaction into a mood of dissatisfaction by his nonrational need to worship humanity. Calamity! Certainly here is an enemy who is *not* us.

Finally, the aesthetic. It's extremely reasonable at the outset, because it suggests that in our "gung ho" attempt to reach certain goals, we may very well ignore the quality that people value in addition to the content. Airports are designed to get people on and off planes; the result may be a very uncomfortable experience for the traveler—even dangerous because his perceptions become distorted. Or an area may be strip-mined, in order to attain the goal of a satisfactory ore supply. But the residents who witness the partial destruction of their natural environment, which is familiar to them, may sustain a psychological shock from which they never recover.

So, yes, there are important values that planning has tended to ignore, and that should be incorporated into our reasoning about change. Even if we can't quantify these important qualities of experience, we should find ways of incorporating them into our design criteria. Our nonfriendly aesthetic critic has become a helpful friend by calling our attention to an aspect of the human system we had ignored.

But our new-found friend turns against us, by pointing out that there must be something to carry this quality of experience, the psychological aspect of the human being which appreciates experience. This is not ego, or the Good Will, or superego, or the archetypes. It is unique, not classifiable. Kant spoke wisely when he told us to act so as to treat *humanity,* either in ourselves or another, never as a means only, but as an end withal. But perhaps he himself did not realize the profundity of his imperative, for the "humanity" to which he refers is that unique quality each of us has, which makes up the reality of our psyches.

But this, too, ruins the game, or work, of the planner. Gone is tradeoff. Gone is adding up values. Gone is any sensible way of assessing change. Everyone's uniqueness is a world in itself, incomparable with any other uniqueness. My God, let's not fall into that trap, so cleverly laid by the aesthetic enemy who is clearly *not* us.

We can readily see the insidious plot that underlies each of these encounters. Above all, the rational planner must be able to respond to reasonable or plausible questions and, indeed, welcomes such questions because they may enlarge his image. Thus politics raises a perfectly reasonable question: Why should we planners try to be holistic, to grasp more and more of the whole system? We planners must respond because the question addresses the epistemology of a guiding principle of our approach. We surely don't want to respond that this principle of holism is a tautology. Furthermore, politics suggests a plausible reason why a nonholistic approach is preferable, because it holds people together and permits action.

Well, why not say the principle is a posteriori and hence testable by experience? And, indeed, we do point to the many instances in which the narrow approach has led to serious—even disastrous—consequences: the auto, drugs, malnutrition, arms—and perhaps even the printing press. But this is not a satisfactory answer, because the meaning of "test" runs into the same paradox. A "test" for the narrow approach is one in which qualified observers can agree on "success" or "failure." But a "test" for the holistic approach is not based on "qualified" observers, because they are probably viewing the problem in a narrow manner. Thus, expert physicists may judge that the "problem" of nuclear waste is minimal, or does not exist at all, because, say, they have no interest in the values of generations, a consideration of prime importance in the holistic approach.

Suppose, instead, we adopt a dialectical epistemology and say that holism and politics are two dramatically different approaches to planning, and that out of their opposition arises a rich and hopefully powerful process for trying to improve the human condition. This is a suggestion, of course, that is wholly holistic: in the planning context we let the narrow, political approach debate "in court" with the holistic approach. But such a courtroom scene spoils the politics, because it has to be conducted in our "impartial" manner. Better— for politics—would be a rigged court—or, in general, politics decides the rules of the debate and the referees.

Matters become worse for the dialectical approach as we consider the other three enemies, none of whom are inclined to debate at all, especially if the debate is based on concepts and information. Sitting down and talking it over ruins the moral spirit, as revolutionaries and oppressors both know; morality abhors reasonableness. For religion, we might debate with images and counterimages of the immense and the small, as the great religions of the world have done. But it's probably absurd to speak of a synthesis of imaginal conflict. And what is there to debate about the uniqueness of the individual?

We need another sign to point to the significance of the systems approach and its enemies, and that sign can be an image, the image of the symbolism of a vision: "in my mind's eye." In my mind's eye I can see a world of human equity, in which the quality of each individual's life is of the highest. I do not mean that everyone in the vision is blissfully happy, because for many bliss may not be the quality that is appropriate to their lives: struggle, frustration, hope, despair may rather be the appropriate life theme. And, of course, the vision need not be so grand and comprehensive. It may be the vision of a better life in a village, or an agency, or even in a single person.

The vision contains all the enemies. It contains community (polis), morality, religion, and aesthetics. It is also symbolic. But "symbolic" means that it is a symbol of something, something real. But where is the reality? The "real" world contains few of the aspects of the vision.

Thus, the problem before us is to put together in a rational fashion the planner's vision and reality—to meet the challenge that the vision is utterly unrealistic, or utterly impractical, apolitical, immoral, and irreligious, or, worst of all, unaesthetic. In other words, I take it that reality includes the claims of the enemies.

It is worthwhile recalling how both Kant and Singer struggled with the question of the real world of the planner. For Kant, there were two worlds of human values—the world of happiness-unhappiness and the world of moral and immoral actions, the world of virtue. It was clear to him that an individual who acts in order to increase his own happiness could not thereby be virtuous. But in principle there was no reason why he who acts with the moral law as his sole motive might not thereby be happy. Only in the real world of today virtue surely does not create happiness; often it seems to create unhappiness for all concerned, as when a poor man in Königsberg stole a loaf of bread for his hungry family. Kant, who thought that the "big idea" behind stealing could not be generalized, regarded the act as immoral, even though the owner of the loaf was hurt very little and the thief's family benefited.

But Kant's vision included the perspective of humanity gradually creating a world in which virtue and happiness begin to coincide—that is, where virtue produces happiness. For this to happen, the vision needed a guarantor, God, the possibility of free choice, Freedom, and an opportunity for the endless struggle, Immortality. But is there any reality in such a vision? Kant calls the three conditions "postulates," as though in effect there was a demand for them, else the whole plot is senseless.

Singer, building on Kant's vision, is somewhat more subtle. He includes in his vision a "heroic mood," which stirs us out of our humdrum life of satisfaction to search for new ways to follow the pathway of progress. Is the heroic mood "real"? Singer thought he could find evidence for its reality in the arts: in comedy and tragedy, for example, or in the *Freude* of Beethoven's Ninth.

Now there is one aspect of the heroic mood that Singer himself does not stress, but that we, his students, did find comforting. If one is driven by the heroic mood, then the "real" world appears disastrous, as though no progress had ever been made, or even as though matters were getting worse and worse. It is up to the hero not to despair when this perspective appears to him. For the time being, he may be blind to a progress that is "really" taking place.

But is human progress "real"? Here again Singer used an ingenious strategy to keep his visionary and his real world together (see p. 90). He early noted that in experimental science no measurement is ever completely precise. Consequently we can never say, "The distance between the points A and B is precisely 3.256 meters." Instead, all we can reasonably respond is something like, "What is taken to be distance from what is taken to be the points A and B, is to be taken as 3.256 meters plus or minus an error factor." We are never really sure what "distance" means, nor are we sure of what a point on the earth's surface means, nor are we sure of the true distance. But what is very neat and clever in his vision is that these imperatives about "takens" can be seen to converge on the "answer" to the question that is the precise response. We become more sure about such matters as distance and point location, and the error factor drops significantly: we can measure within "billimeters" of a meter these days. Finally, we can say that there is a "real" distance between A and B, which is never known precisely but can be approximated by our increasingly accurate estimates. Hence the real becomes the ideal, because ideals are desirable ends (signposts constantly beckoning us on) which can be approximated but never attained.

Thus Singer believed that he had put his vision and reality together: we never know what reality is, but we can explain its idealistic meaning through a vision. If we were to apply this idea to management or to planning, we would say that the manager and the planner never know what is "really" going on in their organization; they need to design criteria that will help them to better their estimates of the reality of their organization.

Thus, if one takes Singer's lesson, gleaned from experimental science, and applies it to the world of human living, then here, too, we may discover a similar progression and a way to bring together the vision and the reality.

But do "we" discover anything of the kind? Not if we are driven by the heroic mood, which colors our perception of the human world with hues of gloom. Who is this "we" that can observe that progress really takes place?

At one time I was willing to give this job to a kind of super anthropologist, who could assess (somehow) how human knowledge and production were related to human cooperation, and thereby (somehow) estimate various stages of human progress, progress that would include retrogressions as well as progressions. But is such an anthropology really possible?

The first signpost points to a human need of all visionaries, the need to integrate the vision with reality, to show what the symbol is symbolizing.

Not "all" visionaries surely. There is another choice: escape the need by retreating either to the vision or to the reality of the enemies. In the first case, for example, one retreats into abstract models that are symbols of nothing but themselves. So when students ask, "What practical value does this model have?" the proud answer is, "None whatsoever!" In the second case one bounds the problem, cuts off a "meaningful piece," does something practical, uses politics, persuasion, and any other tricks of the trade to sell his wares; the vision is gone and often with it the life of the planner.

From all this we can begin to understand the plot of the novel of the hero-planner who does not retreat into his vision or into the specifics of problem solving. It is a modern *Candide*. Whenever the hero recognizes the disasters of the world, usually brought about by the enemies, he says, "But over all there is progress." His statement of faith is like espousing a proposition that fails in every instance but that one believes is "true in general."

Some of the enemies are laughing. For them the words of the old song about Frankie and Johnnie come to mind:

> This story has no moral,
> This story has no end,
> This story only goes to show
> That there ain't no good in men.

CHAPTER XIII

The Positive

OF COURSE, there is no need to leave matters in the depressing state suggested by the conclusion of the last chapter. It is true that reason, through reflection, pushes itself beyond comprehension. It is also true that the world is in a sorry state, and that the cause can likely be adjudicated to be one or more of the enemies at work.

Now when reason creates through reflection its own deep puzzles, it arrives at "paradox"; that is, it arrives at a result that runs counter to its own teachings (para: "contrary to"; dox: "opinion" or "teaching"). Paradox has been one of the driving forces in the history of the codification of logic. Consider the following. It seems highly rational to say that every meaningful proposition is either true or false and cannot be both. Then reflection suggestions that "this proposition is false" is a proposition that cannot be either "true" or "false." Somehow reason needs to unfold its logical theory to take care of this annoying case of the breakdown of its doctrine (i.e., a case of "paradox"). Indeed, this history of logic shows not only different "solutions" of this paradox, but also the way in which the paradox served to create more general logical systems.

There is much to be said, therefore, for purposefully designing paradox, as I'll attempt to do in this last chapter. Returning to the strategies of dealing with one's enemies (p. 149), I suggest that we select the "paradoxical" one, of "being one's own enemy." The prescription "Be your enemy" appears contrary to the teachings of rational planning. What is called for, therefore, is a new teaching of rational planning—that is, a new and more general meaning of rationality, which goes beyond dialectical reasoning.

It is not difficult to see what this new teaching might be. It says that rational humans need to leave the body of rationality and to place the self in another body, the "enemy," so that the reality of the social system can unfold in a radically different manner. From this vantage point he/she can observe the rational spirit and begin to realize not only what has been left out of it, but also what the spirit is like, especially its quality of being human.

It is important (to me) to point out that "being one's enemy" does *not* mean losing one's identity; the rational body continues to exist and to do its life's work. This is why the philosophy of this book is not existentialist nor phenomenological; a philosopher like Heidegger did not truly exist in the rational body. I'm talking about the rational planner who has lived deeply in rationality, in modeling, in conceptualization, in trying to measure some aspect of reality, and who had taken these tasks with deadly seriousness. In "being" the enemy he/she has not lost this "other me" at all but rather has objectivized it. The resultant "being" is neither a loose dreamer nor a hard thinker. To be the enemy means to release the bonds of hard rationality.

I want to end this book with an example of being the enemy.

My example is "organization theory"—that is, the theory of human organizations. I've chosen this topic because it has been so overworked by one kind of rationality, which combines patterns of thinking and observation. The result has been, in the main, a dreary literature which seems to require all too many words to say so little. To me, the little that is said seems not to portray the real life of an organization.

Thus I want to talk about what quality in an organization makes it alive or dead. But I don't yet want to deal with the "biology" of human organizations, as some rationally minded authors have; I want rather to put myself in the body of the enemies. This is best done (for me) by writing autobiography: What has my life in living and dead organizations been like?

As a start, since I'm in the body of the enemies, I don't set out to define "life" and then to apply that definition to organizations. I've generally felt very sure that some of the organizations to which I've belonged were born, had a short life, and then died. The Institute of Management Sciences is one example. I was present at its birth. Then as editor of its journal I felt it begin to grow up and mature, and later as its president I felt it slowly begin to die. The enemy that best describes these feelings is the aesthetic, which can talk about an organization's radiance and its gradual diminution.

But rather than recount the life and times of organizations, I shall concentrate on the political-moral-religious-aesthetic aspects within organizations.

Suppose we begin with something quite close to rationality—"information." I mean not items of information stored in computer accounting and personnel files, but the living process of people informing other people about politically loaded information. Often there is a key figure in this process, who can be called the "informant." The informant himself often has no political ambitions but is highly sensitive to the kind of information that will stir others into forming polis around an issue. Therefore, the information is often "confidential" or "secret" from the point of view of the collective conscious of the organization. When I was much younger, I ran a small section of a research laboratory. One of my group was an excellent informant. I made the mistake of assuming that if he had the information, then it was "public" for the whole organization. No such thing. Three days after my informant informed me, the colonel in charge of the laboratory called all the section heads to his office, told his secretary to disappear, and whispered the "news" to us.

Over the years I've found it relatively easy to identify informants. In my own school I'm more or less brash about it. On greeting the informant, I simply ask "What do you know that I ought to know?" He usually tells me.

Informants also use the moral approach, because, though they don't try or even want to form polis themselves, they're keenly aware of the information that will stir the moral sensibilities of others.

Of course, informants also spread the word of death, marriage, firings, and the like. I'd not label most of them gossips, however. A gossip usually doesn't want to form polis but rather has an aesthetic sense about what stories will catch the fancy of others in the organization.

When I attend advisory meetings for organizations about to design large MIS (management information systems), I'm tempted to ask for the status of the informant, who probably has a much more important function than the computer-based data, or at least a totally different and yet essential function. But I doubt whether most managers want to discuss informants, because it's important that an informant receive no official recognition.

There are lots of other politically based roles in organizations. There are the "instigators," the people who do form polis, usually around the need for change; and there are the counterinstigators who try to kill the polis (one of them put up a plaque in the Berkeley Faculty Club, which has since been removed: "When it is not necessary to change, it is necessary not to change").

One of my favorites is the "embarrassor," who uses a nice mixture of politics, morality, and religion. To understand him/her, you must realize that organizations dearly love to make promises that the collective conscious agrees to and the collective (realistic) unconscious knows is a bunch of malarkey. They make these promises when they are born ("founded"), and occasionally thereafter these promises appear in preambles, at the end of memos ("Above all, let us not forget the principles on which this organization is based . . ."). The embarrassor, using both morality and religion, points out on strategic occasions that the actions just selected—say, by a majority vote—violate the promises. He does not say—but implies—that the actions are therefore immoral. Nor does he have to say that the promises are what give the organization value. They are to be worshiped, but instead the collective conscious has just committed sacrilege. It should be pointed out that the collective conscious does not try to get rid of the embarrassor. Indeed, the embarrassor, more likely than not, will keep threatening to resign, while the collective conscious makes every effort—short of keeping its promises—to prevent his resignation.

There are many other roles I could discuss. For example, the "jester" plays the aesthetic role, using humor, when an organization is beginning to feel overwhelmed by authority. I recall that the colonel in charge of our laboratory once bawled out the head of the physics section because one young physicist had leaked something to the press. "And don't forget, Dr. Smith," growled the colonel, "that responsibility for this mistake goes right up the organization." "I couldn't agree more, Colonel," replied Dr. Smith, looking the colonel straight in the eye. I hardly need mention that the report of this encounter spread very quickly through the lab. I've shied away from hypotheses in this account of organizations, but I can't resist one at this point: the more the collective conscious finds itself under pressure, the greater the need for the jester (who doesn't need to be the same person throughout: Dr. Smith was an "ad hoc" jester).

There is also the "nice guy," the "listener," who encourages the distressed to talk, cluck-clucks at them, shows by his sympathy that he understands. He is the medicine man, alert to any disease that may beset the body of the organization. Since he is a healer, he is mainly interested in the life of the organization—that is, in its aesthetics.

So I want now to discourse a bit on the aesthetics of organizations, and specifically on organizational "life": When is an organization alive, and can it be killed or commit suicide? I will use the research organization as an example.

The broad problem is: How should we humans justify the continued existence of our organizations, or how should we justify ending them? It seems to me that the terms "murder," "suicide," "execution," etc., which we apply to individual humans, work equally well for organizations, although the horror and blood may be absent. Certain individuals may decide that an organization should no longer exist—for example, because it wastes money or is dangerous to the young. They, therefore, take steps toward murdering it. Or, the members of an organization may feel that its continued existence is no longer desirable, and the organization then commits suicide. Or, the nation or the state—for example, through funding agencies—may hold a trial (hearing), or set up a review process, and judge that an organization should be executed, with a specific time, place, and method of execution.

Of course, some organizations—for example, the United States Congress— are so well entrenched that it is extremely unlikely that any group could ever bring them to trial or successfully plot their murder. But here I am dealing with organizations that are more or less continuously either game for their enemies or on trial.

My question, of course, is not only how we justify continuing or ending organizations, but also how we should do these things. Now, the systems approach argues that the justification must somehow be based on our concept of the common good, or else on some principle of equity, or on both. Politics, on the other hand, argues that within certain limits an organization should survive if it has the will and the political clout to do so, and that it should not survive if it lacks either one of these. Or, an organization should not continue to exist if some organization (including itself) has the will and the political clout to destroy it. Religion has another viewpoint: it might say that an organization (e.g., the church) should survive if God so wishes. Morality frequently tries to support or destroy organizations as they arouse moral approbation or indignation. Aesthetics will also have a say, as we'll see. For the moment, though, let's follow the debate between the systems approach and politics.

As a beginning, the systems approach calls for definitions: What is an organization? How can you tell whether it has ceased to be or is really still alive? What are its boundaries? And so on. I admit that these are all fascinating questions—to the rational mind. For example, when the Russian revolutionaries were squelched in 1905, and dispersed over the world, one might have then been tempted to say that the political powers had succeeded in destroying the revolutionary organization, though subsequent history has ruled otherwise.

But I'm not going to yield to my logical urgings and play fascinating word games. It's probably much more difficult to decide whether an organization is alive or permanently dead than it is to decide the same thing for an individual human, but I'll assume that usually common sense is a sufficient guide, with occasional lapses: the Confederate States of America died in 1865, but the organization "lives on" in the hearts of many Southerners.

From the rational point of view, when should an organization exist or die? As we have seen, the systems approach argues that all humanity is tied together by a destiny theme, and that what we ought to choose to do about an organization has to be gauged, as best we can, in terms of the larger system.

For Benthamite ethics, the key ideas are opportunity costs and opportunity benefits, but not in the sense in which cost-benefit studies are made, because these tend to be much too narrow in their perspective. If we raise the question of whether an organization should continue to exist, then we must pursue the systemic question of what the social order would be like without it and with the resources (dollars, manpower, equipment, etc.) that would be released with its demise. It is no easy matter to make this judgment, especially since the long-term benefits of an organization may be obscure. But at least we should recognize that the question, Should the organization exist? means, "Are the long-range social benefits, minus costs, such that the organization's existence is 'better' than its nonexistence?"

The question may appear fantastic, but in fact some people *are* (or should be) asking just such a question when they try to set budgets, say, for support of a research organization. Somewhere in the total social system some people have to judge whether a dollar of research might not better be spent on housing, nutrition, economic development, or whatever. If no one is asking this reasonable (rational?) question, then the country—and society at large— is being terribly mismanaged. Thus, all "zero-based budgeting" must start with the real "zero base"—namely, that all organizations must be judged on the same basis: their contributions to human society. So runs the Benthamite viewpoint.

Of course, if we had a suitable "measure of performance" of human society, then the systemic task might seem realistic. Or, we might want to rely on some surrogate measures, such as the projected number of people dying or maimed by malnutrition, or the number killed by military conflicts, or the number forced into some form of slavery.

If we take a Kantian approach, then we should consider the ethical issue of equity in, say, the destruction of an organization: Are people, as humans, being treated as means only? Organizations are often the playthings of the powerful, and those who play with them must be judged immoral; such judgments are to be used in the ethical determination of the appropriate future of an organization.

Thus the "trial procedure" for an organization, according to the systems approach, should consist of an assessment of the long-range social benefit of its research as well as the equity considerations, where the judges are intelligent people who have read deeply and with understanding in the literature on human destiny, its benefits, costs, and equities.

The charge that the systems approach is utterly unrealistic is both common and strong. The notion that we can seriously and adequately compare the ethical benefits of such diverse organizational activities as research and housing is absurd. Besides, there is a much more plausible and coherent way to proceed, as politics points out: for an organization to exist, it must have the clout to do so.

The political clout of an organization is often based on a design, which for lack of a better name I'll call "submergence." In this design you submerge your organization into one or more "supporting" organizations which you assume to be stable and sympathetic. Your political task is to convince these organizations that your own should survive. You identify your allies, who are also trying to keep their own organizations alive. You try to convince the supporting organizations that your allies are competent judges about your organizational objectives. You also try to build a cadre of people who, though not good judges of the quality of your organization, nevertheless support your survival. You invent political slogans, like "excellence of teaching and research," to be used to characterize your organization's effort and also to murder research organizations that you deem of "low quality."

The nice point in this design is that you have escaped having to compare a research dollar with, say, a health dollar or a housing dollar. It's up to the supporting organizations to fight these battles, the universities, the National Science Foundation (NSF), the National Institute of Health (NIH), etc. The trial—usually called the "review system"—can usually be well rigged to serve the research organization's ends.

All this adds up to the viewpoint that research organizations—and basic research in general—operate through a well-designed political system. The political Weltanschauung, furthermore, goes on to say that this is the way they should operate. To arrive at this ethical judgment, some constraints on the design seem called for. Not every organization with sufficient political clout should exist; for example, some people might argue that the Mafia has the clout but not the justification.

For the research community, the organization and its members should, above all, be honest in reporting their findings. They should not plagiarize. Nor should they conduct specious research using methods that cannot be logically defended. Matters become more difficult if we ask whether the research should be "significant," either to other researchers or to society. In my own field one wants to know whether some of the elegant results of game theory mean anything to anyone except to game theorists. Here the answer is not clear, nor does agreement exist. In any event, the ethical prescription of political design really follows from a long-range prescription: never act so that one's political clout will thereby be diminished in the long run.

Some may feel some uneasiness about the political approach to organizational survival. Of course, politics points out that it is the only realistic way human society can work. People want to do all kinds of things: build roads and buildings, cure others, write novels, fish, love, and watch violence. No one knows which of these things are "best," but the political process, if allowed to work, will allocate resources to those who can muster the appropriate amount of power. Otherwise we live in anarchy or totalitarianism.

Many things could be said about the birth-life-death of organizations: conception, abortion, birth, development, and mutation (through "reorganization," for example), aging, and so on. But I should like to concentrate on one aspect of the life process—suicide—because I think that suicide has much to be said for it in terms of the appropriate management of an organization.

"Suicide" means here the willful acts by sane individuals in an organization which are intended to lead to its destruction. It is true that this definition, as applied to individual humans, has involved drastically different moral judgments on the part of various cultures and religions. In some cases suicide was a "crime," punishable by confiscation of the suicide's property or by prison sentences for his kin. In Japan it was often the only honorable way for a defeated warrior.

But in the case of some—if not all—organizations, the consideration of suicide may be the most appropriate management policy. If an organization has the continuous capability of judging whether it should continue, then society avoids the expense of an external trial or the inequity of outside political murder.

From this point of view, "management development" means developing the talents and attitudes that provide appropriate judgments concerning suicide. It is all too obvious that many organizations survive much too long, and that often society lacks the political power to terminate them. Professor Thomas Cowan wants management scientists and planners to study "dying industries," examples of which he claims are railroads and baseball. Presumably he wants to understand how long they should be in the process of dying, and how their death can be brought about. The implicit suggestion here is that an appropriate method would be to develop or to hire managers with a real skill in planning suicide. Or, in the case of many research organizations, we need "research management improvement" along the lines of developing or hiring directors who are unafraid of suicide and appreciate how to judge when the suicide process is appropriate. Or, in the case of basic research, perhaps we need scientific leaders who can judge when a discipline should come to an end.

How should managers make appropriate decisions about the suicide of their organizations? Of course, they could use either the systemic or the political approach. They could decide reasonably that their organization no longer serves society well, or that their political power has declined rapidly.

But now I want to suggest an aesthetic base for suicide judgment: the spirit, or lack thereof, in the organization, or what I called "radiance." An organization should cease to be if its light has gone out.

Suppose we consider, not the rationality of holism, but its spirituality. Holism traditionally says that a collection of beings may have a collective property that cannot be inferred from the properties of its members. In our example, an organization may have a property that cannot be derived from the properties of its members (and their respective resources). More specifically still, an organization may have a value, which I'll call its "spirit" or "radiance," and which cannot be derived from any function of the values of its membership.

Recall Paul: "For as in one body we have many members, and all members have not the same function; so we, being many, are yet one body in Christ, and everyone members one of another."° Paul's definition of "spirit" is better than mine for all but mathematical minds. The point is that the "body of Christ" means more than the membership of a religious community. The meaning of membership does not derive from the logical relationship of "belongs in a class." Rather, the "body" is basic, and "membership" occurs as one becomes a function of such a body and a member of all other members.

The justification of suicide or nonsuicide now becomes a matter of judging whether an organization has lost its spirit. A research organization may turn into an organization that is simply a collection of research projects. As such, it has no "body" or spirit, because it is nothing more than a function of its individual parts. A wise director may then judge that his organized research unit has died in spirit, and set in motion the process of its suicide. (Of course, he could decide how to revive the body or reincarnate the spirit; these are really options in the total process of suicide.) Why should such action on the part of the director be wise? The only answer I can find lies in morality and aesthetics. The closest moral prescription is "Thou shalt not kill a life," or "Thou shall kill the lifeless," though neither of these really captures the moral feeling.

Now rational or political types may scream and holler at such a justification. "Just because an organization has spirit doesn't mean that it's paying its way," says the indignant systems character. I can illustrate by example the attitude of the political approach. When the National Institute of Education was formed, it asked Professor Michael Scriven at the University of California, Berkeley, to evaluate the educational laboratories that the old Office of Education had supported. Mike went at the job with enthusiasm and asked "experts" to assign numbers to the labs' projects and eventually to the overall

°Romans 12:4–5.

performance of each lab. A "master panel" was created to put all the scores together, in order to make such judgments as "increase funding," "keep the same," "decrease," or "execute." So Mike's approach was political and not systemic according to my definitions; the "scores" very likely did not represent social benefit minus cost. I agreed to serve on the master panel and spent a weekend going through the multitude of scores and subscores. On Monday I called Mike and said I couldn't really go along with his approach. "Besides," I said, "I've worked with Laboratory X, which has a low score, but I admire its spirit and enthusiasm," "We can't fund enthusiasm," Mike replied.

If we can't, then the research community may be in real trouble.

I can end this note on the life of organizations by freely speculating in the moral-aesthetic mode about murder. How does it happen that a group of individuals can openly and deliberately murder an organization, clearly for their own greedy, political ends, and society takes no steps whatsoever to apprehend and punish them? Furthermore, the organization may be young and beautiful, and the killers ugly and malevolent. There's a mystery melodrama for you to contemplate, or even to write a novel about: a lovely, sweet, devoted, unselfish creature is destroyed overnight by a villain, while society as a whole applauds or turns its back.

I hope I have revealed the ways in which the rational mind may free itself and explore the larger land of reality by placing itself in the body of the enemies. Now I want to end with some general thoughts and feelings.

Of course, "being one's enemy" is probably not a strategy at all in the images of the enemies, because strategies are options in a class of alternatives, and the enemies do not usually image their reality in this manner. Otto Rank, in his astute *Art and Artist*,* says that many great artists (e.g., painters and novelists) have a vision they can never realize—that is, in my language, a vision that cannot be the reality of the collective conscious. Naturally, these artists will reflect on whether their visions are not more real than the "other" reality: "Do I wake or sleep?" All deep dreamers have similar questions, especially when the dream material is clearly, even logically, connected, tied together. Rank argues for a kind of "sane schizophrenia": the visionary must at one and the same time and way live his visions and the reality of the collective conscious.

It's not a bad lesson for the ideal-planner, the hero of the systems approach. Above all, he must not give up his vision, even though in reality it fails over and over again. Indeed, his vision *is* a part of reality; and were the human

*Otto Rank, *Art and Artist* (New York: Agathon Press, 1932).

race to lack it, it would die as a species, even though the rituals of daily living went on. You, dear hero/heroine, will perceive day after day the dangerous follies of the enemies and will occasionally be overwhelmed by the enormity of evil and ignorance. The moral is that you must at one and the same time *be* in the reality and the vision.

There is a positive side to this apparently dolorous existence. If you *are* your enemy, you can begin to learn what you yourself are like, as you look on yourself from the vantage point of the enemy: how foolishly you push one point of view, of model building, statistical analysis, game theory, ethics, or holism. Once you are your enemy, you at last see yourself as you really are: a human being, wise and foolish, who has a quirk about the destiny and the improvement of the human condition, just as all the rest of humanity has its quirks.

Finally, consider the gift of freedom the enemies offer us. Sometimes my students ask me if I really believe in the existence of God. Of course, as this book indicates, I've let my rational mind work hard on this question, even to the point of saying that it's badly put, the real issue being how to design a god. But as I pass into the body of religion, I realize how terribly stifling the question is, because reason tends to believe this is the first, or most basic, issue of religion, whereas Saint Paul doesn't even list it in his trilogy of faith, hope and love. That one can have glorious religious experiences without even considering the issue of a divine being's existence is the revelation of religion. One can be intensely political without once worrying about what politics and political power mean, or one can be moral without asking for definitions of the good or the bad, or sophomoric questions like "Who's to decide?"

And enjoy to its depth the aesthetic quality of our life without knowing what it means.

INDEX